THE NEW SOVIET MAN

THE NEW SOVIET MAN

His Upbringing and
Character Development

by

HERSCHEL and EDITH ALT

BOOKMAN ASSOCIATES, INC.

Acknowledgments

OUR MOMENTS of greatest insight and comprehension occurred in talks with Soviet citizens and officials, and it is a matter of keen regret that the political climate in their land forbids disclosure of their identity and appropriate acknowledgment.

We are also indebted to the many students of the Soviet scene in the United States and other countries who despite great odds have devoted years of scholarly endeavor to building up a substantial body of facts about Soviet life. Many of them have been helpful in broadening our perceptions and in sharpening our observations. In this connection we should like to thank Professor Mark G. Field, of the Department of Sociology and Anthropology, Boston University and the Russian Research Center at Harvard University, who read the preliminary notes of our second trip to the U.S.S.R. and encouraged us to write this book.

We also wish to thank Mr. Leo Gruliow, editor of *The Current Digest of the Soviet Press,* for his readiness to share his store of knowledge, as well as for his permission to quote from articles in that periodical.

Mrs. Ina Schlesinger assisted by providing verification of many facts and especially by sharing her knowledge of the roots of Russian educational theory and practice, as well as the present-day organization of the schools.

Our task has been made lighter through the unstinting help given us by Mrs. Ruth L. Tolins in editorial assistance and in the preparation of the manuscript.

HERSCHEL AND EDITH ALT

Contents

Introduction

IN THE REPORT of our first visit to the U.S.S.R., which we made during the summer of 1956, we told of our impressions of Soviet methods of child care and child rearing, and how these mirror the broader social forces which shape the behavior of the average individual in that country.*

We had come away from that trip with many unanswered questions and a variety of impressions and points of view, some highly tentative, some contradictory, but some sharp and clear enough to goad us into a further study of a few basic issues in child rearing in the Soviet Union.

Encouragement to continue these studies came from both within and without. First, we had our own deep interest in finding answers to some important questions we had asked and to note what changes may have occurred in child rearing with de-Stalinization. The second came from students in this field who took our findings seriously and urged us to continue.

We returned to the Soviet Union in the early summer of 1959 to learn more about the everyday life of children and families and to try to understand more fully the apparent contradictions in both ideology and practice which beset education and child rearing in the U.S.S.R.

On our first visit we were struck by the fact that children were highly conforming in official situations—in school, in camp, on the street—but we came away with many questions about the degree of conformity and good behavior in the home. We were concerned, too, about the effect which Soviet child care and educational methods had upon the individual's ability to be creative, capable of initiative, capable of exercising personal

---

* Alt, Herschel and Edith: *Russia's Children*. New York: Bookman Associates, 1959.

judgment. To what extent did the insistent and all-embracing efforts to instill a sense of social responsibility—concern for general welfare as contrasted with individual gratification—achieve their purpose? Was the Russian child, as well as the young person and adult, capable of unselfish behavior, or did he, like our own, respond to motivation grounded in self-interest, in rewards and punishment?

On this second trip we were, therefore, interested in learning more about the theoretical base underlying Soviet educational practices. What were their historical and scientific roots—their guiding principles? To what extent are these different from our own? More particularly, have the Soviets forged new and better methods for socialization? What changes, if any, are taking place in social and psychological theory? How much more, and what new kinds of, research are being carried on in the psychological field, in the study of the behavior of the individual as a member of the group? How profoundly is experience replacing ideology in social policy and social engineering?

We were particularly interested in the opportunity to see children in many different kinds of situations—in the classroom, in the Pioneer organization and, if possible, in their own homes. We wished to find clues to the healthful or unhealthful development of the child.

But we knew that in the Soviet Union an interest in the shaping of the child's personality cannot be limited to study of education and child rearing.

In the Soviet Union, more than in most contemporary cultures, educational theory and practice are direct expressions of the system of control of individual behavior. Education as an integral element of this system, as well as the system itself, is explicitly tied to the national purpose and both are instruments for shaping the behavior of every citizen so that he may contribute most to the common life *as defined by the party and the regime*. That is why the direct connection between education and the system of social control and national purpose is more explicit and clearly drawn in the U.S.S.R. than in societies where so-called "Western" values prevail.

It is for these reasons that no one can adequately appraise what is happening to children in the Soviet Union without understanding the basic goals of Soviet society, how they are being implemented and how far they are being achieved. We have, therefore, undertaken to delineate the system of incentives upon which the regime relies to achieve social behavior, and we have then presented an examination of indicators of success of this effort. This includes such questions as: How far has the Soviet Union achieved a new balance in motivation between egotism and altruism, between self-interest and the common welfare? What is the evidence of the lessening of the competitive spirit among those reared and educated since the revolution? Have Soviet methods of child rearing and social control achieved a new type of motivation or merely more repression and harnessing of individual impulse?

We need to know if some of the usual manifestations of conflict between the individual and the social group have disappeared. We refer to delinquency, crime, neurosis, mental illness, as well as expressions of dissent and opposition to the established order.

We hope our observations will help others to gain a fuller sense of the intricate and varied aspects of the fundamental psychological problem the U.S.S.R. faces in striving toward a new social order.

Developments in the Soviet Union since 1958 continue to provoke our interest. With the ascent of Sputnik and other spectacular achievements, the American people were quickly persuaded that the Soviet regime had been successful in achieving its goals, and this included the shaping of attitudes and behavior of its people in accord with its purposes. The cultural exchange program inaugurated in 1957, which has brought to our shores some of the outstanding musicians and dancers as well as educators, scientists and writers of the Soviet Union, has added to the general conviction of the excellence of the many things the Russians are able to do.

At the same time, American professional workers from many fields have visited the Soviet Union and have reported their impressions of the Soviet scene upon their return. While their reactions differ, the great majority are favorably impressed with what they have seen and are convinced that we would do well to copy many of the things the Russians have done in the field of education. Because of its sharper focus and direction, the Soviet educational program seems to be proving its basic soundness. The Soviets are outstripping us in the training of scientists and technicians. We have come to believe that, in contrast to theirs, our children do not work hard enough; nor do we conserve the abilities of the gifted.

This book can do little more than capture the situation at a moment in time. Events move rapidly and there is always the hazard that under these circumstances some observations may be outdated before they are printed. However, events in the field of social phenomena generally follow a certain hard logical sequence and constitute both causes and effects, so that even when events have been modified by some subsequent change they still can provide clues to an understanding of situations as broad as those with which we are concerned.

While the questions we have raised are those which concern us as workers in the field of human relations, it is important to point out that in a more basic sense they also embody anxiety felt on the part of the Soviet regime. This is particularly so for those entrusted with leadership responsibility in the fields of education and social relations in the U.S.S.R.

During the three-year interval between our first and second visits, and continuing into the present, the Soviet regime itself has expressed its deep concern over the end product of its educational system as represented by the "moral character" of its young people. Leading Soviet educators deplore their lack of success in molding the kind of personality which is a requisite for the society they hope ultimately to establish. In this regard a number of proposals for change in the educational system are being advanced which are intended to achieve more fully one of its principal objectives—a personality with a combination of character traits which in Soviet ideology is identified with the "new" Soviet man.

While it is difficult to say whether the Soviet leaders underestimate the success they have achieved or whether their evaluation of the situation is accurate, the fact that they are anxious and willing to do a number of things to improve their methods is significant. From the standpoint of the world outside the Soviet Union, the question is whether this will mean a recognition by them that there are limits to the modifiability of human behavior and, ultimately, a change either in their goals or in the time allowed to reach them. An official "Commission on Shortcomings in Moral Education" has been at work for several years and, in part at least, the recently adopted educational program reflects the basic concern about the impact of education on the individual's motivation and self-image as a member of the Soviet social order.

Everybody brings to the study of life in the U.S.S.R. not merely a special set of values about life and a special kind of professional experience, but often projected goals and hopes for the Soviet Union itself. In different ways, almost all come away with certain disappointments and frustrations either about the Soviet experiment, which may result in an overcritical assessment of what has happened there, or about life in the country from which they themselves come.

Thus, an outstanding British psychiatrist, who for almost a lifetime has been frustrated by the inadequacies of psychiatric care in Great Britain and other European countries, came back from his "objective" first visit to the U.S.S.R. with almost total approval and admiration for everything there because the ratio of psychiatrists to patients was nearly ideal. In the same way we met American industrialists who, frustrated in their dealings with organized labor in the United States, were completely won over by what they saw in the Soviet Union because workmen there had to be more compliant with management's wishes!

Our own orientation to the Soviet scene is grounded upon the fact that we have spent the better part of our professional lives in activities designed to help neglected and emotionally disturbed children and their families. Because of their life situation, many of these children are in conflict with parent-people or other authority surrogates—teacher, law enforcement officer, etc. Many others in the group of the disturbed have responded to life experience by withdrawal and other restriction in their personality and in fulfillment of themselves. The focus of our efforts has been to establish their confidence in adults as a bridge to the acceptance of adult standards in one instance and release of psychological energy in the other. We have come to believe that confidence in the adult world built upon affection and sustained through consistent support, is indispensable for healthy development of all children.

With this background, it would be surprising if we were not especially sensitive to the way in which the social order, with its arrangements for child rearing and education, affected the fullest potentialities of children as well as adults.

However, in spite of what could be interpreted as criticism of many things in the Soviet philosophy and practice of child rearing, we have not drawn attention to these with any feeling that we in our country are free of serious shortcomings in the same sphere of our common life. A visitor from the U.S.S.R., or from any other country, could easily point to many contradictions in our philosophy and practice of child nurture and education. This, however, does not suggest that we withhold any critical observations of what is going on in the Soviet Union. We would hope that to the extent that these observations are valid, responsible leaders of Soviet education will make use of them in building a happier life for their children.

Answers to the kind of questions with which we have been concerned are hard to come by in any culture, but this is particularly true in the Soviet Union, where much about everyday life is still concealed from the rest of the world, and from the Russians themselves. At best, all we can do is pose the questions and elaborate them in the light of the knowledge we have gained.

It is our hope that even though this study of life in the U.S.S.R. must necessarily be fragmentary, it should be useful not only for ourselves but for the Soviet Union as well which has not yet been able to resolve the question we have posed to its own satisfaction: How much further can it proceed in its program for building a new social order without more realistically facing the basic limitations of human nature—the limits to its plasticity and perfectibility? Moreover, we believe analysis such as this of the impact of radical social reorganization on children and family life has implications for all countries subject to similar experience whether in China, Southeast Asia, Africa or Latin America.

From our own standpoint, fuller knowledge of what is taking place in the U.S.S.R. provides a useful perspective on our own goals, values and direction. The Soviet experience should help us to sharpen our assessment of many focal problems which confront us in child rearing and the conservation of child life.

HERSCHEL AND EDITH ALT

JANUARY 1964

PART ONE

THE INDIVIDUAL
IN THE SOCIAL ORDER

Chapter 1

Theoretical Basis for the Soviet System of Social Control

AT THE CENTER of the communist dream is its unique vision of a society and its view of man in that society. The new social order will be co-operative rather than competitive; altruistic rather than selfish. "From each according to his abilities, to each according to his needs," will be the governing maxim. Man will be motivated by enlightened self-interest that will identify the good of one with the good of all and harmony between man and man will prevail.

This kind of society would come into being as the new economic organization replaced the old; and the new man worthy of the new order would appear as the barriers to his free development were thereby removed.

The leaders of the Russian Revolution, including Lenin, never lost sight of the crucial role for man in the new order, and they devoted time to a delineation of his qualities. They saw him as a man of steel, the builder who overcomes all obstacles, practicing the self-denial of a saint but also the ruthlessness of a soldier in battle; one who unquestioningly follows the leader and fulfills the expectations set for him by higher authority. He must be at one and the same time a "superman" and an "organization" man.

What has happened to one component in the equation of the ideal state and its ideal citizen is the concern of this book. It is difficult to tell which particular part of the equation was the first to be modified—the vision of the society or the vision of man in the society.

While the Marxist concept of the inevitability of the ultimate achievement of the collectivist Utopia has never been surrendered, during the early years of the revolution the pace of its realization through natural evolution was faltering and uncertain. Then too, the original vision did not fully take into account man as he *was,* as distinct from what he might become. His strong self-interest proved more powerful than the rational motivation which identifies individual with social well-being.

The visions of society and of man and how fast they would be realized were both amended, allowing for a transition of indefinite duration from the imperfect to the perfect.

So far as man was concerned, during this transition his self-interest had to be taken into account so as to mobilize his fullest contribution to the building of the new order. To achieve this a system of incentives was instituted, recognizing the proclivities of man as he is: reward him for compliance, punish him for deviation. His profile now lost its unity and became a mosaic of conflicting attributes. The question now was: Was this a portrait of man in the ideal society or merely of one during a period of transition? It was hard to say which from the pronouncements of the official exponents of Soviet policy.

A plausible, though not wholly logical, rationalization of this contradiction between man as he should be and man as he really is, is that one embodies the short-term and the other the long-term objectives of the Soviet plan. Whether one or the other is relied upon as a guide for action depends upon whether the goal is seen in immediate or long-range terms. At the present stage in the evolution of the Soviet social order, with substantial achievement in building a productive economic apparatus and a powerful defense establishment, the vision of an ultimately free and co-operative society is being reintroduced, with greater emphasis on compliance out of conscious realization that the interest of the individual and the common good coincide.

For a clearer understanding of the mainsprings of social behavior in the U. S. S. R., we will trace the streams of thought which contributed to present-day Soviet views of the place of the individual in society and the role of the state in shaping his character and behavior. Although the goal of the revolution was a complete transformation of the social order, and the Bolsheviks believed themselves to be guided solely by the "scientific" principles of Marxism, the historical background of the revolution and the social and economic conditions of the country in which it was launched, as well as the personal *Weltanschauung* of its leaders, cannot be ignored.

Traditional modes of thought and behavior cannot be wiped out overnight by revolution and official proclamation of a new philosophy. Moreover, Soviet ideology itself is not a single logically unified theory, but rather a blend of ideas from many sources. Besides Marxism, it incorporates many streams of thought—from czarist days, from other revolutionary movements—and has borrowed, and continues to borrow, much from the Western world. Nor can we think of the communist sources as purely ideological. The personal experience of the revolutionaries, the ignorance, the superstition, the brutality and the violence, as well as the devious accommodations which human beings made to these conditions, the indomitable personal struggle of Lenin and some of his collaborators, may actually have been as potent in shaping the course of the Soviet enterprise as the ideologies which constitute the communist dream.

Out of this experience has come the emphasis on unanimity of purpose, on strict discipline as an absolute condition of achievement by a small minority, and on a morality whose premise is that the end justifies the means.

It is a basic tenet of Marxist philosophy that every society takes its character from the nature of its economy—its productive forces and the resulting production relations. The Marxist interpretation of history asserts that all other institutions in society are determined by the nature of the economic organization.

Depending on the nature of its productive forces, a society is divided into two or more classes. The particular class in control of the productive forces is the dominant class in the society and controls the secondary institutions—in Marxist terms, the superstructure—as well. These institutions are manipulated by the ruling class with the aim of retaining and consolidating its power. The other classes of society are in inevitable conflict with the ruling class. However, every society carries within it the seeds of its own destruction: the productive forces develop and are perfected to the point where the old organization of production relations is no longer the most efficient one. The system's internal contradictions eventually make it imperative and inevitable that a new social order replace the old, and that new production relations be established to conform to the advanced productive forces. As the ruling class will never surrender power voluntarily, a revolution is necessary to bring about the transition from one system to another. Every society which replaces the outmoded preceding order is a step forward in the history of human organization and must be regarded as progressive until it in turn begins to impede progress in favor of retention of the *status quo*.

Marx identified four kinds of society that existed before the advent of socialism: primitive tribal society, without any organized mode of production; society based on slave labor; the feudal system; and capitalism. Each system is replaced by the next in that order, each representing a higher stage in the development of the history of mankind. This process of development will only cease when socialism is established; a socialist order is a system in which productive forces are controlled by the proletariat which has become so large a class as to constitute the society as a whole. Thereupon, classes would no longer exist and there would be no obstacle to impede the fullest development of productive forces. Marx conceived of this entire process as an inevitable development, determined by the "objective laws of history." Only under socialism, with the disappearance of the class struggle and a just and equitable economic and social organization, can the individual come fully into his own.

Marx discussed the detailed organization of a socialist society only in the vaguest terms. He assumed that after a short period of transition, which would be necessary to impose the rule of the proletariat on the small ruling class of the former capitalist society, a classless society would be established. With the abolition of classes and the class struggle, the institutions of law enforcement would no longer be needed, and the business of the state would be carried on by all citizens. All men would see their duties clearly and perform them willingly for the good of all; the state organization would wither away and social control would no longer be necessary.

Even this brief account of the basic principles of Marxism reveals a great deal in the Soviet brand of Marxism which is in direct contradiction to its own classical principles.

Marx conceived of the socialist revolution as an inevitable event, brought about by the working class of a highly developed capitalist society—the great majority of the population—at a time when economic conditions were ripe for it. But the Bolsheviks organized the revolution while they were a tiny minority in a backward agrarian country.

Marx saw the process of establishing socialism as an *undirected, inevitable* development governed by objective laws. The Bolsheviks insisted on the need for a highly organized and disciplined party which was to be the "vanguard of the proletariat." This party was, in effect, to bring about the revolution rather than wait as bystanders for it to come into being because of inevitable historic forces. Marx saw the future society as the best framework for men as they are; the Soviet ideologists see communist society (the final stage of the socialist society) as an ideal community, which can only be maintained if the very nature of man can be changed to conform to the requirements of the new order.

The origins of many of these principles, so contradictory to Marx's ideas, can be traced to 19th century Russia. An obvious, though perhaps not widely known, source of ideas for future Soviet leaders was a small group of radical revolutionaries who elaborated their views in Russia in the latter part of the 19th century. Throughout that century revolution was in the air in Russia as well as in Western Europe. The Russian revolutionaries, however, tempered and conditioned by their harsh struggle with an absolute autocracy, developed extreme radical and violent theories of revolution. The best known figure in this group was the anarchist and famous adversary of Marx, Mikhail Bakunin.

Bakunin preached the need for the complete and utter destruction of existing society through a universal—political, social, philosophical and economic—revolution. Only if all existing institutions were destroyed would it be possible to abolish the political and social inequality which, he held, caused all immorality in contemporary society; only then would it become possible to build a new and better society. Bakunin believed man to be entirely conditioned by his environment and thus not responsible for his actions as long as the environment was imperfect. Only when an ideal society was established could mankind expect disharmony and antisocial behavior to disappear.

The destruction of the old order and the building of the new, according to Bakunin, should be entrusted to a revolutionary organization which would operate on three levels. The mass of members would be led by a small central committee whose membership would be secret. This committee, in turn, would be directed by an absolute "czar" with autocratic powers.

The concept of revolution led by an organized and highly disciplined minority who would bring about the utter destruction of the old society was also advanced by other "Machiavellian" revolutionaries of the period, the most interesting of whom were Sergei Nechaev and Peter Tkachev. Both were active revolutionaries who were imprisoned by the czarist government for their subversive activities.

Nechaev's only concern was the destruction of the old order and the organization of the revolution. He drew no blueprint for a society of the future. To organize revolution, he believed in training a small group of dedicated revolutionaries whose only profession would be revolution. In his *Catechism of a Revolutionary* he envisions a "consecrated man . . . all of him is absorbed in the single exclusive interest, in the one thought, in the one passion—revolution. . . . Moral for him is everything which facilitates the revolution. Immoral and criminal is everything which hinders it." *

His contemporary and accomplice, Peter Tkachev, was a more constructive thinker. Called the "forerunner of Lenin," he must certainly have greatly influenced the Bolshevik leader. Tkachev was as much concerned with mapping the new and better society as he was with destroying the old order. Although much influenced by the Marxist idea of gradual progression toward socialism through various stages of economic development, he contended that in Russia a bourgeois-capitalist phase of development as a step toward socialism might prove unnecessary. He developed the theory of the historical "jump" by which it would be possible for a country to make a transition directly from one phase of development to a much higher one, without passing through the intermediary stages. Thus, he argued, Russia might pass directly from her then semifeudal and agrarian stage into socialism. The very backwardness of the country would facilitate this changeover; with a weak and inefficient government and a backward economy, it would prove easy to overthrow the regime and establish a socialist system. If the revolutionaries waited until political and economic reforms

---

* Reshetar, John S., Jr.: *A Concise History of the Communist Party of the Soviet Union.* New York: Frederick A. Praeger, 1960. (Published under the auspices of the Foreign Policy Research Institute at the University of Pennsylvania.) Page 5.

had strengthened the established state, the socialist revolution might have to be postponed indefinitely.

A necessary element in Tkachev's plan for immediate revolution was the organization of an enlightened and clear-sighted minority which would be highly disciplined, and both willing and able to act in the name of the masses. He considered that the people, if left to themselves, lacked the decisive force and the power necessary to organize and carry out a revolution. He also considered them incapable of recognizing their own best interests and of planning the new order after the old one had been overthrown. In Tkachev's plan, the revolutionary minority would have to blueprint the new society and set up new institutions after they had achieved the victorious revolution. Thus, a possibly prolonged period of transition to the new society would be needed. During this time it would be a task of the new regime to re-educate the people because the new society would require a new type of man. The revolutionaries would have to "reeducate man and change his very nature." *

The one central idea which the radical revolutionaries of 19th century Russia held in common was the need for an informed, disciplined and organized minority to lead the masses toward the future which they were too slow to realize was in their own best interests. Further, this minority had to plan and act for the people as a whole.

Most of these men were guided by a Utopian vision of the perfect society and by the conviction that they were called upon to destroy the old order and establish the new. This missionary belief explains their conviction that the end justifies the means and the fact that they sanctioned and even stressed the importance of subversive and conspiratorial activities. Terror to them was an accepted means of furthering revolutionary ends, and tricks, ruses, suppression of truth, outright falsehood,

---

* Counts, George S.: *The Challenge of Soviet Education.* New York: McGraw-Hill Book Company, Inc., 1957. Page 28.

and even serious crime, became moral in this context. In this respect, also, the radical revolutionaries were forerunners of the Bolsheviks who viewed their dealings with opponents as total war, with the complete destruction of the enemy as the only possible outcome.

Their concept of what this better world should be like owed much to the liberal ideas prevalent in Russia in the 19th century. In spite of the oppressive intellectual atmosphere in Czarist Russia, neither a wall nor a curtain separated East and West Europe. Rather was there a permeable membrane through which contemporary Western liberal ideas penetrated into the country without great difficulty. Many great Russian writers and intellectuals went abroad to study and work, bringing back with them the philosophies then current in other countries. Many elaborated these concepts to adapt them to Russian conditions and to spread their ideas by legal or illegal means. Although persecution was incessant, the intellectual ferment could not be suppressed. One result of the constant attempts at the suppression of ideas and at thought control was that the need for revolution and change in Russia came to be almost universally accepted. Thus intellectualism and revolutionary thought became closely linked, so that literary figures—critics, great poets and writers—became leaders of political thought and agitation.

Four outstanding representatives of this group must be mentioned: Alexander Hertzen, Vissarion Belinsky, Nikolai Chernyshevsky and Nikolai Dobrolyubov. These authors are all still highly regarded in the Soviet Union today and are considered to be the forerunners of the "true" revolutionaries, the Marxists of a later day.

All these men believed a socialist society to be the best possible system for the future Russian state. Their concept of the socialist society was, however, quite different from that of Marx. They visualized it as based on an agrarian rather than on an industrial economy.

The middle of the 19th century saw the liberation of the serfs in Russia and with it the dawn of a period of enlightenment. Thinkers were exhilarated by the heady air of liberal political ideas and enthusiasm for reform. Political liberalism in the Western sense, however, did not take root in Russia, where there was little fertile soil for democratic ideas. Rather, it took the form of a romantic faith in the potentialities of the common people and the desire to be of service to them. This philosophy was best expressed in the *narodnik* movement, led by men who wanted to achieve reform in Russia by "going to the people," by living with them and trying to better their lot through work with them on the spot.

At the same time, there was a growing sense among the intellectuals that Chekhov's "Cherry Tree" upper classes were useless, and that their lives were wasted unless they performed some service for society. The theme of the "superfluous man," the useless member of society who suffers through idleness and boredom, is a recurrent one in 19th century Russian literature. Work and be useful to the people; this is the theme of many of the great Russian classics of that period.

None of the Russian liberals who advocated a change in the economic and social organization of the country believed in bringing it about by violence or by terroristic methods. Their concern was with the dignity of the human personality which would have been violated by the use of these revolutionary tactics.

Although the Bolsheviks claimed to represent the very antithesis of czarism, the influence of the autocracy cannot be omitted in discussing the trends of thought that make up Bolshevik philosophy. In fact, a closer look at the two systems strikingly highlights their similarities. Both czarist ideology and Soviet Marxism proclaim a uniform and absolutely proven system of thought, the one based on religious principles, and the other on the "objective laws of history." Both systems advocated an absolute form of government which claimed its right to power on its exclusive authority to interpret and implement the ideology. Both systems insisted on complete and unquestioning adherence to the philosophy, and on unquestioning obedience to the authority established in its name. The intellectual "climate" might change under every czar, depending on the character of the ruler. The individual sovereign might change his policies from extreme liberalism to extreme repressive measures within the period of a single reign; similarly, the policies of the Soviet government might fluctuate, veering from comparative freedom to extreme intolerance, as short-term goals might dictate. The basic principle, however, that the central authority had the power to dictate in intellectual as well as political matters, was never abandoned in either system. In both ideologies, and under both systems, the state was paramount and it was the duty of the individual to serve it.

It is clear that Lenin and his party brought to power with them a body of ideas gleaned from more diverse sources than they themselves perhaps realized. Although officially they acknowledged their indebtedness to Marxism, they also owed a great deal to both the political philosophy of the czarist autocracy and the non-Marxist revolutionary thinkers and liberals.

Like the radical revolutionaries, Lenin believed in the need for a revolution which had to totally destroy the old institutions before the new society could be built. He believed with them in the need for a highly disciplined and centrally directed party of dedicated revolutionaries which would organize the overthrow of the old regime and direct the establishment of the new. Like his predecessors, Nechaev and Tkachev, he believed that in the good cause the end justifies the means and anything which furthers the revolution is moral, anything which hinders it, immoral. He agreed with Tkachev that the semifeudal agrarian state which was Russia could "jump" from this stage straight to socialism, and with the 19th century liberals that any future society in Russia must take into account the vast peasant masses. Like these thinkers, he believed in the possibility of a better world, where all men could live in freedom, and he and his followers were imbued with ideas of serving the people and establishing a better society for them, even if the people did not wish it or realize that they needed it. With Tkachev he believed that men would first have to change their nature before they were fit to live in the new society created for them. All these elements were present in the reservoir of ideas which Lenin and his followers used, even if all of them were not always propagated at the same time.

How this aggregate of political philosophy was transformed into the dynamic rationale for practical programs is one dimension of the story of the revolution. As we will see, what happened was a process of interaction between ideas and stark realities—the stage of the Russian economy in 1917, the level of its technology, the resistance of the population to revolutionary goals and the personal equation reflecting the life experiences of revolutionary leaders.

We must not overlook the fact that the admixture of contradictory elements in their ideology has afforded the leaders a choice of principles with which to rationalize changes in policy they have found necessary to adopt to meet changing realities. Thus they have always been able to reverse courses of action and still affirm their loyalty to accepted ideology. It has also, as we shall see later, enabled them to reverse their official positions and the idea content of their indoctrination activities without seeming to contradict themselves—as, for example, their espousal of equality and democracy on the one hand, and of unequal rewards and class distinction on the other.

Immediately after the seizure of power, the Bolsheviks moved ahead to implement their theories and achieve the long-awaited Utopia. Industry was nationalized and its management was placed in the hands of the workers. Similarly, steps were taken to socialize agriculture and abolish all capitalist institutions.

There was an attempt to equalize wages and introduce payment in kind and distribution "according to needs."

In the movement from theory to life, however, the altruistic and benign features of the Utopia had to be left behind on the assumption that the present was a transitional period and that only after the economic and political structure had been rebuilt could the original vision be reinstated. Utopia has since been projected as the long-term goal.

On the road to this ideal society the benign approach has been replaced by relentless and hard-headed realism and by unflinching determination to achieve the practical objectives at all costs. The dream of altruism and harmony was set aside and the bitterness engendered by the imprisonment and persecution of czarist days characterized the practical measures to achieve compliance and conformity.

The drive to the future millennium had to be amended because of present harsh realities. So the immediate socialization of all industry had to give way to the New Economic Policy, which reintroduced a measure of private enterprise into the economy. Collectivization of agriculture was postponed and the restrictions on the *kulaks* (prosperous peasants) were relaxed. The administration of industry was taken out of the hands of the workers and entrusted to trained administrators of the old order. Inequality in wages was reintroduced, and payment in kind was again replaced by money wages.

However, all these measures were considered merely as so many concessions on the road toward socialism—tactical retreats on the road to ultimate victory. The Bolsheviks never abandoned their doctrinal position as their guide to action.

Throughout the 'twenties this dogma was discussed, argued and interpreted in various ways by different factions of the party, according to the differing *Weltanschauung* of the individual leaders. It was not until the beginning of the 'thirties that internal and external conditions reached a point where Soviet doctrine could crystallize. Only then were the country's political and economic goals definitely determined and a clearly formulated body of dogma proclaimed.

Lenin's death set off the struggle between the major factions in the leadership group. This proved to be as much a struggle for the succession as for the definition of future goals. On the one hand, Trotsky and his followers stood for the "orthodox" wing of the revolutionaries. They asserted that although the advent of socialism was inevitable, socialism could not be achieved in Russia without the help of the industrialized Western European countries. Nothing could be done in Russia, they contended, until a socialist revolution had taken place in the rest of Europe. Therefore, Trotsky advocated the fomenting of revolution in Europe as the most urgent task of the Bolsheviks. Stalin, on the other hand, who had none of the "cosmopolitan" experiences which had molded Trotsky's views, and those of Lenin as well, favored the "immediate building of socialism in *one* country." He felt himself to be in control of the party apparatus and believed that he could transform Russia with this tool. A third powerful group in the party believed in a gradual transition to socialism within the country and advocated development of the economy in a balanced way, with agriculture keeping pace with industry and light industry with heavy industry, change proceeding as a slow, evolutionary process.

It is superfluous here to examine the arguments that were used by the various factions. It should be pointed out, however, that the struggle between the "rightist" faction and Stalin carried implications which went beyond the field of mere economic theory. At the heart of the conflict was the question: Is it possible and desirable for man to change his society by taking active measures to achieve the predetermined goal? Or should he wait passively for evolutionary changes to take place? Stalin's opponents argued that socialism would develop inevitably, even without any active help by men. They were content to wait for events and let them come slowly. Stalin, on the other hand, argued that socialism must be brought about by conscious and active measures, that it was fruitless to wait for evolutionary developments or for revolution in other parts of the world: socialism must be built *now* and *in Russia*.

The resolution of this struggle between conflicting views was embodied in the first Five Year Plan, adopted in 1928, which called for the "building of socialism in one country" regardless of developments abroad. This meant priority for development of heavy industry to give the country an industrial base. To enable the country to finance the new plans, agriculture had to be regimented and private property forfeited. This demanded collectivization of agriculture as rapidly as possible and the abolition of all remnants of private enterprise.

The economic goals that were projected could not be achieved without relentless regimentation of the population. Obviously forcible and rapid industrialization of a country will entail enormous social upheavals. By the same token, stringent measures of social control become urgently necessary.

This is not the place to trace the political and police measures which were used to bring the population into line and to achieve fulfillment of the succeeding Five Year Plans. However, the consolidation of party control and the inauguration of the new policy in economic construction were also accompanied by a crystallization of doctrine in all other fields. All intellectual endeavor was now made subservient to the overriding purposes of the state. Above all, the attitude of the authorities toward the individual citizen had to change to conform to the new policies.

The replacement of the Marxist doctrine of inevitability by that of activism brought a change in the official view of the nature of man. In the early days of the revolution man had been regarded as the product of his environment, basically good, but helpless in the grip of forces beyond his control. He could thus not be held responsible for his actions. Now this concept of man as the victim of social forces gave way to a view of man as having considerable freedom of choice in his behavior and therefore to be held responsible for his actions.

These two assumptions furnished the basis for a system of relationships between the state and the individual which would fully mobilize the energies of every citizen in the advancement of national goals. An activist economic policy and the conscious transformation of society required an active but obedient citizen, a man who would be willing to subordinate his personal interest to the greater good of society, who would be willing to sacrifice immediate advantage for future happiness. It also required men who would work to the utmost of their ability. As a result, Soviet authorities soon found themselves in a contradictory position. While trying to develop the "new Soviet man" who would perform his duties for the joy of being a useful member of society and whose interests would be in complete accord with the interests of that society, they had to resort at the same time to a system of personal incentives and punishments to get the necessary performance. On the one hand, they encouraged the "collectivist" attributes in their subjects, on the other, they encouraged the desire for personal gain. This conflict, which had its origins in the years of the first Five Year Plans, has not been resolved in the Soviet Union to this day.

The basic social philosophy embodied in the first Five Year Plans remained the foundation for Russian life until after the death of Stalin. Since then the system of control of human life and conduct forged during the absolutist period has been relaxed but not basically transformed.

The new party program, approved by the 22nd Congress of the Communist party in 1961, proclaims that the present generation will live under communism during its lifetime. The new order will mean new relations between man and man, and between man and society—new relations that are said to be visible in Soviet society even today. The consciousness of the individual that his duty is to society is increasing constantly and in the new order less and less coercion will be necessary—trends embraced in the concept of the "withering away of the state."

Although in the period since 1956 we have witnessed relaxation of the terror and some sorties into liberalism, thus far, however, the changes have not been sufficient to indicate a firm trend. While they add up to a significant change in the psychological climate, the frequent manifestations of reaction shake any confidence that there has been a basic change in goals or methods.

*   *   *

The chapters that follow will show how the basic realities of public policy have been articulated into a concept of relationship between the individual and the state, and this, in turn, translated into a system of social control for conditioning individual and group behavior.

We will proceed to consider the fruits of this system in the material achievements of the revolution and in the kind of social structure which is a by-product of these achievements. We will also try to assess the response of the people to the system of conditioning to which they have been subjected. How has it influenced their personality, their character, their mental health and general attitudes? Have any specific characteristics resulted which make them different from people living in other cultures and subjected to different influences?

Chapter 2

The Carrot and The Stick

As SUGGESTED IN the preceding chapter, the leaders of the Soviet state soon recognized that the frail structure of authority born in the revolution could not be sustained and defended from the dissenters within and the enemies without unless certain essential goals were realized. The building of a productive economic organization that would sustain the population, and an effective defense establishment that would yield security on the world scene were absolute requisites if the revolution was to succeed. To accomplish this called for the harnessing of all productive energy and skills to the national purpose. It was important to get everyone to study, to work, to carry responsibilities appropriate to his role as husband, parent, citizen; to obey the law and to identify with the party ideology.

Social change, according to Stalin's strategy, was to be accomplished by the most direct route, with only secondary consideration for the cost involved. It meant "running roughshod over individuals and groups which stood in the way, and exacted a maximum of exertion out of the Soviet citizen." * This resulted in painful deprivation and much suffering for the Soviet population: "a frenzied pace of life, which was called the 'tempo'; extreme physical exertion and hardship; scarcity of food and shortage of clothing; deterioration and frightful overcrowding of housing; forced population movements and disruption of family life." * *

Human effort became a key resource in the industrial effort. To maximize the yield from this resource—the human material

---

* Inkeles, Alex and Bauer, Raymond, with the assistance of David Gleicher and Irving Rosow: *The Soviet Citizen.* Cambridge, Mass.: Harvard University Press, 1961. Page 255.

* * *Ibid.* Page 256.

—the regime recognized that there were limits beyond which it could not be exploited and that the citizen's health had to be protected and his skills and abilities increased. Though this meant concern for the welfare of the individual, it is a concern which has been dictated by the direct connection between general welfare and the accomplishment of the long-range goals of the regime.

At the heart of the far-flung apparatus instituted to achieve the kind of behavior the regime considered necessary to accomplish its goal was a well-developed scheme of rewards and punishment.

Far more than our own or similar systems, that of the Soviets relies on coercion as a determinant of human behavior. But coercion is to be resorted to after rewards, persuasion and propaganda have failed. In 1917 Lenin wrote:

The proletariat needs state power, the centralised organisation of force, the organisation of violence, both for the purpose of crushing the resistance of the exploiters and for the purpose of *guiding* the great mass of the population—the peasantry, the petty-bourgeoisie, the semi-proletarians—in the work of organising socialist economy.*

Although emphasizing persuasion and positive identification with national purpose, the Soviet regime did not basically concern itself with the intimate feelings or thoughts of the individual or his complete approval of its program. It took for granted that some of its citizens would be opposed to its policies, and consequently the system of control which it created was aimed to isolate discontent and to suppress open disloyalty. Stalin was not concerned with how people felt, but only with how they behaved. Accordingly, every effort was made to so structure the life situation of the Soviet citizen that "he would do what

_____
* Lenin, *Collected Works* (London 1927-1930), XXI (2), 169.

was expected of him *regardless* of his feelings toward the regime." *

In examining the motivational system built into the Soviet social order, we encounter a series of paradoxes and contradictions which have their roots in both ideology and practical compromise. It becomes obvious that the system is divided within itself: on the one hand, there are appeals to self-interest, higher pay and honors for achieving the norm; and, on the other, appeals to altruism which take many forms, including a part in building a Garden of Eden on earth. As one writer has put it, it is the story of the donkey with the carrot dangling in front and the stick at the rear. We see the same contradiction in the unique quality which pervades human relationships and which we have described as mutual aid and surveillance—helping your colleague when he is ill or otherwise disadvantaged, but combining this with surveillance of his behavior to make sure that it conforms to social norms.

Before describing the principal components in the Soviet motivational system, we must bear in mind certain historical and contemporary facts about the sources of authority in the Soviet Union.

In the monolithic and hierarchical political structure of the present-day Soviet Union, authority comes from the top down—the Central Committee of the Communist party, the Presidium of the Supreme Soviet, and the Council of Ministers. The party and its leaders are the only ones in a position to interpret what is right and what is wrong, and it is the individual's duty to comply with the truth as enunciated by the party. Khrushchev has explained it this way:

Our opponents in the bourgeois countries try to claim that Party spirit in artistic creation fetters the workers of literature and the arts, limits freedom of creation and the free presentation

---

* Inkeles and Bauer, *op. cit.* Page 282 and Page 283.

of their views and convictions. Of such persons it should be said that they are simply incapable of understanding either our social system or the new relations, born of socialism, of monolithic unity of the Communist Party, the Soviet government, the working class, the collective farm peasantry and the people's intelligentsia; it is not given to them to comprehend the indisputable truth that the Communist Party is the leading force of our society, the embodiment of the will and aspirations of the people, that it enjoys the unlimited trust and gratitude of the fraternal commonwealth of all the socialist nations of our country.*

This hierarchical character of the political and social structure is consistent with the absolutist monarchical government of the czarist days and the bureaucratic structure of the Communist party both before and since the revolution. It is worth repeating that many of the features of the system of social control derive from the lessons which the leaders of the present regime learned as revolutionaries. This is true of the uncompromising insistence on obedience from subordinates, on the doctrine that the ends justify the means, and on the necessity of retaining the initiative at all costs, not only in planning and implementation but also in their inseparable concomitant—indoctrination.

One cannot help but observe in this connection that not only does the system of control have its roots in czarist days as well as in the party apparatus, but the way in which the Russian citizen comes to terms with it is likewise a product of centuries of accommodation to tyranny.

During centuries of oppression, the Russian peasant developed skills in dealing with his overlord—the nobleman-landowner whom he served. He learned how to flatter him, how to

---

* "Khrushchev's Remarks to Writers and Intellectuals." *The Current Digest of the Soviet Press,* Volume XIII, Number 17, May 24, 1961. © Page 5. (*The Current Digest* is published weekly at Columbia University by The Joint Committee on Slavic Studies, appointed by The American Council of Learned Societies and The Social Science Research Council.)

placate him. He also learned how to live with the officials who cheated and exploited him. This capacity to accommodate to arbitrary authority, as we will see, manifests itself in many different ways: avoidance of responsibilities which may touch on those of others; shutting out certain knowledge and information which might carry with it involvement with the authorities, such as reporting misdeeds on the part of others. It is interesting that the words *nachal'nik* (petty bureaucrat) and *khozianin* (patron, seigneur, master of the estate), have not only continued to be widely used in the U.S.S.R. but continue to carry the same overtones as in the czarist days.

As we examine the Soviet system of social control we find that its principal components fall into three broad categories: the more positive motivations and incentives—love of country, tangible rewards and honors (the carrot); the negative—denial, punishment, and repression (the stick); and a third which can be seen as an admixture of both of these—persuasion and propaganda commingled with many forms of social pressure.

A. Differentials in Material and Other Rewards

Faced with the need to harness human energy, the Soviet Union gave up the concept of equality and adopted a system of differentials in material and nonmaterial rewards. The concept "from each according to his abilities, to each according to his needs," has been replaced by one which says "to each according to his contribution," and "he who does not work does not eat." Thus, pay ranges from 80 rubles a month for the ordinary workman to 200 or 300 rubles at the other end of the scale for the industrial manager, musician, political leader.* The whole concept of equality has been thrown out the window as unrealistic and perverse.**

---

* At the new rate of exchange of 10 old rubles for 1 new ruble.

** Stalin himself, in his famous speech on "New Conditions—New Tasks in Economic Construction," delivered in June, 1931, had started the trend by

In addition to the differences in the basic wage, some workers are paid on a piecework basis. Then too, almost without exception there are bonuses at the end of the year for exceeding or even fulfilling the norm, so that the man in charge of the greenhouses on a government farm may earn 900 or 1,000 rubles a year as his regular pay and get an additional 400 or 500 at the end of the year as a bonus.

Unequal pay obviously makes for inequality in material comforts and this, in turn, must make for differences in self-esteem and in the individual's sense of well-being—freedom and psychological elbow-room. Some members of the population have savings in the bank; some have been able to buy or build their own homes. An increasing number own automobiles, and highly placed officials, artists and scientists employ maids. Some can afford to travel. These are all part of the things one gets by either being more skilled, more inventive, or a better producer.

However, other considerations besides money wages enter into the possession of these privileges. Unequal rights derive also from one's status, particularly one's membership in the Communist party. This is an important factor in getting and holding favored positions; in the opportunity to buy in special stores; in the right to better housing; and in the chances of a child being admitted to the right school. In other words, such factors as membership in the party, the holding of a responsible post in industry and government, etc., confer special privileges far beyond the differential in pay as such.

---

attacking the practice of wage equalization or equality-mongering as a leftist deviation and by pointing out how absurd it was that "a rolling-mill hand in a steel mill should earn no more than a sweeper . . . a railway-locomotive driver . . . only as much as a copying clerk." He argued, furthermore, that such a situation deprived the unskilled worker of the motivation to acquire skills (the improvement of skills and the acquisition of knowledge being precisely what the Soviet Union needed for the industrialization drive). From: "Some Sociological Perspectives on Soviet Education" by Mark G. Field (Pages 175-191) in *The Politics of Soviet Education*. Edited by George Z. F. Bereday and Jaan Pennar. New York: Frederick A. Praeger, Inc., 1960.

There are other positive incentives besides the amount of salaries and wages which are held out to the population. We refer to the wide variety of benefits—in medical care, education, housing and social services. There is constant reiteration of the theme that if everyone works hard and produces to his utmost, the regime will be in a position to liberalize these benefits and will move closer to the ultimate achievement of the communist dream, which is "from each according to his abilities, to each according to his needs."

Closely related to tangible rewards is the wide variety of honors conferred on all those who contribute in exemplary ways to the national purpose. In every trade, in almost every profession and in all industries there are special marks of distinction for exemplary performance. Through the newspaper accounts and through the visits of musicians and dancers we in the United States have learned of the many kinds of honors the artist may earn. He may move from one level of distinction to another. So, the opera singer may be a distinguished artist of his own republic or, what is greater, of the Soviet Union itself.

At important thoroughfares one may see elaborate and beautifully designed bulletin boards surrounded by floral beds very similar to the outdoor memorials we erect to honor our war heroes. In the U.S.S.R. these are called *Doska Pocheta,* and the names listed are either of individuals or industrial plants or institutions that have, over a specific period, achieved an extraordinary record in production or earned distinction in other ways. On the walls of the waiting rooms of the pediatric clinic one sees many photographs of staff members who are presumably best liked by the patients, and who have otherwise carried out their duties loyally and with distinction.

We visited the cemetery behind the *Novi Dochii* nunnery in Moscow. Here we found another incentive for social effort. The cemetery abounds in beautiful headstones ornately inscribed, many of them marking graves of people who had died since the revolution. Poets, artists, musicians, political, industrial and military leaders are among those interred there.

Not only distinctions that are earned, but marks of professional status are of tremendous importance. It was almost pathetic to have a very intelligent middle-aged man tell us how he finally achieved the diploma of "economist." He had had various posts, was a skilled millwright, and because of his knowledge of languages was engaged as a translator in a government bureau. But in spite of the work he was doing he had no professional degree or rank and he was under constant pressure from his colleagues to do something about it; it was incongruous for him to be an intellectual worker without being qualified as a professional of some sort. He finally found that the easiest way he could achieve the status of a professional was to take courses in accounting. He eventually completed his training and has been qualified as an "economist." The importance of having achieved this is revealed by the fact that he carries his diploma in his pocket at all times.

B. Persuasion, Propaganda and Identification with National Purpose

Education conceived in its broadest terms remains a basic instrument in the system of social control and is more consciously employed as such in the Soviet Union than in the Western democracies. This could also be said of authoritarian nations such as Germany under Hitler and Communist China.

Education is not only a distinct instrument by itself, but is an aspect of all the other elements in the system of control we are describing. It is part and parcel of the system of control in the industrial plant, in the organization of the collective farm and the tenants' committee, and almost every human being is subjected to these at all times except for his most private moments. As Khrushchev put it:

After all, through the best works of literature and the arts people learn to understand life correctly and to change it; they assimilate progressive ideas and develop their character and convictions as naturally and unnoticeably as a child learns to speak.

We need books, films, theater productions, works of music, painting and sculpture that educate people in the spirit of communist ideals, stir their wonder at all that is splendid and beautiful in our socialist reality, inspire in people a readiness to devote all their efforts, knowledge and abilities to boundless service of their people, the desire to follow the example of the heroes of these works and make them uncompromising toward all that is antisocial and negative in life. We need skillful, vivid books that people will read and films that people will view with pleasure, music they will listen to with delight.*

There is little question about the effectiveness of Russian efforts to educate the masses. The achievements of the regime would not have been possible without the consistent and almost overpowering emphasis on indoctrination of every human being in the nation.

In other words, education in the Soviet Union is conceived of not only as a medium for shaping the minds of children in the desired pattern, but also in molding the attitudes of adults. Beyond providing a channel for communication, which all media of information provide in other countries, in the Soviet Union the nature of what is communicated is very carefully designed. Thus, the regime not only controls the instruments of education but carefully formulates what it wishes each individual to know and believe. This sometimes becomes both amusing and annoying to the visitor unaccustomed to this feature of the social scene. For instance, when we boarded a plane in Sochi to go to Moscow, it turned out that this was one of the new Turbojets that had only recently been put into service. As soon as the passengers were seated, the chief hostess began

---

* *The Current Digest*, Vol. XIII, No. 17, May 24, 1961, *op. cit*. Page 5.

a detailed explanation of all the extraordinary features of this plane—an account that lasted about fifteen minutes.

If one visits a park, one invariably finds many groups of children and adults standing around in circles being instructed about the unique beauties and special virtues of the place. This is also true in every museum.

Because in covering simple facts the lectures also continuously interweave much propagandist moralizing, they no doubt add up to an important influence on the thought and behavior of the people.

Propaganda is not limited to positive comment about government policies and expectations or tributes for exemplary behavior and achievement. These ingredients are balanced by a great deal of scolding for all violations of good form as well as all malefactions, including egotism, parasitism, speculation and ordinary criminal behavior. In short, every form of unsocial conduct is held up to scorn.

Special devices have been developed for giving preachments the appearance of spontaneity and originality. A questionnaire may be circulated among a Komsomol group soliciting the views of each member on the virtues and faults of present-day youth. Are they proud of the Soviet Union? Or are they disappointed? These surveys provide an opportunity for youngsters to present their point of view and scold others who disagree with them.

Such a recent survey posed the question: Why do young people leave the farms and how is this connected with their goal in life? While most of the answers ran true to form ("I want to be a good engineer," "I want to serve society and help to build communism," etc.), one Moscow girl confessed that her goal in life was to amass as much money as possible, for money is happiness. The succeeding issues of the paper published numerous indignant replies to this letter, extolling the approved communist virtues and condemning such an incomprehensibly selfish attitude.

Posters and satirical poems are hung in prominent places in public parks and recreational institutions, condemning such "Western decadence" as the Hollywood shirt, narrow pants for boys, the exaggerated hairdos of girls in imitation of Western styles, or the "bourgeois" custom of "necking" in public.

Another interesting device for expressing disapproval of unacceptable conduct is the institution of correspondents whose business it is to write letters to the press pointing out various kinds of weaknesses on the part of groups as well as individuals, including officials who misuse their authority.

Love of country, pride in its achievements, glorification of its historic figures, are being increasingly cultivated and are apparently relied upon to create a firm basis for identification with national purpose. One of the extremes this takes, for example, is the glorification of czars like Ivan the Terrible who helped to build Imperial Russia by conquering neighboring provinces, even though the methods they resorted to made them infamous for their brutality and oppression.

A phenomenon of another kind is the reverence paid to the remains of Lenin resting in the Mausoleum in Moscow.* We, as well as many others, have drawn attention to the daily stream of human beings from all corners of the Soviet Union—people of different races, often garbed in their national costumes—standing in line for hours to get a glimpse of the revered leader; in all respects similar to the pilgrims at world-renowned historic, religious shrines.

Another expression of this same social phenomenon is the adoration of Lenin which is not too different from the deification of god-figures in religious practice. In a prominent place in the rotunda of every public building—and you must remember that with the exception of apartment houses most buildings

---

* When we first observed this phenomenon, Lenin's and Stalin's bodies were both on view. Since then, Stalin's remains have been removed from the Mausoleum.

are public—is to be found a bust of Lenin. Almost without exception there is a spotlight playing on his head and face. Permanent decorations in the form of multicolored ribbons and artificial wreaths surround the base of the pedestal. Formal adoration ceremonies, in which children participate in groups, take place in front of these statues.

Love of country precludes loyalty to any other nation or group or ideology. It means loyalty to the regime, excluding all others. Some of the minority nationalities, who the regime still suspects may have interests or kinship beyond the Soviet orbit, pay a price. This is the only logic for the continuing discrimination against Armenians and Jews, as well as the Baltic peoples.

Love of country is not only an affirmative sentiment; it also involves hatred of the nation's enemies. The United States is still cast in the role of the principal enemy and the one fact about which everyone in the Soviet Union is still unanimous— and this includes people in varied walks of life with different educational backgrounds with whom we talked—is that we are planning war and seeking justifications for starting one.

Later in this book we will tell how the children are taught very early in their ideological "catechisms"—oaths of loyalty— to love their country and *hate* its enemies.*

C. PUNISHMENT, REPRESSION AND FEAR

In the report of our first visit to the Soviet Union we spoke of fear as an ever-present reality of Soviet life, and we considered it one of the most important determinants of social behavior.** While its extent and depth may have lessened since the death of Stalin, there is no doubt that it still remains one of the most important forces, if not *the* most important, in shaping human personality and behavior in the U.S.S.R. We also

---

* See Chapter 9.
** Alts, *op. cit.*

believe that fear is more pervasive and deeper in its impact there than in most other civilized nations.

The range of prohibited and punishable behavior is without doubt more extensive in the Soviet Union than in Western countries. Not only does the criminal law provide punishment for the usual types of criminal offenses, but aspects of living which are regulated only by public opinion in other countries are explicitly prohibited by law in the U.S.S.R. Recent decrees dealing with idlers, petty hooligans, and persons appearing drunk in public places are an example of this.*

Manifold regulatory provisions are built into the work situation so that there are extensive schedules of penalties for being late to work, breaking machinery, etc.

It is not in our province to describe the far-flung and complicated apparatus which the Soviet regime has established to impose its policies upon the individual, to punish dissidence and disobedience. Nor do we propose to detail the operations of the law enforcement agencies, the activities of the secret police (MVD), the labor camps, the practice of transportation to remote parts of the Soviet Union. Such measures presumably have played a diminishing role in achieving conformity since the death of Stalin, and it is more pertinent to the basic purpose of this book to describe fear as we encountered it in our talks with people we met and in our observation of their behavior.

The American visitor to the Soviet Union encounters manifestations of fear at every turn. Whether this is a residue of response to the repressive measures enforced during the Stalinist regime, some of which no longer exist, or a reaction to measures now in force, most Russians are still fearful of fraternizing with Americans. The ones who are willing to come to see you at your hotel are either highly placed officials, and therefore more secure than the ordinary citizen, or a few more venture-

* See Chapter 5.

some than the average. Very few Soviet citizens will invite Americans to their homes.

On our last visit we had a good deal to do with a mature Russian woman—a senior official. She was very friendly to us on a personal level, reached out to learn about our way of life, and in many different ways displayed great personal warmth. Alone with us she seemed very comfortable, shared many of our views about family life and child care, and we developed a sense of mutual trust and confidence. It came as a shock to us, therefore, to find that when one of her superiors walked into her office while we were present her face and manner immediately displayed a great deal of anxiety and fear. We could only conclude that warm trustful relationships with Americans were still suspect.

We found on this visit, as we had earlier, that an official would be friendly and generous in talking to us about his work and in arranging visits to establishments under his direction. But any inquiry about matters falling within the purview of a colleague who might be the head of another department set off a reaction of obvious discomfort. This was frequently accompanied by an appeal to be relieved of any involvement in matters outside of his immediate jurisdiction and the suggestion that we present our request to Intourist.

The way in which fear is expressed in the behavior of the individual citizen has been almost universally reported by every visitor to the Soviet Union, and will be more fully discussed in a later chapter when we consider Soviet personality.*

The plight of the Jews in the U.S.S.R. illustrates the reliance on fear to achieve compliance. In this instance it takes the form of social discrimination amounting to persecution, and remains one of the gross contradictions between the vision of the ideal society and the actual form it has taken on the road to its realization.

---

* See Chapter 4.

Khrushchev's own confusion about the place of the Jew in the Soviet Union is well-illustrated in his interview with Serge Groussard, which appeared in *Le Figaro,* April 9, 1958:

. . . What is the explanation of this unhappy phenomenon [failure of Jewish colonization in Birobidjan]? In my opinion, it is to be found in historical conditions. In all ages the Jews have preferred the artisan trades: They are tailors; they work in glass or precious stones; they are merchants, pharmacists, cabinet makers. But if you take the building trades or metallurgy, you can't find a single Jew, to my knowledge. They don't like collective work, group discipline. They have always preferred to be dispersed. They are individualists. . . .

. . . The Jews are essentially intellectuals. They never consider themselves sufficiently educated. As soon as they can manage it, they want to attend the university. . . .

. . . The Jews are interested in everything, probe deeply into everything, debate everything and end by having profoundly different opinions. . . . *

For obvious reasons—the most tangible being that we ourselves are Jews—we were in a position to gather more information about special attitudes toward Jews in the U.S.S.R. than other phenomena of the same character. Some facts are incontrovertible; one is the irrational persecution of Jews in the last days of the Stalin regime, which took the form of deportation, loss of jobs, and murder. While the situation has improved since the death of Stalin, and many of the extreme expressions of anti-Semitism seem to have moderated, discrimination still remains as one of the punitive elements in the social scene. What is difficult to determine is how far the fear that we found besets almost all the Jews we talked to is still a residue of the Stalin era and how much of it is a consequence of present policies.

---

* Reprinted in *The New Leader,* A Report by the Editors, Special Issue, September 14, 1959. Page 8.

Anti-Semitism in the Soviet Union may have multiple roots, and no doubt some of it is an extension of the attitudes prevalent during the czarist regime. It does derive rationale, however, from the insistence of the present regime on undivided loyalties. And since it is presumed that Jews have some sense of kinship and identity with Jews in other nations, they have been branded as "cosmopolitans," and are suspect as not totally identified with the aims of the regime.

A universal expression of discrimination as well as an instrument in perpetuating it is the designation of "Jew" in the space for nationality on the internal passport or identification card that every individual must carry. While it is true that the passports of all members of the nationalities that constitute the U.S.S.R. likewise indicate the nationality of the bearer, the difference is that in the case of the Jews, they do not occupy a territory of their own. Moreover, expressions of their cultural heritage have almost entirely been restricted. Therefore, in their case there would seem no rationale for their identification as Jews. It only serves as an instrument for discrimination. We were told that on all employment application forms Question #6 is: "What nationality are you?" and if the applicant writes "Jew" he may not get a job.

On our first visit we learned much about the plight of the Jews in the Soviet Union; how many of them had been downgraded in their trades and professions; how they met discrimination in many of their personal relationships.

It is true that Jews still occupy important places in the professional life of the nation. This includes the fields of medicine, teaching, engineering and science. On our way into the Soviet Union we met the wife of a top official of the Institute of Nuclear Energy, a Polish Jew. We also learned that one-fourth of the inventors who had recently received Lenin Prizes were Jews. But it is well-established that even today Jews are not appointed to important posts in government or the professional fields, although where they have held such posts, they are allowed to keep them.* Then, too, while there is no proof of this fact, it is generally understood that there are quotas for admission of Jewish students to institutions of higher learning.

What is indisputable is the presence of great fear among the Jews still living in the U.S.S.R. Discrimination has had one result opposite to what it was intended to achieve. Inevitably, it has brought greater consciousness on the part of Jews of their own identity and their kinship with other Jews. Many told us that a large proportion of the Jews in the Soviet Union would be willing to migrate to Israel if the doors were open to permit them to leave. We encountered many other expressions of this identification.

One of our most dramatic interviews was with a 61-year-old Jewish professional whom we met while sitting on a bench at a resort city.

He told us that he had worked at his profession up to the age of 58; then he was retired because of disability—a facial paralysis.

He said that he had suffered much because he had remained a dissenter. "If you speak openly, you sit." ("Sit" in this context means "You are imprisoned.")

This man showed more evidence of fear than anyone we spoke to. He often used the Yiddish word *mereh* (fear); as we sat talking together he would turn around every minute to see if anyone was coming, and if someone was approaching, he would stop talking. Later he asked that we move to a more secluded place under the nearby trees, but he continued to look around, and he would ask every few moments: "Do you see anyone coming?" As did many others, he told us how Jews were culturally deprived and vocationally discriminated against. He too referred to Question #6 on the application blank. It is

---

* Since this was written Benjamin Dymshits, a Jew, was appointed supreme dictator of the Soviet economy.

the Jews who have more to fear than others because they remain a group with some sense of kinship and tend to express themselves more openly to each other.

This man clung to us as if we were messengers from a world of kindness and generosity. At the same time, this did not dissipate his fear. When we had to leave him to check on something at the hotel and said we would return in five minutes, he agreed to wait. When we came back, he was not there.

D. SOCIAL PRESSURES

We can think of social pressures as embodying all the forces, negative and positive, which condition individual and group behavior and interpersonal relations in the Soviet social order. This would include fear and punishment, honors and rewards, commendation and criticism. However, we are disposed to use the term in a more limited way to describe a set of special devices and media utilized in the Soviet Union perhaps more than in any other nation. In all countries the individual is exposed to public opinion, to the opinion of his fellows in his church, his lodge, in his political club, and even in the bar. With growth in mass communication, he is also subjected to the influence of popular notions of good taste and good form as well as social responsibility.

The differences in the way social pressure is exerted in the Soviet Union lie in the relative uniformity of ideas and in the intensity of the indoctrination process. The Russians have created and are actively utilizing in a planful way many media for exerting pressure on the individual to comply with the declared purpose of the regime. To this end there has been developed a tight interlocking transmission apparatus moving from the central government down to the plant and collective farm, to the tenants' association in the apartment building, to the sports club, to the political organizations for children, youths and adults.

As we will see in later chapters, the elements in this process are identical with the ingredients of "collective education" as incorporated into the student organization in the school and into the Pioneer and Komsomol circles.

In the report of our first visit we designated an important dimension of the process of social pressure in the U.S.S.R. as a combination of mutual aid and surveillance. We believe that its force in maintaining and establishing social control of individual and group behavior may be equal to that of the penalties embodied in the criminal law.

What we have learned since then entirely confirms our previous impressions. While we have not gleaned anything different, we have gained a more realistic sense of the process itself than we had before—its greater intricacy, comprehensiveness and impact. We have come to understand more fully the use of various devices for transmitting pressure both in general community life and within the educational organization itself. Thus, in the apartment building sanitary committees are established which regularly inspect the apartments and make sure that acceptable standards of decency and cleanliness are maintained. The comrades' court, which may be established by the tenants' organization, may be convened to try a mother who neglects her child.

Within the organization of educational and other children's activities we became familiar with various devices for exerting influence upon the child in the classroom, in the Pioneer organization, in the club—the use of *aktiv* pupils to spur lagging students, to act as *starshi,* or monitors, to enforce discipline and report violation of rules or misconduct, and to mobilize approval of conformity and disapproval of deviation.

We will consider these methods of conditioning individual behavior as they are embodied in educational theory and practice when we address ourselves to the social interaction within the family and the school and the children's political organizations. At this point we will limit ourselves to examples of this process as it involves all human beings, and particularly adults.

On one occasion we spent the greater part of a day with the chairman of the tenants' committee of a large apartment building. She was the wife of a physician, had no children of her own, did no remunerative work, and devoted most of her time to her duties as chairman of the committee. The vice-chairman of this committee was a retired railroad conductor living on a pension. He explained to us that the committee busied itself with efforts designed to raise the level of public and private behavior, as well as to increase mutual aid activities on the part of the tenants. These efforts include such matters as the maintenance of a high standard of upkeep of the apartment building itself and participation by the tenants in the *Agit* center located in the building; the care and supervision of children while their mothers are at work; the provision of emergency first-aid and home-nursing. It is important to point out, however, that running through all these mutual aid activities is a thread of moral discipline which may extend as far as referral to the comrades' court.

The same pattern of organization exists in the factories, where there are many employee committees. Service on these committees is not entirely voluntary, but represents response to many pressures from management and the party.

The factory committees may, on the one hand, be engaged in such things as operating the cafeteria, acting as sponsors of the orphanage, the residential or day care centers for preschool children; or they may be concerned with necessary safety measures and the elimination of accidents; and they may also carry the duty of visiting any member who reports himself ill. The nature of this two-pronged interest in both mutual aid and surveillance is illustrated by the fact that the visitor to the sick employee has two major concerns—one, to see if the family is in need of groceries or medical care; the other, to ascertain whether the member who has reported himself as sick is actually ill or is just malingering.

The reliance upon social pressure as a form of social control, and more recently as a substitute for legal measures, seems to be growing in the Soviet Union. Interestingly enough, it is theoretically and logically associated with the concept of the "withering away of the state." It takes the form of an extension of the use of "volunteer" citizen organizations to achieve social control in various areas of life. We have already cited the tenants' committees, the large number and variety of union committees and employee groups in the industrial plants.

In line with this newer policy, the number of these volunteer groups, as well as their authority and the areas of life over which they are to have supervision, are being extended. One example is the youth brigades which were organized about three years ago to help control delinquency among youth—what the Soviets call "hooliganism." These youth brigades, working in close co-operation with the police, patrol the streets, arrest any young people suspected of hooliganism, and turn them over to the police. The brigades are made up of Komsomol members and this volunteer police function is one of the Komsomol activities. More recently, the theory behind the youth brigade and the utilization of this kind of organization to deal with conduct in the twilight area between nonconformity and actual violation of the law was discussed at great length in one of the Soviet journals. The writer argued that clothing the average citizen with a greater degree of responsibility for enforcement of socially acceptable standards, including enforcement of certain laws, could be seen as a step toward the reduction of the area of governmental activities. One could very well question whether this represented any true beginning of the "withering away of the state," or whether it was not really the opposite —the extension of state authority into the more intimate aspects of the average citizen's life.

This phenomenon of mutual aid and surveillance which is a focal expression of the whole system of social pressure, must be a source of great anxiety to the individual. How does it feel to know that the man working next to you in the plant is also watching you and possibly reporting your behavior to the committee, or political cell? How does it feel to realize that the neighbor in the apartment next door is in a position to visit your apartment to see if you keep it as clean as it should be kept, if your garbage can is properly covered? How does it feel to know that your next-door neighbor has the right to pass judgment upon your methods of rearing your child?

Privacy, as we know it, is practically nonexistent in the Soviet Union. For the time being the lack of privacy is intensified by the overcrowded living quarters. Though this may be remedied as the general housing situation improves, what will remain, however, is the attitude that has been established, and is constantly reinforced, which holds that each individual has the responsibility to judge his neighbor, his co-worker, his fellow-student, his friends as to their loyalty, their social conformity, their social contribution, and this extends even to the relationship between parent and child. The anxiety that this engenders —expressed in various forms of deception, evasion and concealment and the inevitable distortions of personality—can hardly be measured.

Any consideration of the underlying assumptions of this system of social control leaves us with many questions about individual rights and individual expression, individualism balanced against social conformity, restriction and surveillance. How much individual expression is compatible with the system of control we have described?

If we sample the general run of contemporary Russian fiction, or the formal discussions of social relations which appear in the Russian press and magazines, we are left with a concept of individualism different in many respects from our own. There is little open talk of the individual and individualism, a great deal more of social responsibility and socially approved behavior. The rights of the state are elementary and absolute. The state is all-powerful. In contrast to Western political philosophy, the individual does not delegate rights to the state; it is the state which defines the rights of the individual and protects him. "Individualism" is often used as a term connoting disapproval and is equated with deviation.

In many contemporary Russian novels the protagonist who stands out as a leader, and therefore as an individual, is usually depicted as one imbued with the highest social ideals, who devotes his life to the perfection of some machine or technological process which will improve the lot of mankind or advance the goals of the party or the state. He may be depicted as struggling against great odds and overcoming great obstacles, even as fighting bureaucracy. But there are few characters in novels written in recent decades who are portrayed as individuals displaying psychological discomfort in complying with group pressures or removing themselves from group participation. In different ways they are heroes in the struggle to achieve communism. The Kremlin's violent disapproval of *Dr. Zhivago, The Trial Begins,* and similar writings of dissent published only outside the U.S.S.R., makes clear the official fear of portraying characters who dare to be different. It would be inaccurate, however, to assume that this is a true picture of the psychology of the Russian people. The scant reference to psychological discomfort in fiction and in other portrayals of Russian life—which reflects official policy—does not necessarily mean its absence from the life of the population.*

It may be worth recalling our conversation with a leading Soviet child psychiatrist during which we pointed out the

---

* Psychological issues occupy a more important place in poems, stories and novels appearing in the early months of 1963; although most of these appeared without the open sanction of the regime, publication was permitted. However, in May of 1963, Khrushchev condemned such works as "deviations from socialist realism."

differences between our view of the individual and that which prevails in the Soviet Union. The professor agreed that there was a real difference. But while we are preoccupied with the self-realization of the individual, with the release of his potentialities for living as almost an end in itself, and while we stress the uniqueness of individual development as having great spiritual value, she pointed out that in the Soviet Union they are interested in the development of individual talents for social ends. While they believe in the fullest release of the psychological energy of the individual, she emphasized, this is to be directed toward socialist purposes.

The discussions of educational theory and practice appearing in technical journals reveal a growing concern for safeguarding the autonomy of the individual. But this is still stressed as a means of fostering creativity. Moreover, this concern is far outweighed by the concern of leading educators over manifestations of individual behavior which do not advance social purposes.

Although one might well characterize Khrushchev as an individualist, no concern for individual rights or autonomy is evident in any of his pronouncements. This is illustrated in a detailed report of a conversation he had with the villagers while on a visit back to his own village in Belorussia. His tone is that of a nobleman-landowner telling his serfs in a kindly way what they should do, or of an adult talking to young children. He praises them and scolds them patronizingly: "You have done well." "You should do this, or that." They should use their "indivisible fund"—the end-of-the-year surplus—to build a creche, a boarding school, a home for the aged, etc. Never is there an inkling that he cares about what *they* might want.

In an article by an economist on bringing more women into the labor force, the writer never questions whether women will rejoice or be unhappy about giving up the care of their children and becoming industrial workers rather than housekeepers. He limits himself to two desiderata: more women in the labor force;

more children in the boarding schools. To this writer, the individual woman is an instrument for production.

In certain areas of life we are beginning to get some cracks
and air vents in ideological thinking, and increasingly the Soviet
Union seems to be on the way to a more realistic approach,
taking into account human values as well as national purpose.
Our discussion of the Soviet family shows the growing recognition that stringent divorce laws, tantamount to prohibition, have
resulted in the separation of husbands and wives and the breakup
of families, as well as an increase in illegitimacy. In many other
areas of Soviet life we will see steps being taken to afford the
individual more opportunities for self-assertion and greater
Lebensraum.

We will see that within the educational sphere individualism
is being reborn in the concern for creativity and teaching the
child to think. We will also see in our projection of Russian
character traits that individualism continues to break through
in spite of restrictive ideology.

It would be pertinent to consider how the basic principles
of control we have described are translated into the guidance
of all aspects of human endeavor—in the arts, in literature and
sciences, and in religion itself. Suffice it at this point to reiterate
that all human endeavors remain tools for the furtherance of
broad national purpose and specifically defined goals for each
area of activity, and this applies equally to the arts as well as
the sciences. Art, as any other human expression, must advance
the basic purpose of the state. The result of this thesis is social
realism. All the arts must be the handmaidens of official doctrine. Consistent with this thesis, the contemporary painting
one sees displayed almost exclusively is in the form of posters,
propagandist in subject matter, intended to glorify and advance
the immediate purposes of the regime. While music, to some
degree, is an exception, even here much that is outstanding in
musical composition is, in the main, the product of men whose

artistic roots, as well as personal experience, go back to pre-revolutionary or early revolutionary days.

As this book was being completed, a battle for greater freedom for individual expression in art and literature seems to have been launched by a growing group of writers, and it is generally agreed that there has been some relaxation of the control of the arts. However, there apparently has been no basic change in the ideological point of view about the place of the arts as a tool in national policy. The advance to greater freedom is still characterized by many reversals, contradictions and compromises. This is well-illustrated in the conclusion of an interview which Ilya Ehrenburg gave to the correspondent of the *Literatura i zhizn:*

The writer can derive inspiration from the construction of a mammoth dam and from a child's first sorrow, from all the thoughts, feelings and works of Soviet people.*

And Khrushchev asks, for example, whether one can

. . . imagine an organized human society without community norms and rules binding upon all its members? If each person were to insist upon foisting his subjective concepts, his personal tastes and ways upon everybody as obligatory, life in such a society would be simply unbearable and would resemble the tower of Babel.**

Khrushchev holds that since the party ideology is identical with mankind's noblest ideals, there is no conflict between the views and aspirations of the writer and those of the party. The two are in harmony and therefore the writer has the only kind of freedom that any creative person should have.

---

* "The Canons of Art." *The Current Digest of the Soviet Press,* Volume XI, Number 37, October 14, 1959. © Pages 28-29.

** *The Current Digest,* Vol. XIII, No. 17, May 24, 1961, *op. cit.* Page 5.

He goes on to say

First of all, to be of the Party in artistic creation means to dedicate oneself, one's efforts, one's talent to the great cause of the struggle for communism, for carrying out the policy of the Communist Party, and consequently the cause of the people. This is the essence of the matter, . . . *

---

* *Ibid.*

Chapter 3

The Fruits of the System I

WHAT ARE SOME of the fruits of the Soviet system of social control we have described? How are unequal rewards, propaganda, coercion, social pressures, reflected in individual and group behavior, in traits of personality and character structure?

From the standpoint of this book, more specific questions are: How far does the average person exemplify in his attitudes, behavior, modes of thought, the attributes of the idealized Soviet man? Or how far does he remain unregenerate, like the bulk of humanity? What clues point to contentment, to self-fulfillment, or to personal discomfort, to protest, to disharmony and conflict?

In describing the results of this system in psychological terms, we must ask ourselves how successful the new system has been in terms of both the short-range and long-term goals which constitute its rationale and justification, the building of resources necessary for civilized living in a contemporary world and, ultimately, the establishment of a communist society. And to the extent that it has been successful, what price has had to be paid in terms of human values and in the character of the social order which is taking shape?

Obviously answers will be hard to come by. Who can determine with any precision whether the Soviet system is producing a new kind of man, one whose behavior is differently motivated and which reflects a new balance between egotism and self-interest on the one hand and altruism and the common welfare on the other?

Measurement in the psychological field is still an uncertain undertaking. Thus, it would be difficult to establish with certainty the connection between coercion and individual and mass behavior, or distinguish between selfish and altruistic motivation. At the point where the individual acts, these opposites may have already become one, and neither that individual nor anyone else can separate them. The middle-aged childless wife of the doctor who serves as volunteer chairman of the tenants' committee is engaged in a socially useful effort, but undoubtedly enjoys the status as well as the other privileges this function yields. The same might be said of the intelligent, articulate adolescents on the collective farms who write letters to the newspapers criticizing their colleagues who leave the collectives for life in the city.

Whether the motivation be self-interest or the common welfare, or a mixture of both, there is no doubt that the Russian has been spurred to self-improvement and acquisition of skills, so that in 45 years the U.S.S.R. has progressed from the status of a backward nation, industrially and educationally, to one that has substantially achieved the requisites of civilized living as these are understood in Western Europe. It has been able to create an industrial establishment with a progressively increasing output, and with a potential for continued liberalization of the standard of living; an educational system that has produced a comparatively large number of professionals—scientists and administrators—a number almost sufficient to the present needs of the nation; a system of social security and health protection as comprehensive as any in the civilized world; and finally, a position of strength among nations.

We do not know what price for these achievements has been exacted by the terror—its toll in human suffering, total destruction and denial of freedom. We know that repression and coercion have played an important part. No one knows, including the Soviet leaders, how far continued progress in realization of their goals will be possible without continued resort to punitive measures.

We do know that the appeal to self-interest has resulted in a class system, class consciousness and inequality; that there is also much evidence to show that it has resulted in a struggle to "get what you can" and readiness to exploit any avenues—both the weakness and the greed of others.

We know too that the Russians themselves are deeply disturbed at what they consider expressions of individualism and egotism and their failure to achieve more fully the kind of character structure which they have identified with the Soviet man.

There is no indication, however, that those in authority entertain the possibility of any less reliance on the appeal to self-interest. Mr. Khrushchev publicly affirmed this in a speech in Moldavia a few years ago which was published verbatim in the Soviet press. He was reporting on Governor Averell Harriman's surprise when on a visit to a Soviet reformatory he found that the prison inmates were being paid for their work. Commenting on Mr. Harriman's reaction, Mr. Khrushchev said: "We have long learned that slaves do not produce. Neither persuasion nor coercion alone, it seems, is as effective as coercion combined with self-interest." And as we have seen, while the Russians insist that in the ideal society which they envision self-interest and the common welfare will be identical, this has obviously not yet been realized. An incentive plan inaugurated late in 1962 carries beyond anything in the past the principle of extraordinary compensation for an extraordinary measure of production. In fact, the American press has hailed this step as an introduction of the profit system. Although the increased compensation under this plan would go to the enterprise rather than to the individual, indirectly the individual would benefit because the employee's share would ultimately be greater.

Before proceeding with a more detailed account of the fruits of the system as these have been institutionalized in certain features of community life and incorporated into personality and character structure, it seems in order to draw attention to some of the problems involved in any assessment of results of social change which takes place on a vast scale.

It is difficult to assess whether the amount of change is sufficient relative to the price paid, or whether the rate of progress is in keeping with the economic and social situation that existed at the beginning of the period in which the changes being measured occurred. In assessing the progress the Soviet Union has made, we must not forget that prerevolutionary Russia had already built the foundations for an industrial society; and one might assume that considerable advancement might have taken place in the past 45 years even if no revolution had taken place.

In other words, one needs to take account of the rate of movement from one level to another—the denominator of time. Given natural resources and manpower, and a certain measure of physical vigor and technological skill in the population, has the progress in the Soviet economy been greater than it might have been under other kinds of economic organization and incentive systems which exact less toll in human suffering?

A. RESOURCES FOR SURVIVAL

Since Sputnik, Soviet achievements and technological progress in building an impressive defense establishment and industrial machine producing both capital and consumer goods, an improving level of social services, as well as manifold cultural amenities, are achieving widespread acknowledgment throughout the world. There is a growing acceptance of the Soviet claim that it will soon outstrip all other nations in lifting universal standards of living. This is cited as proof that the Soviet system of social control, economic planning and administrative process is superior to all others. The exception to this achievement is the comparative lack of success in the agricultural sector of the economy which has remained a mixture of collective and private enterprise, with the worker being both wage earner and entrepreneur.

While evaluation of economic phenomena is beyond our special area of competence, we cannot bypass consideration of the economic situation because, as we have already pointed out, in Soviet ideology it constitutes the foundation of the social order, and all aspects of the common life and individual behavior are shaped by and toward economic facts. It may be said to be "the proof of the pudding" of the Soviet system in the current phase of its evolution.

We find there is a consensus, not only in statements by the Russians themselves but authorities from other countries, that there has been a general improvement in standards of living in the past decades. The supply of food has increased since Stalin's death and the Soviet housewife is now likely to find a more adequate supply in the shops. Clothing, too, is not as scarce as it had been. The stores that carry what might be considered luxury goods—shirts, ties, leather bags, suitcases, etc.— appeared to have much more stock in 1959 than they did in 1956. At the same time, while up to the 1963 crop failure bread was plentiful and cheap, the price of meat and butter has always been extraordinarily high in relation to the average earnings, and the same has been true of clothing and shoes.* It is not clear how far real wages—the equation between money earnings and prices—have increased in the last decade. We know that in spite of inequality in wages and other factors which make for wider differentials in the standard of living, for the vast majority it remains meager and constricted.

Even though most students of Soviet life agree that the foundations for a productive economy have been established, and that it is likely to yield progressively improved standards of living, there is not basic agreement among these authorities that more progress might not have been achieved under another system

---

* See Chapter 8.

functioning in a different social order, relying on different incentives for individual effort.

Some authorities contend that given the level of prerevolutionary economic and social development, more might have been achieved in the last four decades under a different system, and perhaps at less human cost. They point to the fact that by 1917 Russia had already established the foundations for universal education and professional and technological training. In addition, Russia was and is a nation extraordinarily endowed with natural resources and with a great reservoir of manpower.

Moreover, this contention gains support from the fact that implementation of Soviet economic objectives reveals the same duality of purpose as in other aspects of organized life. Progress in the economic area is often utilized to further noneconomic objectives: the strengthening of party control, the reward for party loyalty. Too, priority among national goals determines the allocation of the fruits of the increased industrial production, whether it be for guns or butter.

We are not in a position to assess how far the economic master plans and the bureaucratic superstructure required to implement them interfere with efficiency; to what extent defects in the character of the industrial managers, as well as the system of bonuses, are limiting factors.

Observers cite many instances to illustrate how factors extraneous to the basic goal have interfered with the building of a balanced economy. Thus, the declared intention of the regime to increase the supply of consumer goods has had to be set aside or seriously modified because of the need to provide help to the satellite countries, to divert energy for achievements in space technology or for more military equipment. The result is that the production of consumer goods is accorded a lower priority.

A recent published appraisal of progress in housing is another example of the extent to which noneconomic considerations influence economic activities.* The author feels that special objectives—"strengthening the controls of the Communist Party, and shaping the contours of Soviet society according to party blueprints"—have significantly handicapped the housing program, citing allocation as well as management of new housing.

Living space, as previously reported, is allocated as a reward for real or presumed service to the state, i.e., for excellence in production. Party membership or influence are other vital factors in determining the amount and quality of the housing assigned.

The personnel selected to manage public housing has been of low quality. The more able individuals are not attracted to the field because it has held such relatively low priority for many years. Even more serious, from the standpoint of efficient management, is the kind of responsibilities assigned to housing managers. From the beginning of the revolution, the Communist party has relied heavily on them for political surveillance of the population and their appointment has always been subject to police approval. Many of their duties are of a police character. Reporting on the activities of all tenants and their visitors takes up a sizable proportion of the time and energy of the housing manager.

Since it is part of our thesis that the psychological and human situation in the U.S.S.R. will be influenced by the degree of economic and technological progress that has been achieved both as an end in itself and as the basis for national security, it is pertinent to take a look ahead. We are warranted in two assumptions, both of which are grounded in a conviction that the industrial base of the country has been well established— that dire scarcity and drastic rationing of materials no longer exist or are likely to recur, that the extreme shortage of skilled personnel is fast disappearing and is being replaced by a supply

---

* "Non-Housing Objectives of Soviet Housing Policy." Alexander S. Balinsky. *Problems of Communism,* Vol. X, No. 4, Jul.-Aug. 1961.

of workers of competence and experience at all levels and that in place of confusion and contradiction there is a relatively stable system of communication and command.*

The two assumptions are that the occupational environment in the Soviet Union is being materially changed and that the distinctive features of the Soviet occupational setting will take on more and more the general characteristics of modern industrial society; and these two changes may have major consequences for the whole tone of occupational life in the Soviet Union and hence for the social system at large. The Soviet factory and large-scale farm will have substantially the same structure of authority relations as the large factory or farm in Europe or the United States.**

The consequence of the economic progress achieved to date is predictable. Since its "tempo" (as Inkeles and Bauer call it) —the stringency of the labor discipline and frequency of arrest for violation, the heavy emphasis on unusual devices such as Stakhanovism to raise labor productivity—will have disappeared, there is likely to be less fear and more freedom for initiative, experiment and innovation.

These optimistic projections, according to their authors, apply only to the industrial worker; they do not touch the worker on the collective farm, which remains a relatively unstable and only poorly integrated social and economic institution. As recently as November 1962, at a meeting of the Executive Committee of the Communist party, deep concern was expressed over the failure of agricultural production to meet the norms which had been set. The importance of greater attention and the deployment of more capital resources to this aspect of the Russian economy was emphasized.

Assuming that the regime can achieve its objective of converting the collective farm into a factory-like organization and

---

* Inkeles and Bauer, *op. cit.* Page 125.

** *Ibid.* Page 124.

the farmer into an industrial worker, assuming further that this will significantly strengthen the weakest part of the Soviet economy, it is difficult to predict how and when the other factors inherent in the economic structure and incentive system that hamper economic progress will have been minimized or eliminated. One may still safely predict that it will take decades before the supply of consumer goods is such that the hunger for material things is satisfied and the strong acquisitive and competitive drive of the Soviet population is seriously diminished.

B. Classes in a Classless Society

The growing social stratification in the Soviet Union in recent years can be seen as one of the inevitable consequences of the need to offer unequal incentives to achieve the economic and social progress which are the goals of the regime as embodied in its Five Year Plans and in its aspiration to outstrip the capitalist powers in standard of living and in general national achievements.

Yet ever since Stalin denounced "petty-bourgeois equalitarianism" there have been unmistakable signs of the emergence of a new social hierarchy:

Beginning with the reappearance of the felt Stetson hat in the thirties, the predictions of Orwell's *Animal Farm* began to take shape before the eyes of an astonished world. The abandonment of the principle, "from each according to his ability, to each according to his need" and the resultant growing disparity of incomes have led not only to a return of military epaulettes, academic rank, and bureaucratic titles, but to a widespread differentiation in the standard of living. Nor is income inequality the most significant aspect of the new situation. In the Soviet system, those in power combine the privileges of our politicians, business captains, trade-union organizers, and academicians. It is natural that such concentration of power should favor elitism.*

---

* "Class Tensions in Soviet Education," by George Z. F. Bereday (Pages 57-88) in Bereday & Pennar, *op. cit.* Pages 58-9.

Class stratification has become a basic and dynamic feature of the Soviet social order. This is particularly brought home when one visits a place like Sochi where the more favored groups come with their families to enjoy a holiday. They stayed at the same hotel we did, ate in the same dining room and lived at a relatively expensive level, far beyond the means of the average workingman, even the skilled ones, or the average teacher or white-collar worker.

We were also struck with the degree of class consciousness which seemed to prevail. This characterized the attitude not only of our guides, but of others we met. The unwillingness of one of our guides to have the chauffeur eat with us shows how far class consciousness influences social relationships. We had driven out from Sochi to Lake Ritza. This is a difficult drive which takes about four hours. The chauffeur was a very agreeable young man who was an excellent driver and who seemed very sensitive in his relationship with us. There were, altogether, five in our party: the driver, our guide, another American visitor and the two of us. When we walked into the dining room for lunch, we suggested that the chauffeur eat with us; there was a good deal of whispering between the guide and the chauffeur, and we were finally told that he was unwilling to eat with us.

Mr. B., the white-collar worker in whose home we spent a day, told us that he would not allow his wife to go to work because she had not finished her course at the Textile Institute and therefore had not achieved status as a skilled or semi-professional worker. The only thing she could do was sew, and a man in his position—he has a diploma as an economist and works as a journalist—could not have his wife engaged in such lowly work as sewing in a factory.

The existence of class consciousness is generally recognized. We were often told that the reason for the new educational program was the snobbishness of the budding intelligentsia and their distaste for common work. "You think I would go to school for eleven years and then drive a tractor?"

The possibility of moving into a higher class, with the privileges and status that this promises, is an important incentive for conformity, for increasing one's skills through education and for being as productive as possible.

To summarize some of the advantages that membership in one of the more privileged classes carries with it: In addition to higher wages, there is the right to a better apartment, access to special stores that serve only the more highly placed members of the Communist party and the upper level administrators, the greater chance of one's child being admitted to a professional school (almost two-thirds of the young people who succeeded in entering these schools have come from the favored classes).

An American observer told us that when he visited a Pioneer Palace in an outlying part of the country he was told that about 3,000 or 4,000 children would be using the clubs and activity rooms of this beautiful new building. "But," the American said, "there are thirty or forty thousand children in the age group who are Pioneers and thereby eligible." The explanation he got was: "Not all of them could be allowed to use this building." While the basis of selection is not clear, excellence in performance and deportment must obviously play a part. The class to which the parents belong must also be a factor. The chances of being admitted to a rest or vacation home are greater if you belong to the right class in the "classless" society.

Membership in the right class—and this includes certain strata of the Communist party—is tantamount to a guarantee of tenure in favored posts in spite of poor performance. Examples are cited in the Russian press of *apparatchiks* who continue to move from job to job but are never really demoted despite poor performance because it is assumed that a place has to be found for them. To a certain degree, the same applies to their offspring. In other words, class consciousness not only means an immobility hampering movement from a lower to an upper class, but also the reverse.

Since there is no status based upon hereditary rank or accumulated wealth—although there are some beginnings of both of these—most students of Soviet society agree that at present class hierarchy largely conforms to the occupational scale.* This scale does not include the aged and handicapped, nor does it in our opinion fully reflect class differentiation as this betokens privilege and well-being. For this reason we have constructed a class scale of our own which we believe reflects more completely the social and personal advantages and disadvantages of the total population.

The *first class* would be the rulers—often described as the elite: Khrushchev and his aides; the heads of the various governments in the republics; the members of the primary policy-making and implementation groups.

The *second class* would include the first line below the top— those who carry out policies as well as those who provide the extraordinary creative and technical skills which are indispensable to successful planning and execution. These would include not only the higher officials and technicians below the elite, but also artists, writers and scientists.

The *third class* might be described as the middle class; chief engineers, professors, heads of hospitals, heads of various second-line agencies.

All members of the first three classes would enjoy special privileges—higher incomes and general preferment as to housing, education for their children and travel.

The *fourth class* would consist of two occupational groups: the white-collar and the skilled worker. These would include teachers, some of the second level professors in the universities, doctors, and the large group called "engineers," many of whom are skilled

* See Page 77.

technicians rather than professionals. The earnings of those included in this class are much higher than the unskilled city worker or the farmer.

The *fifth class,* and this is the largest group, is what we have referred to as the "humble" or the "downtrodden." This is the group that used to be called the proletariat and which is still the proletariat. It includes women working on the roads, workers on the collective farms, the people we saw in the waiting rooms of the Central Communist party submitting petitions, or who, as relatives of the accused, fill the seats in the people's courts; and last, and least, those older and younger people with their air of submissiveness and hopelessness whom you see in the churches.

It should be noted that in the table on Page 77 the "professional-administrative" category cuts across our classes one, two and three, and only constituted 2 per cent of the population in 1939. While our class four includes three classes in the official scale—the semiprofessional, white-collar and skilled worker—our class five includes the last two categories plus others outside the occupational group, the older people and the handicapped.

Though the privileges that inhere in class status are beyond question, the issue still remains as to how membership in a particular class influences the chances of improving one's lot and status by moving into another class. Or, put in other words, will those born into the more favored families have an undue advantage or does the Soviet situation alter what is the usual pattern in other social orders and give the children of workers and peasants, the "humble or the downtrodden," an even chance to move to the top?

The Harvard project, which included an analysis of the occupational data of émigrés living in Western Europe and the U. S. whose fathers were adults in the Soviet Union in 1940, addressed itself to this question. The project established the connection between the father's occupation and the one which the son followed. The finding was that the young men, in the main, remained at approximately the same occupational level as their fathers. And wherever occupational mobility took place, the move was usually from one category to an adjacent one, that is, from semiprofessional to professional or vice versa, or from semiprofessional to white collar, and not from collective farmer to professional.*

An important finding was that, by and large, the same situation prevailed in the Soviet Union as in other countries. Children of professional fathers almost completely fill the available professional jobs. If only 2 per cent of the available jobs were in the professional category, assuming equal opportunity, then only 2 per cent of the children of professionals would in turn become professionals themselves. The sample studied by the Harvard project, however, indicated that two out of every three children, or 66 per cent, of those born to a professional father became professionals.

It is obvious that the ultimate occupational placement of a child, although not absolutely sealed at birth, was heavily determined by his father's position in the occupational structure. Two out of three male children born into a professional or administrator's home could count on attaining to the same level as their father did, whereas only one in twelve of the children of peasants could realistically have the hope of reaching the professional-administrative level. Less than one in five of the sons born into the favored homes was forced to toil with hands, whereas almost eight in ten of the peasant children earned their living in the "dirty, hot, and hard" jobs. We must repeat that this pattern developed in the face of an early social policy deliberately designed to turn the old social order upside down by selective encouragement of the mobility of the children of workers and peasants.**

---

* Inkeles and Bauer, *op. cit.* Page 81.

** *Ibid.* Page 83.

OCCUPATIONAL FATE OF SONS AGE 21-40 IN 1940 BY FATHER'S OCCUPATION*

Father's Occupation

Respondent's occupation	Professional administrative	Semi- professional	White- collar	Skilled worker	Ordinary worker	Peasant	Percentage of 1940 labor force
Professional-administrative	65%	47%	40%	26%	9%	8%	2%
Semiprofessional	8	27	14	17	6	6	4
White-collar	9	17	30	9	11	10	11
Skilled worker	7	0	4	25	16	15	33[a]
Ordinary worker	7	9	10	23	55	29	
Collective farmer	4	0	2	0	3	32	50
Total number of respondents	76	41	70	76	359	343	

a. Skilled and ordinary workers are combined in this figure.

* *Ibid.* Page 81.

In weighing the implications of the findings reported in the above citations, one must bear in mind that the situation has been rapidly changing in this decade. With an increasing rate of industrialization and a growing demand for skills, there is more room at the top. Taking this into account, however, there is still general agreement among students of Soviet society that the basic situation reported by Inkeles and Bauer remains.

With the death of Stalin the regime appears to have acknowledged the incongruity between the existence of the class structure and the more idealistic aspects of Soviet goals. There have been a number of efforts made to reduce class differences and achieve equalization.

In the early days of the revolution, drastic measures were taken to eliminate classes—the nobility, the more privileged intelligentsia, and, subsequently, the independent landowner. By the time Stalin came into power, the nobility had been forced to emigrate or had been driven under cover and had virtually disappeared as a privileged group. The same was true of the intelligentsia in the early days of the revolution. On the other hand, the practical problems of the administration of a country as large as Russia and the need to keep the wheels of industry moving forced the regime to turn more and more to the former intelligentsia to reassume a leadership position.

Efforts to stamp out the privileged classes came to an end when Stalin established the system of incentives which took into account the differential contributions of the individual. In the 25 years from Stalin's pronouncement affirming the necessity of unequal rewards until his death, the class system was undisturbed. The more recent efforts to reduce class stratification have taken many forms and have included an increase in the minimum wage, a reduction in the disparity between the wage of the rural and that of the city workers, as well as a reduction in the income of the more privileged groups—officials, top administrators—thus narrowing the gap between the extremes of the upper and lower rungs of the economic ladder.

Another group of measures is intended to upgrade the social condition and opportunities of the ordinary citizen. The discontinuance of fees for secondary education is one such measure, thus increasing the opportunity for education of children from poorer families. The new education program, with its requirement that all children do some manual work and with more emphasis on achievement and ability rather than on family background as the basis for admission to higher educational institutions, represents another such attempt.

Despite the measures aimed at reducing class stratification, there is a good deal of difference of opinion as to how far this represents a reversal in the basic trend and how far a natural readjustment reflecting less acute need on the part of the regime to buy the co-operation of the gifted and the able, as well as to harness the productive energies of the average person. The improved economic situation makes it also possible for the regime to improve the lot of the ordinary person without necessarily reducing the major effort to build capital resources—the tools of production and the weapons for defense.

Another consideration, which may be seen as a reaffirmation of the motivation that introduced inequality and which now seeks to reduce it, is the continued authority of the Communist party. It has been suggested that those individuals who wield power need to be curbed if the authority of the party is to be maintained; in other words, a balance between the party and those who serve it must be restored.

What is being done should redress the balance somewhat but does not necessarily mean the elimination of inequality as a reality of Soviet life. What a continued attack on inequality and positive efforts to bring about equalization will ultimately achieve is difficult to predict.

The Soviet experience over the past 45 years warrants this question: Can an industrial order which seeks to keep pace with growing scientific knowledge and technological skills dispense with special rewards for the effort needed to acquire such skills and technical knowledge?

Rewards and privileges inevitably create class differentiation and a class hierarchy. Moreover, inherent in class structure are forces which work for its perpetuation—special privilege at the top and social immobility at the bottom. The likelihood of class structure being seriously modified in the near future is slim in spite of equalitarian ideology.

Chapter 4

The Fruits of the System II

C. Images of Soviet Man

Is there any discernible connection between the demands and pressures to which the individual in the Soviet Union is subjected and any particular single or group of character traits which he displays? In what respects, if any, is he different from man in the West?

We are aware of the difficulties which beset any attempt to speak of personality or character traits as being more generally applicable to the members of a particular race or nation. Such efforts are always open to challenge; there is always the risk of projecting characteristics which are only true for a limited number of individuals as if they applied to everyone. Moreover, it is even more difficult to connect personality and character traits with any particular culture or social situation. We do not know how far personality qualities reflect biological endowment and instinctual needs and how far, cultural influences and life experience; how far specific traits are peripheral and transitory and how far, basic and fixed.

Furthermore, even when we identify certain qualities as more characteristic of the Soviet man than of men living under other social systems, we do not know how far these differences reflect the system of social control to which the individual is subjected and how far the heritage of Czarist Russia or more recent historic events, as for example, the social disorganization following the revolution and the Second World War. Thus, no one has studied the adults who were members of the bands of homeless children in the early 'twenties, or who were rendered parentless by the last war and lived for many years in children's institutions.

81

Recognizing the inconclusiveness of such impressions, we will attempt to bring together some of our own, as well as those of others, that highlight the differences in Soviet character traits from those in social orders where more individualism is sanctioned. We will try to gauge how far the Soviet ideal is realized in the character of present-day Soviet man.

On both our trips we saw people either in groups or individually in different parts of the country. Besides a number of the principal cities, we visited a collective as well as a state farm, and gained an impression of the lives of the people living there. We went to Sochi, a resort by the sea, and from there to Lake Ritza, another resort in the Georgian mountains. The visits to these resorts, which attract holiday-seekers from all parts of the country, enabled us to see members of the many nationality groups which comprise the peoples of the U.S.S.R.

We saw people in the church at Zagorsk as well as in other churches; we saw them on the highways, in the theaters, on the street; children and teachers in the schools; doctors in clinics; officials up to the rank of cabinet minister.

We encountered striking differences between various social strata—various levels of sophistication and self-assurance; we noted differences in the psychological mood of the population in the three-year interval between our two visits. As we watched the young people, particularly those of the more sophisticated, white-collar classes—including the students at Moscow University—we got a sense of more animation, more gaiety, more release of psychological energy. There was more conversation, and more life in the air.

When we came back to Moscow in May 1959 we were first struck with a new kind of girl elevator operators at the hotel. They were younger; they were more flashy in their use of cosmetics; they were flirtatious with the male guests. As a matter of fact, we were startled to see that there appeared to be less self-discipline and decorum among this group of young women than there would be in our own country under like circumstances.

The appearance of girls on Saturday nights at the National Hotel was much different than it used to be. Dresses were low-cut and revealing, excessive use of make-up was the mode. The young men, too, were better dressed than they had been. There was kissing in the hallways.

There was an eagerness about it all that made it seem pathetic compared to the attitude of our youngsters who take these freedoms for granted. We also noticed among this group of young people an extraordinary amount of drinking, even though many of them did not look more than 16 years old. A group of four couples, eight boys and girls, would "stash away" numerous bottles of wine, beer and vodka, and proudly exhibit the empty bottles on their table.

The adolescent girls one saw in the streets could no longer be described as "convent-bred" in their appearance. They did not all wear the same ribbons in their hair and the same little frocks, as they did on our first visit; there was much more individuality and variety in their dress. There was also more freedom shown in deportment on the streets by both boys and girls.

In sharp contrast to the scene in the hotel, we noticed on our trip to Zagorsk (seat of the monastery of the same name, about 40 miles from Moscow) a number of boys and girls on the roadways, girls in slacks, members of hiking groups, a great deal of naturalness and easiness in their manner, neither noisy nor overdecorous.

In still sharper contrast to the girl elevator operators and the girls in the hotel dining room on Saturday night are the women working on roads, not only cleaning streets in Moscow but also repairing roadways in the cities and the rural areas. What we noted on this visit, which had not been so clear before, was that these women were not all old, many young ones were engaged in this kind of work. Our impression was that some were girls not much more than 14 years old, and when we expressed surprise that girls so young were occupied in this way, our guide told us that these were youngsters who did not apply themselves in school.

To continue these impressions, the one that seemed most striking to us was the contrast between the more privileged with the simple people or the proletariat, those we have described as the humble and downtrodden. This class includes the women working on the roads, and the men and women taking part in religious ceremonies. It also includes the petitioners in the office of the president of the Soviet Union and the Central Committee of the Communist party, requesting redress of grievances of many kinds: denial of claims to pensions, housing, etc. Then there are also those whom we saw on the benches in the *prejom* of the Ministry of Internal Affairs, pleading for the right to visit their youngsters in youth colonies or asking for advice about a young daughter who runs away, or is incorrigible, or keeps undesirable company, as well as the relatives we saw in the people's court where four men were being tried for stealing a coat, selling it and using the proceeds to buy liquor.

These people all looked different and behaved differently from the officials we met, and from the people we saw in the hotels and theaters. The women in the less privileged groups were simply dressed; they used no make-up, wore no modern hairdos; there was less laughter and the general demeanor was one of anxiety and submission.

The impressions just recorded should be contrasted with our impressions of the holiday crowd at Sochi which seemed more individualistic in manner, even though its members still presumably follow the ideological line which stresses the duty to rest rather than play in order to strengthen one's health. The clothes of the men and women were more individual, more colorful and of somewhat better quality. These people could afford the same dinners in the hotel that we ourselves had; they danced energetically and with pleasure; they participated in the

competitions for prizes that were staged by the hotel in order
to attract more diners.

Here we encountered a number of people whom we dubbed
"individualists." The one we called the "troubadour" was an
operatic tenor who lived in Sochi and made his living by singing at local concerts and at the various sanatoria. Here, too, we
met the young woman he introduced as his "wife and not his
wife," while pinching her hips. She was a nurse in one of the
sanatoria. In Sochi we also met a sculptor from Odessa, with
his two young children and his wife, who announced that he
was self-employed and his earnings were his own, although to
be allowed to operate this way he had to belong to an artists'
cartel. He added that he was a "free man."

Here, too, we met our guide Nadja, who came to embody
for us the freest expression of individualism we encountered
on our visit, and whom we will describe more fully later in this
chapter.

It was at Sochi that we met a rebel spirit from among the
simpler people. He was an agronomist on a state farm and
was in charge of the greenhouses. When he told us that he
received a bonus at the end of the year of 300 or 400 rubles
if his hothouses fulfilled their quota according to the plan, we
asked him what he did with the money. Holding up one hand
as if pouring the contents of a bottle down his throat, he said
he took a trip to Moscow and bought a lot of vodka.

Here, too, sitting on a bench we met the prototype of the
old-line Communist party member. She was a retired schoolteacher who had taught English and French. She could admit
nothing wrong in the Russian scene and was the perfect apolo-
gist for the rightness of all the accepted ideology and practice.
"The [Russian] children have been given too much freedom
and need to be held to stricter account. They will never grow
up properly unless their care is taken away from the parents
and put in the hands of professionals." She was so uncompromising in this view that we were finally prompted to ask

her "since parents did such a poor job, perhaps they should be forbidden to have any children at all?" She had no answer for this.

As we proceed with our impressions of personality traits in the Soviet Union it will become clear that some are the product of the influences embedded in the Soviet view of life, its social order and child-rearing and educational arrangements, while others reflect the persistence of basic human drives and motivations. Without discounting the importance for the future of the result of Soviet methods of controlling behavior and shaping personality, on balance we believe the Russian has remained very much as he was before the revolution and very much like the inhabitants of the Western world.

The taxi driver in Moscow, with whom we sat in the front seat, does not restrain his natural curiosity about life in the United States. He wants to know how much we earn, the kind of house we live in, what our family is like, the opportunities our children enjoy, and then goes on to check some of the things he has read in his newspaper or heard in lectures about the United States: its intentions with respect to peace or war, etc. He proceeds to discuss some of Khrushchev's latest pronouncements and does not hesitate to express his opinion on subjects where he differs with him.

The porter at the Ukraine Hotel in Moscow appeared untouched by all the preachments of good form and was as ungracious as ungracious people are everywhere. He took our suitcases on his handcart from our room down the front steps of the hotel where our car was waiting. When he put them in the car we handed him a tip.

The practice with regard to tipping had changed between the time of our first and second visits. During our visit in 1956, most of the waiters refused to accept tips. The old waiter (a relic of czarist days) who brought our breakfast to our room always took a tip, the amount he received being about what a waiter would get in our country for such services. On our second visit we had noticed in the dining room that tips were generally being accepted, especially if one bought vodka and paid cash for it. Also, we discovered later, in paying for a meal with coupons one allowed more than the amount of the check. Occasionally, however, a waiter would refuse.

To return to our porter, when we handed him the tip he shook his head, and we assumed he was one of those who spurned a gratuity. We gesticulated, indicating that we thought he should accept it. He then frankly told us the tip was not large enough. Since the amount was equal to what we would have given under similar circumstances at home, we declined to increase it. Thereupon a considerable altercation ensued, which ended with his cursing us, but accepting the tip.

Human nature asserts itself in the Soviet Union despite powerful contrary influences—social pressures and punishment. The common phrase the regime uses to designate this expression of attitudes out of line with official dictates is "survivals of the past." The mass of the people cling to many traditional ways and thoughts reflecting prerevolutionary values, even though these are strongly disapproved. It is hard to say whether some of this behavior represents a more basic expression of human need, or a phenomenon in cultural persistence, or both. Thus, after 45 years the Soviet regime has not succeeded in suppressing "middle class and bourgeois" values, has not stamped out love of family, has not changed parental indulgence and love of children, and has not changed the Western pattern in which males still to a great extent dominate females. Nor has it eradicated the acquisitive and self-seeking proclivities.

One of the conclusions that stands out from the reports of numerous observers of Soviet life in the last decade is the extent to which behavior in Soviet society today is a response to fear—a pervasive fear that envelops wide areas of thought and activity.

In *Russia's Children* we reported a conversation with members of the Intourist staff in Kiev. We had asked these young, apparently intelligent workers why they were so reluctant to let us see certain things in their country. We pointed out that they had much to be proud of and we could not understand why they were afraid to let us observe freely and inform ourselves of certain aspects of their community life. This brought heated and indignant replies. "We are not afraid. We work under strict rules."

We have encountered instances of avoidance of responsibility lest one exceed one's prerogatives and incur disfavor. It is safer to close one's eyes to official misdoing than risk reprisal from the bureaucracy.

We read a story in one of the Russian papers involving criminal behavior of two men, one of whom was the director and the other the business manager, of a *dietski dom,* an institution for orphans. Their arrest brought to light the fact that for a number of years they had misused government appropriations, buying liquor with the money intended for the children and going on wild drunken sprees. They had also confessed to having inflicted cruel and barbaric punishments on their charges. One of their inhuman practices was to strip a child of her clothing and lock her in a closet overnight, even in cold weather.

When it was asked how this could continue in the light of the fact that a government inspector visited the school at least twice a year and reported on conditions as a basis for continued support by the government, the answer was that the inspector limited himself to interviews with the managers, to the acceptance of their report which he signed. They were then asked, "Surely the principal of the school which the children attended would have known about these conditions?" When the principal was asked about this, his reply was that he did know there were many things wrong in the orphanage, but he felt that he had problems of his own and he was not going to get himself mixed up in what might prove to be a difficult situation with unpleasant consequences.

Many instances of what can only be described as defensive lying undoubtedly are a product of fear. Some were reminiscent of experiences on our earlier trip, such as the stock excuse for not permitting a visit to a particular establishment because it was *remont,* "under repair." Visitors to the U.S.S.R. during 1961 reported the same kind of evasion. For instance, during a call on a woman official holding an important post in the Soviet government, a staff member of a noted international organization suggested that she would like to visit the official's home. The latter replied that it was not possible because her child was suffering from a severe cold. The visitor remained in Moscow for at least a week; two weeks later she returned to the city for another week's stay. But the excuse remained the same and she was never invited to the official's home even though she had entertained the Soviet official when the latter had been in her country.

Rigidity—reflecting fear of making decisions and taking responsibility—is encountered by almost everyone who has visited the Soviet Union in recent years. In February 1961 a relative of ours spent several days in Yalta. She was with an American tour traveling by ship. It was the practice, when the tourists left the boat, for some to stay in town to eat and some to return to the boat for lunch. On one of the days of this visit, the guide was in charge of a group of 14 adults. When it was time for lunch, some wanted to eat ashore and others wanted to return to the boat. The guide was thrown into a panic, not knowing what to do. The hurdle she could not seem to clear was the fact that there was disagreement within the group—some preferring one thing and some another. After at least a half-hour of discussion, during which the guide seemed completely immobilized, she finally came up with the idea that they should vote, and the desire of the majority should prevail. Only when the group took things into their own hands and said that those who wished to go back to the boat should do so, and those who wished to remain in town should remain, was the deadlock broken.

Two of the guides who were with us on our last visit present sharp contrasts in personality traits; one might very well consider Nadja the individualist and Vera the conformist.

Nadja's father is a scientist and her mother is a retired educator. Nadja herself is 24, attractive, has had a good education, speaks English well, and is married to a doctor. In spite of the fact that she has served as a leader in the Pioneer Youth movement for many years, she is as spoiled as many girls in our country coming from a similar environment. She is self-indulgent, with a disdain for the common people. She is interested mainly in maintaining the perfection of her complexion and in assuring herself of enough amusement to avoid being bored. This is not to say that she is not also a quite delightful person with a charming sense of humor and with perhaps more realism in her view of life than many others we met.

Nadja's young husband, instead of being assigned as many doctors had been to some distant place—the virgin lands of Siberia—for his three years of compulsory residency, had been given an assignment in one of the most beautiful resorts in the south of Russia. Her vacation, she told us, would be spent during November and December in Moscow so she could go to the opera.

Nadja was continuously pointing out to us how crude were the Russian clothes, cosmetics, etc., and how much superior were the sweaters, dresses, cosmetics from Germany, Czechoslovakia, even from China. She loved jazz and begged us to teach her slang and beatnik phrases.

At the opposite extreme was Vera, our other guide, a 23-year-old schoolteacher with whom we spent a great deal of time, at least six or seven hours a day for two weeks.

Vera was rigid and constricted, rarely able to make a statement that represented her own view. Knowing the official position on every issue—from education to modern art, from religion to Americans—one would always get from her a carbon copy of it. This was so much a part of her character that she could not restrain herself from so acting. One day she scolded the woman chauffeur whose 6-year-old boy seemed shy, and said to her: "He is shy because you did not send him to the state nursery school."

When we asked her to take us to the famous monastery at Zagorsk, she scheduled the visit for Sunday afternoon. When we insisted on being present during the morning religious services, she reluctantly agreed. All during our visit there she seemed uncomfortable and kept talking about the bad health of the people attending the service and the danger of the spread of disease by their being crowded together at the mass. Her disdain of the place and her intolerance of the people were so great that she had a hard time listening to our enthusiastic comments about certain things we liked. She complained of feeling physically ill.

Vera had another problem. As a dutiful daughter of the regime, indeed a granddaughter of the revolution, she was continuously preaching to us about the virtues of her country. However, in this she was faced with a serious dilemma. A child reared in a household where some vestige of Jewish folklore was still present, she seemed caught between two pulls— her loyalties as a member of a distinct ethnic group and her loyalty to the communist ideology and values. She told us that if she ever married she would marry a Jewish boy, since Jewish men were good family men; in the next breath she would go on telling us how unreliable, from an ideological standpoint, Jews are. Hardly a day went by when Vera did not present us with another of these situations where she praised the Jews on the one hand and voiced very strong anti-Semitic views on the other.

We have used Vera as an example of what we feel is a consistent product of the Soviet scheme of personality development, and she is but one of many such young people we met. The fact that she is a highly successful teacher underscores the point.

The picture she presented so completely was that of a person who lacked critical faculty; she hardly seemed capable of ideas of her own, repeating over and over again in a parrot-like way the official point of view. Here we see rigidity, complete lack of initiative and ever-present fear deeply incorporated into the personality.

It is difficult to say which of the two—Vera or Nadja— represents the past and which the future.

Whether their judgment is an accurate one or their anxiety is out of proportion to the situation, the fact remains that despite the magnitude of the efforts to mold the Soviet child, Russian officials are plainly disappointed in the results. From Khrushchev down, their criticisms are increasingly outspoken. They freely express anxiety about the evidence of breakdown in the character of Soviet youth. This includes such traits as laziness and poor work in school, prompting and cheating in examinations. They find young people absorbed by a love of pleasure, a distaste for hard work, reluctance to make sacrifices for the common good. They bemoan the imitation of Western ideas in dress and social behavior.

There is a striking universality about the complaints. They come from all sections of the population, not only highly placed members of the regime and the Communist party, leading educators, a highly placed official of the Komsomol organization, the head of the Pioneers, but also from the man on the street, the individualist as well as the conformist. Whether the standards the regime has set for behavior among children and young people are too high and unrealizable and therefore any deviation, even though relatively slight, gives cause for disappointment and concern, whether there is any substantial amount of the kind of misbehavior which is condemned, is hard to tell. Even those who believed that the Russian child was better behaved and was capable of more social responsibility than children reared in Western societies, still bemoaned the amount of unsanctioned behavior which exists and conceded failure of the Russian educational system to curb individualism.

One of the persons with whom we discussed the problem was a highly educated woman who was born in the U.S.S.R. and has lived there for most of her life. But because she had also lived for several years in the U.S., she combined in a unique way an understanding of the American as well as the Russian point of view.

She began by expressing the view that Russian children are in some respects better educated than American children. The problems of everyday living are very real for the Russian child. He knows that he has to keep quiet when his brother is engaged in his studies in the same family room. He knows something about the basic economic problems which his family faces: he knows he cannot tear his pants because he only has one pair.

When we moved on to a discussion of motivation and personality development in her country, she conceded that though the Russian children are notably capable of doing things for the common good, nonetheless, in the final analysis the ruble remains the incentive for the Soviet child as well as the Soviet adult.

As we will see in later chapters, the anxiety about the character of children and their behavior had led to many kinds of action on the part of the Russian regime, including basic changes in educational programs. There are many indications of further changes which are likely to be carried out in the years ahead.

In 1959 we spent a good deal of time with one of the members of a commission on shortcomings of collective education. The commission consists of a group of educators, members of the staff of the Academy of Pedagogical Sciences who are assigned the responsibility of evaluating the problems and suggesting remedies. One of the things they have been doing is to study educational methods in other countries, including the United States, particularly those methods focused on the development of qualities of character, on the implantation of correct moral values in the child. Interviews with this educator, as well as with others, made it quite clear that the Russians were now becoming more keenly concerned about the personality of their children.

Her comment was that "We have been busy building schools, training teachers, and we have not had time to get close to the child himself."

D. Perspectives on Soviet Character

Now that we have reported our impressions, as well as those of other observers, of those character traits of the Russian people that suggest some differences between them and people in other social orders and cultures, it may be useful to examine these impressions within the context of a classification of character traits and personality types recently formulated by a group of American psychologists and social scientists.

One of the latest and most complete attempts to develop a typology of character is described in a recent book by Robert F. Peck and Robert J. Havighurst.* In this study, character is defined, following William James and Sigmund Freud, among others, as a "pattern of acts, rather consistent through time, which may be said to 'characterize' and define the human individual. In both its general sense and its specifically moral aspects, [these authorities] emphasized the inward elements of motivation and intent as the major determinants of character."

---

* Peck, Robert F., with Havighurst, Robert J., and Ruth Cooper, Jesse Lilienthal, and Douglas More: *The Psychology of Character Development*. New York: John Wiley & Sons, Inc., 1960. Pages 1-2.

And, ". . . character is to be defined by the intent as much as by the deed: 'As [a man] thinketh in his heart, so is he.' "

The authors posed this question: What constitutes character and what are some of the major manifestations of character and personality? In an attempt to find an answer, they formulated a typology of character grounded in two basic postulates: the kind of control system the individual uses to adapt his personal drives—his search for satisfaction—to the requirements of the social world, the operational patterns of behavior which he consistently employs, and the stages in psychosocial development to which these patterns presumably are most appropriate.

The authors fully recognized that few people actually operate exclusively and consistently in one way throughout their lives, so that there are few pure character types. In applying the classification the study formulated, subjects were labeled as one type or another on the basis of the relative proportion of each person's personality structure and modes of behavior which belongs in each of the categories. The authors found that one component tended to predominate and make the person a reasonably clear-cut example of a particular type. This was true even though there were some times when the person acted according to other type patterns.

The character type, together with the developmental stage with which it is identified, is described in the following table.*

Character Type	Developmental Period
Amoral	Infancy
Expedient	Early Childhood
Conforming	
Irrational-Conscientious	Later Childhood
Rational-Altruistic	Adolescence and Adulthood

---

* The table and following definitions are from Peck and Havighurst, *op. cit.* Pages 3-10.

Amoral. This type corresponds to what is often classified as the psychopathic personality. The distinguishing trait of such a person is that he "follows his whims and impulses without regard for how this affects other people. . . . He has no internalized moral principles, no conscience or superego. He feels no need to control his personal impulses, and exhibits no control. . . . In a real way, this is a picture of an infant, in his first year."

Expedient. Like the amoral type, the expedient is also self-centered. He considers other people's welfare and reactions only as a way of gaining his personal ends. "He tends to get what he wants with a minimum of giving in return. He behaves in ways his society defines as moral, only so long as it suits his purpose." He is willing to conform to social requirements on a short-run basis in order to achieve long-run advantages. "Such a motivation-behavior pattern is characteristic of many very young children, who have learned to respect the reward-punishment power of adults, and to behave correctly whenever an adult is around. External sanctions are always necessary, however, to guide and control their behavior, and keep it moral."

Conforming. This kind of person observes "one general, internalized principle: to do what others do, and what they say one 'should' do. He wants to and does conform to all the rules of his group. . . . He is kind and loyal to his family and tribe, because he is rewarded for acting in such a way on this occasion, punished for transgressing the rule on that occasion. . . . He follows a system of literal rules, specific for each occasion," without reference to moral implications. A "violation is not wrong in itself, . . . but because other people say it is wrong and their approval is at stake. . . . It differs from the Expedient approach in that social conformity is accepted as good for its own sake. . . . In a sense, such a person might be said to have a crude conscience, since he may feel very uncomfortable about departing from the rules. . . . He defines 'right' as acting by the rules. . . . The rules he lives by may call for kindness to some people, cruelty to others. . . . This kind of pattern is visible in middle and late childhood."

Irrational-Conscientious. In contrast to the conformist, this is a person who judges a given act according to his own internal standard of what is right and wrong. "In the adolescent or adult of this type, conformity to the group code is not the issue. Rather, it is conformity to a code he has internalized and believes in." This type can be identified as the obsessive neurotic; he is moralistic, has a strict conscience, is anxious, guilt-ridden, often self-punishing. "An act is 'good' or 'bad' to him because he defines it as such, not necessarily because it has positive or negative effects on others. This is the 'blind,' rigid superego at work. It is characteristic of children who have accepted and internalized the parental rules, but who have not attained awareness that the rules are man-made and intended to serve a human, functional purpose."

Rational-Altruistic. This type "describes the highest level of moral maturity. Such a person not only has a stable set of moral principles by which he judges and directs his own action; he objectively assesses the results of an act in a given situation, and approves it on the grounds of whether or not it serves others as well as himself. . . . He is as much concerned with assuring the well-being of others as with assuring his own. He is capable of self-sacrifice, but only if it genuinely helps others, not for neurotic self-satisfaction. . . .

"He wants to work constructively in some area and produce results useful to everyone. He sees his relations with others as a pleasant, cooperative effort toward mutual goals, whether vocational, social, or recreational. As an adult, he assumes an appropriate share of responsibility in his role as member of a family, community, nation, and the human race. His moral horizon embraces all mankind, as his behavior demonstrates.

He is honest with all, kind to all, and respects the integrity of every human being. . . . His public and private values are just about identical. . . .

"This picture of the Rational-Altruistic person represents an ideal goal, of course, to be sought, perhaps to be approached by adulthood, but probably never to be perfectly achieved and unfalteringly maintained by the best of mortals . . . it is in the nature of this character pattern to continue to grow, to experiment, to incorporate new facts, and to develop new depths of understanding as long as life permits."

Turning to the question as to whether we have more young people who fall into the Rational-Altruistic category than the U.S.S.R., we believe the only basis for an answer is either inference from the child care methods employed or from the fragmentary observations like our own, and the answer would have to be that Soviet methods are calculated to produce a conformist type of character. At the same time, so many different dynamic threads enter into character formation that it may very well be that other forces would cancel those that are calculated to produce the conformist.

On a long-term basis, the goal of the Soviet educator, like that of our own, is to achieve a rational-altruistic character. The immediate effort in the Soviet Union, however, which has been dictated by pragmatic and short-term considerations, is focused on the *conforming* who often becomes the *expedient* character. Reliance on external influences, overemphasis on the intellectual and the minimization of feeling and parental influence, and pressures to conform to group standards constitute the core of Soviet child-rearing methods.

What the Soviet leaders do not seem to realize is that the course they are pursuing will create serious obstacles to their ultimate goal. While they clearly perceive the connection between a certain kind of human being and a certain kind of society, they have not faced the fact that so long as they keep producing the expedient or conformist character, they are perpetuating a society different from the one they have set as their goal. The changeover to other kinds of motivations and controls is bound to become increasingly difficult, if not impossible. Moreover, the Soviet leaders still do not know by what method the rational-altruistic person can be achieved, and certainly, for the time being, they are holding on to a system of social control and child education which militates against such an achievement.

The impressions we have gathered warrant the conclusion that there is no evidence that the U.S.S.R. is more successful in producing a mature individual who identifies self-interest with the common good than other nations relying on other sanctions and methods. There is no evidence that there is any greater altruism among its population than that in other industrial societies.

At the same time, although it may be logically assumed that pressure for conformity combined with a rationalistic approach to child rearing will produce fearful and constricted personalities, many—if not most—of the Soviet citizens contradict this expectation. It is difficult to tell whether this is due to imperfections in the system itself, whether there has not yet been time enough for its effects to be fully realized, or whether any system yet designed can guarantee the character of its products. The constellation of life forces which play upon the individual is so diverse—basic human proclivities, the persistence of social attitudes, the multiplicity of significant personal relationships, all of which escape any design for shaping human personality— that so far Soviet man seems to have escaped the impact of the Soviet system and remains an imperfect product of the official cookie cutter.

Chapter 5

Social and Personal Maladjustment

THE DEVIATIONS IN character and personality that we have thus far described may influence personal happiness, self-realization and the individual's capacity to contribute to the common welfare, but they do not remove him from participation in ordinary daily activities as student, artisan, laborer, husband and father.

There are, however, other forms of maladjustment which seriously impair the individual's capacity for participation in the life around him or remove him entirely from ordinary activities. We have in mind open conflict with constituted authority—which may range from political dissent to serious crimes—as well as psychological disabilities which manifest themselves in full-blown neuroses and psychoses.

Crime and mental illness represent social waste and therefore run counter to the Soviet goal of fullest conservation of human resources. If the Soviet vision of the future is to be realized, conflict and disharmony between the individual and the social order must be eliminated because where these exist, compliant behavior can be achieved and sustained only by repressive and restraining measures. Moreover, crime and mental illness as gross expressions of social or individual maladjustment challenge basic Soviet theories as to the way in which the social order evolves with growing harmony between the individual and the group.

Although crime and mental illness are prevalent in all contemporary cultures, most other theories of society acknowledge the imperfection of the social order itself and the imperfect adaptation of the individual within it. A state of disharmony between the individual and the social order is taken for granted.

In this respect there are two basic differences between the point of view of the Soviet Union and our own. The first is the assumption by the Soviet leaders that social maladjustment is basically the product of inequality, exploitation and discrimination which characterize the capitalist social order; the second is that with the establishment of socialism man's better nature will assert itself and these phenomena will quickly disappear, although for the time being man must be held accountable for his conduct.

Another closely related difference in the two orientations is in the underlying assumptions as to how the instinctive drives of the individual are socialized. By and large, there is a difference between the two philosophies in the extent to which external pressure is relied upon to tame the individualistic drives.

Along with pressure to meet social expectations, to live within the law, the sublimation of individualistic drives into the more socialized is acknowledged by both as part of the process of social maturation—growing up and becoming a responsible member of society.

The difference between the two points of view is in the nature of the psychological process through which socialization is achieved. In the minds of many in the West, socialization is rooted in the quality of the intimate interpersonal relationships between the young child and his parents. This leads to the identification of the child with his parents and his assimilation of their values as the representatives of the social order. Social pressures and community values become important influences later, when the child moves outside the family into the broader community.

In Western—and particularly American—culture there is a premium on diverse cultural expression, on individualistic "spiritual" values; the pioneer who transcends conventional attitudes and values is honored.

The balance we in the West seek to maintain is between the requisites for fullest realization of the individual self and the growing adaptation to demands of community life. Both remain primary goals.

In the Soviet Union there is a *different* balance, with the weight on social adaptation—the kind of behavior that will yield a more powerful nation and ultimate victory of a clearly defined ideology and social order.

A. CRIME AND DELINQUENCY

In the Soviet Union today a stream of condemnatory invective is continuously aimed at many forms of behavior which fall into a twilight zone between deviations that are tolerated and offenses that are punished. These include irregular sexual behavior, separation of husband and wife, idleness, and unsanctioned practices, short of bribery, for securing the good will of officials and persons in power.

In the chapter dealing with the family we will discuss in some detail the phenomena of divorce and illegitimacy, the reliance on formal and informal regulatory devices which would limit these and other expressions of personal discomfort, maladjustment and social disorganization.

Alcoholism, even though it is often the precursor to serious crime, falls within this borderline area. It remains a social phenomenon inherited from the old regime. It is well-known that in old Russia alcoholism was prevalent among the rural as well as the urban population. It is also true that in those earlier times, crimes of violence were usually committed by persons during states of intoxication. Russian literature abounds in accounts of alcoholic excesses and violence.

But alcoholism is the antithesis of the model conduct of the Soviet man. It represents uncontrolled, impulsive, wasteful and socially dangerous behavior. The Soviet press carries many stories of crimes committed during periods of intoxication and many discussions on what to do about the problem. The fact is that 10 per cent of the admissions to mental hospitals, as compared with 3 per cent in the United States, are diagnosed as alcoholics.

While drunkenness is not now a crime in the U.S.S.R. there is a great deal of talk about making it one, and much is being done in other ways to discourage alcoholism. Wine, beer and liquors can be purchased only in package stores or eating places where food is consumed. The price of vodka is high—two days' pay of the average worker for half a liter.

Mr. Khrushchev himself often speaks out about the disgrace of alcoholism: "We cannot shut our eyes to the fact that there are still drunkards, thieves and scoundrels in our society. . . . Drunkenness undermines a person's health, but this is not all; drunkards ruin family life and harm society."

As he condemns drunkenness in public places, Khrushchev also speaks out strongly against the brewing of liquor in one's own home.

The medical profession, particularly its psychiatric members, has been concerned with methods for treatment and rehabilitation. On our last visit we were told by the head of the Institute of Forensic Psychiatry that the specific treatment for alcoholism includes the use of drugs—Antibuse and others.

Prostitution, another form of disapproved behavior which falls into this borderline area, while rarely discussed as a social problem is sometimes referred to in studies of the reformation of the young prostitute.

The Soviet Union seems no more to have abolished crime than the Western democracies it condemns, and does not seem to be any nearer a solution of the problem. No one knows the extent of crime in the Soviet Union. It may very well be less than ours because the forms of social control hold the individual much tighter in their grasp, and more and more every man is not only his brother's keeper but the policeman in his apartment, in his plant and sometimes even in his family.

While no definite statistics on the incidence of crime are available, we know that crime is a topic of discussion in newspapers, magazines, educational journals, speeches and, more recently, at conferences on measures for combating it.

One impression that stands out in high relief from this spate of words is the greater degree of attention that is given to offenses which hamper the achievement of economic goals.* A great deal of indignant writing is expended on the condemnation of idling, parasitism, black market operations. The articles are replete with examples of how private property is built up through devious and unsanctioned means: through speculation and black market trading. This, it is explained, is made possible because of imperfect distribution of consumers' goods, so that the marketeer can buy commodities where they are available and resell them where they are scarce. Another practice falling into the same category as black marketeering is the renting out of *dachas* and private homes beyond what is legally permitted.

Bribery is another offense which comes in for strong condemnation. From the published accounts one may conclude that it is frequently utilized to secure such favors as admissions to educational establishments of young people whose low academic achievement would otherwise make them ineligible.

Recently an article in *Kommunist* addressed itself to the issue of "why parasitism exists under socialism." It consisted of a digest of letters from workers, collective farmers, housewives, etc., commenting on an editorial which had appeared earlier entitled, "He Who Does Not Work, Neither Shall He Eat."

---

* The death penalty is now imposed for crimes of this type, i.e., currency speculation, black market activities.

The overwhelming majority of the correspondents supported the fight against parasitism and other manifestations of private property tendencies. Those who try to "grab" all they can from society, either without working at all or working as little as possible, were castigated.

All the letters called for strict public and state control over the "measure of labor" and the "measure of consumption."

The article reports that some of the letters questioned why the pursuit of money still occurs under present-day Soviet conditions, and some of the writers disagreed with the editorial which categorized these reprehensible tendencies as "an expression of bourgeois psychology and ways inherited from the exploiting system."

Those who challenge this view argue that the desire for a parasitic existence can be observed among individual young people who have never lived under capitalism. "Where did they get the attachment to private property, the thirst for profit, individualism and other habits and traditions of capitalistic society?"

The answer to this question runs something as follows: Materialists have held, and hold quite justifiably, that ideas and ethical norms are rooted in objective social conditions and so Soviet man in his social and ideological nature is a new man, an active builder of communism. Therefore individualistic, selfish attitudes reflect errors in upbringing and education and the persistence of prerevolutionary attitudes and values.

The discussion of the problem shows no recognition that expression of individualism may be rooted in man's instinct for survival and self-protection, nor is there any recognition that the state itself may have contributed to these individualistic tendencies by encouraging competition through a system of unequal reward.

An article in the *Literaturnaya gazeta* of September 27, 1960, reports a conference on the writer's responsibility to combat parasitism.* In a discussion of how volunteer groups can help control crime, it tells a good deal about official attitudes toward prohibited behavior:

The community's war on parasites may assume exceedingly diverse forms. And it must be said that so far we have been making nothing like full use of them. One need but take the case of the people's volunteers. In many places their work adds up to patrolling "from pillar to post." Why not channel the efforts of the people's volunteers into re-educating the parasites in their neighborhoods, into preventing thievery? And how rarely do we enlist the assistance of the apartment house collective in dealing with loafers and parasites! A striking example was cited at the conference. A young girl had "gone wrong," as they call it. She wouldn't get out of the restaurants and kept hanging around foreigners. No amount of remonstration could tear her away from the "sweet life." Then the apartment house residents—and they were a harmonious and wholesome group—decided to hold a comrades' court. The proceedings were really impassioned and angry. And a "pedagogical miracle" occurred. The girl at once broke off everything she had been doing. No more restaurants or dubious acquaintances. Since then more than a year has gone by. She has graduated from an institute, received her diploma and been married.

"It is time also to get after the people who avail themselves of the parasites' services and in effect create the conditions enabling them to lead a parasitic existence." These words of G. Nikitayev's met with general approval. Yes, an atmosphere of public scorn, of *boycott, should be created* [our italics] around parasites and their accomplices. L. Gromov's advice that the papers carry the names of those using the services of speculators merits attention.

A decree enacted early in 1961 to strengthen the criminal laws provides for deportation of those leading a "parasitic life."

---

* "Writers Confer on Combating Parasites and Idlers." *The Current Digest of the Soviet Press,* Volume XII, Number 41, November 9, 1960. © Page 20.

. . . in cities and in the countryside there are still individuals who are stubbornly opposed to honest work. Such people frequently hold jobs for appearance's sake while in actual fact living on unearned income and enriching themselves at the expense of the state and the working people; or, although able-bodied, they may hold no job at all but engage in forbidden businesses, private enterprise, speculation and begging, derive unearned income from the exploitation of personal automobiles, employ hired labor and obtain unearned income from dacha and land plots, build houses and dachas with funds obtained by non-labor means and using illegally acquired building materials, and commit other antisocial acts. On the collective farms such persons, enjoying the benefits established for collective farmers, avoid honest work, engage in home brewing, lead a parasitic way of life, undermine labor discipline and thereby harm the artel's economy.

The parasitic existence of these persons is as a rule accompanied by drunkenness, moral degradation and violation of the rules of socialist society, which have an adverse influence on other unstable members of society.*

Reading these statements we could not help but recall the British vagrancy laws promulgated in the 15th and 16th centuries to stem the break-up of the feudal system by forcing laborers to continue to work on the lord's estate.

Out of the mountains of affirmation of the correctness of the Soviet ideology and theory of social evolution, and the error of the capitalist and bourgeois societies, out of the plethora of adjurations and scolding, some changes in the Soviet approach to the phenomenon of crime are emerging. It is at the same time pertinent to indicate that in our opinion the level of understanding of the causes and cure of crime, as reflected in Soviet writings and practice, is naive and the rationalizations

---

* "Decree of Presidium of U.S.S.R. Supreme Soviet . . ." *The Current Digest of the Soviet Press,* Volume XIII, Number 17, May 24, 1961. © Page 8.

relied upon are oversimplifications of the complex phenomena involved.

What may represent a break-through to a newer approach to the problem of crime is presented in a recent article by A. A. Gertsenzon in the magazine *Soviet Legal Administration,* entitled "The Study and Prevention of Crime." He stresses the importance of study of the nature of the crime, the circumstances under which it was committed, and the personality of the criminal. He also advocates a greater degree of participation by the average citizen in the prevention of crime.

Like most writers of articles dealing with social problems in the Soviet Union, the author begins by establishing the correctness of the Soviet point of view and the error of the bourgeois assumptions, theories and practice. He begins by referring to Lenin's writings, restating some basic propositions which Lenin formulated relating to crime prevention:

(1) Under socialism progress in all spheres of life takes place with the participation of the entire people;

(2) the entire people exercises supervision over the conduct of those persons who are the bearers of survivals of the past;

(3) the people themselves have the possibility of directly stopping and preventing various excesses that might be committed by individuals.

The writer then points out that crime in the Soviet Union is a residue of its presocialist era: "It is a survival of the past" and has no logical place in a socialist society. He addresses himself to two problems: the concept of crime prevention and the study of the causes of crime as an aid in implementing crime prevention methods. We will see later that *prevention* is used to designate secondary prevention or early treatment, as well as what in our terminology might be called *control* of crime.

The author scorns the bourgeois criminologists for using the concept of prevention for "apologetic" purposes and employing it to designate various kinds of "bio-criminological" measures, and for speaking of "the criminally inclined" to describe the adaptation of individuals to the conditions of life in bourgeois society. He adds:

But is it impossible to speak of the causes of crime in capitalist society without disclosing the organic link between capitalism and crime? Obviously not. Yet if bourgeois criminologists disclosed this link, they would cease to be bourgeois criminologists. And it is not surprising that the overwhelming mass of bourgeois criminologists prefer to speak of "criminal personalities," if only to avoid touching upon the real roots of crime. Similarly, is it possible to speak of preventing crime in capitalist society if, by capitalism's very nature, the entire essence of capitalism and the entire development of capitalism are opposed to crime prevention? What can the preventive recipes of bourgeois criminologists yield when the entire capitalist way of life determines the growth of juvenile crime and intensification of the moral decay of society and the family? Obviously it should be recognized that the problem of crime prevention in capitalist society in general cannot be solved within the framework of this society.

The "bourgeois criminologist" projected by the author recalls a prototype of the Positivist category of this profession no longer extant.

In the light of his condemnation of bourgeois criminologists, it is interesting to see that the writer ends with almost the identical approach to the problem as the one he condemns, including the study of the personality of the criminal. It is also significant that while in his view there is nothing basic or fundamental in the socialist society that would cause crime, and every step in the development of communism contributes to the complete eradication of crime, he goes on to say that it would be a great mistake to count on "drift"—on the assumption that crime will disappear of its own accord in a communist society. A struggle is needed to eliminate it and this struggle involves Soviet society, state agencies and the broad Soviet public.

The writer's analysis of the causes of crime reveals an appraisal very much like our own—interaction between environmental factors and a particular kind of individual. The recognition that there are differences in the way in which individuals react to similar circumstances represents a break with the earlier explanations of behavior. In explaining differences in individual reactions he points out that while individuals are not born criminals,

Yet it must be borne in mind that various unfavorable conditions in which a person may find himself by no means exert an *automatic* influence on his psyche, mind and behavior. These unfavorable conditions are perceived by a person in his own way and are subjected *to his own processing*. [Our italics]

Also significant in the author's discussion is that he admits to interpersonal problems as causative factors: experiencing a "complicated family situation one person may come out of the situation with honor, another as a criminal." He also cites facts derived from studies of criminals, showing that many of them are individuals who have been reared outside the family or in a family without a father or a mother.

At the same time, however, the writer does not seem to grasp the implication of these findings for social control or for child-rearing philosophy and methods. He continues to adhere to the official thesis. He reaffirms the importance of a wholesome environment without special emphasis on the parent-child relationship. He stresses the importance of the work of the children's commissions as instruments for protection of children by removing them from unwholesome life situations. He also looks to the new educational laws as a reliable means of eradicating crime among young people.

Turning to his recommendations for dealing with the problem of crime, the author points out that there is no adequate organization for the study of crime and its causes in the U.S.S.R. Neither the public nor the scientific community has been drawn into the search for solutions. He then outlines approved methods for study and research as a first step. "Study" is to include the study of the criminal act and of the factors which contributed to its commission, as well as of the *personality* of the given law violator. Following this kind of study, he would proceed with the classification of criminals and causes and conditions which contribute to the crimes in specific situations—city, village, trade institution, collective farm. In studying the personality of the offender he wants to make it clear that this must not proceed from any biological or bio-social theories, thus ruling out heredity; that the study he has in mind would move from the assumption

that the influence of external causes, conditions and circumstances takes place not mechanically but as *refracted* through a person's psyche, character and temperament. Therefore in deciding the question of whether a criminal punishment should be applied to a guilty person or whether his re-education can be achieved by a suspended sentence or by handing him over to the custody of the public, it is always necessary to have sufficiently complete information about the given personality.

The writer also devotes a good deal of space to a discussion of the way in which the average citizen can help prevent crimes: through people's courts, children's commissions, volunteer brigades, through service as volunteer neighborhood policemen.

Russia's conception of child delinquency and its treatment is another illustration of its approach to problems of social maladaptation.

Child delinquency in contemporary society has often been spoken of as a barometer of social health. This is borne out by studies of the causative influences which reveal a constellation of etiological factors cutting across many aspects of the social order: economic, political, social mores and value systems. Increase of delinquency during periods of rapid social change or social dislocation is evidence of the large part that social factors play in its etiology. Within our orientation, the recognition of social factors, however, does not ignore the part that individual attitudes and values may play in the specific situation. We see the delinquent act as a response of a given individual to a set of life experiences.

In comparison, the professional workers in the Soviet Union place greater emphasis on social forces as producing the delinquent behavior, minimizing the individual's psychological make-up and limiting their acknowledgment of the personal component to "bad upbringing." Because of this interpretation, they are deeply troubled about delinquency in their country and their first reaction to an inquiry from the foreigner is to deny the existence of this phenomenon. "We had a good deal of delinquency after the war, but it is fast disappearing." Confronted with the concrete fact of current delinquent behavior, they respond that it is the result of faulty methods employed by parents in child rearing. Sometimes they observe further that the Soviet Union is still in transition toward the ideal social order and delinquency will disappear when that order is established.

On our first visit to the U.S.S.R., in 1956, we tried to learn what we could about the problem of delinquency and the answer to the question of how much child delinquency there is in the Soviet Union and whether this is greater or less than in our own country.

As is true for many other manifestations of social disorder in the Soviet Union, statistics are unavailable on the extent of child delinquency. Although the newspapers carry many stories of delinquent behavior by young people and there is much anxiety about "hooliganism," the official position remains that both delinquency and homelessness among children were postwar phenomena only and have now disappeared.

This, however, is contradicted by the fact that there are very carefully formulated legal provisions for dealing with the delinquent; and many agencies are charged with responsibility for detection of delinquent behavior and disposition and re-education of the delinquent child.

As a matter of fact, although we did not get to visit a colony for delinquent youth, the equivalent of our training school, we did discuss the problem with a number of leading workers in this field and visited a number of establishments engaged in dealing with it. Among our informants were two judges of the people's court, a people's advocate, a professor who is an authority on civil law, an assistant procurator-general at the All-Union level, a children's inspector in the school system, two juvenile police officers, several educators and psychiatrists and, lastly, and in many ways the most important, the official responsible for the administration of the colonies for children and youth in the Ministry of Internal Affairs.

By piecing together the facts we gleaned in our interviews and visits, we got some impression of the extent and character of delinquency in the U.S.S.R. For instance, the professor of civil law, who is one of the highest-placed authorities in the field, said that 30 per cent of all crimes were committed by children. The juvenile police officer who dealt with delinquency in one Leningrad district with a population of 25,000 estimated that she was involved with about six cases of children a year in which the disposition was commitment to a colony. This did not include the much larger number of cases she herself disposed of or which were handled by the Children's Commission and the people's courts, in which commitment was not the final disposition. We learned that in Leningrad there were two disciplinary schools, each of which cares for about 300 children, operated by the Office of Education of the municipality.

Our observations lead us to the conclusion that while we still do not know how much child delinquency there is in the Soviet Union, or whether the incidence is greater or less than that in Western countries, we do know that there is a substantial amount of such behavior. We are inclined to believe that it is somewhat less than in our own country or other Western countries. This is borne out by our personal observation in moving about Moscow streets. Except for a few drunken boys and an occasional group of girls much like American bobby-soxers loitering around street corners in the early evening, children and young people on the streets and in the parks and youth clubs were unusually well-behaved.

At the same time, when we take into account what is reported by the professor of civil law and the juvenile police officer, and when these facts are added to the arrangements for the care of the delinquent—the number of disciplinary schools, the number and bed capacity of youth colonies, the number of reception centers in the city of Moscow—we can only say that while comparison with other nations or societies is impossible, there is no question but that the Soviet Union is faced with a substantial problem of juvenile delinquency.

We also learned something about the kinds of children who are delinquent. Although the theory espoused by many of the officials with whom we talked is that delinquency is a product of social deprivation, this was not borne out by the stories of the children they reported. These more often involved privileged rather than underprivileged youngsters. The cause seemed more often to be pampering rather than deprivation. This is consistent with what is now a widely publicized phenomenon—the misdeeds of pampered youth.

B. Mental Illness

The attitude toward mental illness in the U.S.S.R., as toward many other social problems, is ideologically at some midpoint between the assumptions implicit in the revolutionary ideology and the growing acknowledgment of the stubborn realities of social life.

As late as 1956, leading psychiatrists we interviewed minimized the existence of neuroses and mental illness, affirmed that it was declining and propounded the theory that mental illness would disappear with the disappearance of war and with increased collectivization of living. By 1959, the same professional leaders discussed with us the need for additional hospital beds for mentally ill patients. More facts were now available on the number of beds in use; there was a great deal of curiosity about our methods of treatment and the degree of success we achieve.

Although we are primarily concerned with the incidence of neuroses and mental illness as a symptom of disharmony between the individual and his environment rather than how the Soviet Union goes about dealing with the problem of mental illness, nonetheless the Russian view as to the causation of mental disorders compared with our own is pertinent to any attempt to get at the problem of incidence.

Though there are substantial differences between the theories of causation held in this country and those in the U.S.S.R., what is important for us is that they both admit the influence of life experience or environmental factors. Both recognize the concept of predisposition—the Soviets, consistent with Pavlov's teaching, emphasize the weakness of the central nervous system; we accept limitations in endowment and resultant weakness in development and personality structure. While there may be more emphasis on the organic by the one and the psychosocial by the other, both assume that some individuals are more likely than others to become mentally ill. What is also interesting is that they both rely on psychological and physiological methods of treatment, on soma and psyche. The Russians probably put greater stress on a series of remedies or therapies to strengthen the physiological processes—vitamins, drugs, exercises, etc. However, work, sleep therapy and psychotherapy, which are also included in the Russian treatment armamentarium, are primarily psychological therapies.

With this background in mind, we are willing to try to answer parts of the question as to how much mental illness there is in the Soviet Union as compared to that in the United States. As might be expected, no total answer to the question is now possible. An exact comparison could be made only if all factors that enter into measurement, especially case finding, diagnostic and treatment methods and definitions and statistical reporting, were similar. This possibility is ruled out for the present.

To begin with, an important difference lies in the over-all organization of the medical care services in the Soviet Union. Coverage for all types of medical needs, including psychiatric, is available to the population from birth to death through a vast and tightly integrated network of regional polyclinics, specialized dispensaries, hospitals and medical services in the home.*

Combined as these services are with the system of mandatory home visits by doctors and nurses from the regional polyclinics to families where there are infants, and the firm requirement that their records reflect any observations they note with regard to health and family attitudes, the case-finding apparatus accelerates and brings to light many psychiatric problems that might otherwise escape early detection. Psychiatric consultation is woven into pediatric care and is available, therefore, to the mother and child from infancy on.

Psychiatric care as a specialized service is available within a variety of facilities: consultation in general polyclinics, in specialized dispensaries, day hospitals; emergency and follow-up care for the patient in his own home, in hospitals for the acute and more treatable conditions; in foster homes and in colonies for the chronic ill. It is our impression that among the patients in the many large sanatoria on the Black Sea and similar re-

---

* Alts, *op. cit.*

sorts there are thousands receiving "convalescent care" who have already been treated for psychiatric disorders and are sent there on an aftercare basis. Still others who are ill are sent there as a preventive measure.

The more comprehensive organization of medical services and coverage for the average Russian, as compared to the system in the U.S., strongly suggests that patients are found at an earlier stage of mental illness, therefore more accessible to treatment while remaining in the community. The Russians have been more consistent in their emphasis on keeping the psychiatric patient at home and helping him to continue at work at his usual place of employment. Encouragement is given to families to care for these patients at home in many ways, chiefly through making available needed medical nursing services, through disability insurance to which the patient is entitled and additional compensation if it is proven that the patient's illness causes hardship to the family.

Earlier detection of mental disturbance might very well mean that fewer persons require commitment to hospitals as mentally ill. It could also mean that a larger ratio are sent to hospitals during periods of acute stress and for briefer periods. There is a sharp division between the mental hospitals treating persons on an acute basis and the colonies, or work villages, for long-term chronic psychotic patients.

In Moscow, for example, there are 11 psychiatric dispensaries which treat a total of about 500 patients a day on an outpatient basis. There are also eight specialized psychiatric hospitals with approximately 6,000 beds for the treatment of the short-term, not chronic, patient with mental illness. These figures exclude patients in the long-term chronic facilities, or at home and not under outpatient care.

Dr. Nathan S. Kline, noted American psychiatrist who visited the Soviet Union in 1957, concerned himself chiefly with the same question of the relative amount of mental illness in the Soviet Union and in the United States.* At the time of his visit there was a total of 115,000 beds for psychiatric patients. This is in contrast to about 770,000 beds in the United States. However, his conclusion was—and this reflects the opinion of most Soviet authorities—that the estimated rate of psychoses in Soviet Russia is between 3 and 7 per 1,000 which is not different from the rate now prevailing in the United States. This would mean that in the Soviet Union, with a population of 200 million, there are roughly from one-half million to one and a half million psychotic persons. After including beds for epileptics, oligophrenics (mentally defectives), and those in hospitals under ministries other than the All-Union Health Ministry, adding the patients maintained in their own homes, as well as those in foster homes under supervision of the mental hospitals, he found the total number of psychotic patients at any one time in hospitals and colonies amounts to 225,000. This would still mean that the Soviets had about one-third the number of beds we have in the United States. However, the factor that equalizes the ratio of psychotics in the U.S.S.R. with that of the United States lies in the *utilization* of, rather than merely the *number* of, beds.

To quote Dr. Kline:

Our public prolonged-care hospitals for mental disease with 550,000 beds had 122,585 first admissions, 58,892 readmissions, and 12,098 transfers. In other words, the ratio of admissions to beds is about 1:3 [in the U.S.] as contrasted with the Soviet hospital ratio of 3:1. This is a ninefold difference. The turnover of patients is infinitely greater than we are accustomed to in our state hospitals. Almost without exception, these patients are referred back to the dispensaries, and there is virtually no static

---

* "The Organization of Psychiatric Care and Psychiatric Research in the Union of Soviet Socialist Republics." By Nathan S. Kline. *Annals of the New York Academy of Science*, Vol. 84, Art. 4, Pages 147-224. April 22, 1960.

population. Presently, almost none of the patients is referred to the *colonia*.*

To restate Dr. Kline's findings: One bed in the Russian psychiatric hospital is used by three patients each year, whereas one bed in the United States is used by one patient every three years—a ninefold difference—which would seem to indicate that while the number of beds in the U.S.S.R. is strikingly less than our own, the ratio of incidence of mental illness (psychoses) in the Soviet Union is the same as in the U.S.

When we turn to consideration of neuroses, we find that while Soviet leaders in psychiatric care hold that neuroses, like psychoses, are accompanied by changes in the central nervous system, at the same time they recognize the importance of environmental factors, particularly various kinds of "traumatic" experiences. As we will see in our discussion of the interpretation of neuroses in children, emotional experience in the etiology of neurotic states is acknowledged.**

The description of life in the Soviet Union as depicted here should leave no doubt as to the burden of anxiety carried by the Soviet citizen. This observation, it should be noted, is in sharp contrast to the superficial impressions of tourists, many people in our own country as well as in other parts of the world, whose views have been shaped by the official Soviet interpretation of the superior advantages of life in the U.S.S.R.

For instance, there is a general acceptance of the fact that insecurity stemming from fear of loss of one's job, incapacity or illness of the breadwinner, or failure in business, no longer exists in the Soviet Union. The facts, however, support the finding that anxiety about the material requirements of living, though it may take a different form in the U.S.S.R. than in the Western capitalist societies, is nevertheless very real to most people in

---

* *Ibid.* Page 158.
** See Chapter 9.

Russia. In spite of the fact that medical care, housing and the usual types of insurance such as old age, accident and disability are provided, nonetheless there are other counteracting circumstances which may engender anxiety about earning a living as serious as, or more serious than, that which the individual faces in Western countries.

Every Soviet employee carries a workbook in which the manager of the plant records his rating of the man's work capabilities, skill, fulfillment of norms, etc. The worker has no absolute assurance of getting another job, and the kind of job he gets will depend on what is in his workbook. He may actually find it necessary to accept work thousands of miles away from the city in which he has lived or worked, and at much less pay, if his rating is unfavorable. He is also under constant pressure to live up to certain norms and certain canons of perfection, very often beyond his ability. His status depends upon fulfillment of the norm, upon performance as good as or better than that of his fellow-worker at the next bench. He can only lift himself to a higher status or greater comforts by improving his education and his skills. He probably faces more difficulty in "getting by" than the individual in the same occupational niches in our own country. Moreover, his earnings are still relatively meager and the problem of making ends meet remains with him.

But even if we assume that within the economic area he is more secure, in other phases of his life he is surrounded by many anxiety-creating conditions and forces. He lives under almost constant surveillance by his fellow-worker, fellow-tenant, fellow-member of the sports club or political organization. From childhood on he lives in the company of the potential informer, sometimes even within the bosom of his own family.

The restriction on physical and psychological privacy must be another source of irritation and psychological discomfort. No one has been able to assess the psychological price for conformity which the Russian pays and to what extent it is greater than that of the citizen of other social orders.

Any true assessment of the amount of neuroses in a culture would have to go beyond the numbers of individuals diagnosed as neurotic. It would have to include those whose symptoms are obviously psychosomatic in nature, or viewed more broadly, those whose everyday functions in various roles—husband, employee, citizen—are impaired. With the increase in psychological insight this category is an expanding one.

We are in a position to estimate the amount of neuroses in the Soviet Union because, unlike the experience in our own country, neurotics are hospitalized.

Dr. Kline discovered that patients with primarily neurotic difficulties comprise 25 per cent of the population in sanatoria.

The official figure is 284,000 beds in such sanatoria and over 160,000 beds in rest homes. This in turn would mean 111,000 beds for neurotics. Once every 2 years the government arranges through the trade unions a 28-day stay at a sanatorium (for 1 of each 30 Soviet citizens). This would mean approximately 26 different sets of patients during the 2 years. If 111,000 of each shift of 444,000 are neurotic, the over-all figure would be 26 x 111,000, or 2,886,000 such patients. This is close to 1.5 per cent of the total population. . . .*

The most common neuropsychiatric diagnosis is neurasthenia. One of the neuropathologists to whom I spoke indicated that there are also cases of hysteria and emphasized that the neurasthenics, of whom there were about 100, may have had other concomitant conditions. The order of diagnoses in the sanatorium was: (1) heart disease, (2) gynecological conditions, and (3) nervous diseases.**

From the foregoing it may be concluded that even though the differences in methods of diagnosis and treatment, as well as recording, preclude any explicit comparison between the

---

* Kline, *op. cit.* Pages 167-8.
** *Ibid.* Page 169.

United States and Soviet Russia as to the amount of psychoses and neuroses which exists in each country, on the basis of whatever knowledge we now have, we have a right to conclude that the extent of these manifestations of individual and social maladjustment is probably the same in both countries.

Chapter 6

Dissent and Accommodation

IN OUR DELINEATION of the interaction between the individual and the social order, we have drawn attention to certain manifestations of social and personal disorganization, such as crime and mental illness. We would now like to address ourselves to the presence of open dissent and deviation from social demands, as well as the reverse, accommodation to such demands. In doing so, we will note the changing balance between these two phenomena since the death of Stalin.

On our visits to the U.S.S.R. we encountered expressions of disagreement and criticism of public policy. Young adults accosted us on the streets or in the parks and seemed to be searching for the opportunity to voice their disappointments and dissatisfactions as citizens of the Soviet Union. Some were ready to resort to circuitous methods of communication with us after we returned to the United States.

We met with expressions of difference with official policies on such topics as the care of children, the attitude toward Jews, the role of the secret police and many of Stalin's policies, etc. These emerged in conversations at the airport, on the plane, in taxicabs, in public waiting rooms, and even in governmental offices.

Those expressing such differences included persons in many walks of life—not only the taxi driver but also the loyal member of the Communist party. A young man finishing his first year at the medical school in Moscow seemed to have little hesitation about telling us how deeply he resented having to go to one of the undeveloped sections of the Soviet Union, the virgin lands, as soon as his examinations were finished. He felt strongly that it was unjust to deny him the right to visit his family before beginning his summer "hitch" as a construction laborer in the far distant provinces.

Two incidents show the obvious contradictions between the open expressions of approval of the regime and the resentments that lie just below the surface.

The woman who boarded the plane with us in Odessa, en route to Sochi, was a middle-aged seamstress who soon told us she was going to this resort for a rest. She stressed how generous the government was in making it possible for her to have a vacation without cost. No sooner, however, had she registered these positive views than she launched into a series of querulous complaints about how hard she worked, how her heart was weak, how she should be given disability insurance and be allowed to remain at home entirely.

The other more dramatic incident took place in the waiting room of the MVD reception center. Among those waiting was a mother who had brought in her 14-year-old daughter, complaining about the child's misbehaving. While we were all sitting there, the woman turned to address an elderly man who was worried about his petition for special consideration for his son who was in a colony for delinquents. In a loud voice, so that everyone in the large waiting room—including the officer in charge who sat within earshot at his desk—could hear, she proclaimed that she was sure his request would be granted because "our country is a kindly, generous one that looks after its people." She undoubtedly recognized us as foreigners, and perhaps this was said also for our benefit.

She then proceeded to prove her point by telling how she, a widow, had been helped by the government. However, as soon as the officer went into an inner room to talk to his superior, the tenor and substance of her remarks changed and she went into a tirade of complaints about the manifold problems she had faced in bringing up her daughter, and what little help she received from the authorities.

At a deeper and more subtle level is the conflict disclosed in the comments of a member of the Communist party with whom we discussed many questions about life in the Soviet Union. He told us that during the late 'forties, the latter years of the Stalin regime, he was vice-principal of a school and it was his responsibility to open the school for the day. This meant that he was there as the first children arrived. He told us that during those years a child would often say as he arrived in the morning, "My father was taken away last night." In relating this, the vice-principal's comment was, "I *had* to believe *it was right.*"

As we move from the impressions we ourselves gained in these personal encounters to an analysis of the observations of other students of the Soviet scene, we find general agreement that there is widespread disapproval on the part of Soviet citizens of many phases of Soviet life, particularly as these existed during the Stalin era. Although the secret police are the target of the sharpest and most general hostility, strong disapproval is expressed of the collective farm system and the manner in which it has functioned: the Communist party and the men who operate the bureaucracy; the many forms of regimentation of daily existence—regulation of family life amounting to violation of privacy, restrictions on travel and the disciplinary features of the work situation, as well as the scarcity of comforts of life, i.e., the shortage of housing and consumer goods.

As may be expected, there is a difference in the quality of dissatisfaction between members of different classes as well as individuals in different personal circumstances. Obviously the officials, who are also members of the Communist party, are less likely to express any criticism; the same is true of those enjoying a more privileged status and thus more of the amenities of life. Those at the bottom of the occupational scale—the peasants and the unskilled workers—are more dissatisfied. As a matter of fact, criticism may extend not only to those aspects of life which come in for general disapproval but also to the privileges which the more favored group enjoys and which the less privileged are denied.

The question which has puzzled the Western world is the absence of any known organized opposition in the U.S.S.R. To what extent this phenomenon represents the potency of repression or to what extent relative satisfaction on the part of the populace, no one can say. The organized forms of dissent one encounters are such relatively mild expressions as the reproduction and distribution of forbidden literature and other printed matter.

Those seeking an explanation for this apparent harmony between the government and the population point to Russian history and the historic place of the average individual in Russian society. Oppression was always a feature of Russian life; its citizens have always lived under autocracy. While aspiration toward a greater measure of individual liberty and democracy, as we have seen, came to the surface in various ways during the 19th century and culminated in the Russian Revolution in the early part of the 20th century, the Russian people have never actually experienced life in a democracy and do not have any concept of civil liberties as these are understood in Western democracies.

What the situation appears to add up to is that to a substantial degree the indoctrination has been successful and Soviet citizens have accepted the thesis that the Soviet system is the best; that it has already achieved great things and more are in store. They feel very positive about free education, which they have been told is not available under any other system. The same is true of other aspects of their welfare state—medical care, social security, the promise of more adequate housing and consumer goods. It is true that they would like more freedom in family life and fewer restrictions on the job. However, they do not challenge the thesis of state ownership of the tools of production and they accept the values of a strong government, albeit they would like it to be more gentle. The hostility seems to be projected on the men who run the society, rather than on the institutional forms of the system.

The attitude of the people of the Soviet Union toward the United States is an example of how the thesis of the regime is accepted by the population. This attitude may be seen as a product of fear, effectiveness of propaganda and basic human impulse and, like most psychological attitudes, it is not without conflict.

Obviously one cannot be definitive or dogmatic about an attitude of a large group of human beings. The feeling about the United States as we and others have encountered it represents a mixture of distrust, hostility, respect, envy and, sometimes affection.* The U.S. remains the nation that has the greatest influence upon the thought and feeling of the individual Soviet citizen.

The simple folk in Russia are friendly, almost affectionate, toward American visitors. We found this to be true of the people on the state farm, of almost all the taxi drivers with whom we shared the front seat of the taxi. This is true of many of the servants in the hotel, of the "troubadour" whom we referred to earlier and who, when he learned we were Americans, got up from the park bench, walked over to where we sat and vigorously shook hands.

Late one night in Sochi, when we were out for a stroll, we passed a high iron fence and heard sounds of music and singing. We looked through the iron gate and saw a group of adults sitting in a circle playing guitars and singing. The building near which they sat looked like a hotel, but as the singers came forward and started to talk to us it became clear that this was a sanatorium for mildly disturbed mental patients. As we stood outside the locked iron gate that first evening two of the men standing on the other side of the gate, on learning that we

---

* See Inkeles and Bauer, *op. cit.*

were Americans, became very friendly and begged us to come inside or return the next day and have lunch with them. They spoke at great length about how much they wanted peace, and hoped very much that all of us in America also wanted peace. This was the message that, they pleaded, we should take back to our country.

On the other side of the coin, it is pertinent to cite an illustration of the extreme kinds of misinformation resorted to by the regime to instill an unfriendly attitude toward the U.S.

The official Economic Geography, the textbook for the middle grades of the public schools, has a section on each country of the world, including the United States. We were amazed to find that in the reference to World War II the United States was not credited with giving any assistance to the Soviet Union in the winning of the war. Nor did we ever encounter any positive reference to the United States in any of the news digests that were handed out for tourists, nor in the *Moscow News,* a paper printed in English.

The conviction that the influential people in the U.S., as well as the government, want war with the Soviet Union, a conviction that was shared by everyone we encountered including members of minority groups who were critical of the regime, is proof of the extraordinary effectiveness of the process of indoctrination in a closed society with total control over all communication media and education.

In searching for an explanation of how the degree of accommodation by the average person to the Soviet political and social situation which now prevails has been achieved, we are compelled to recognize the effectiveness of the system of social control which Stalin erected, with its emphasis on external behavior rather than inner thoughts: not how people felt but only how they behaved in conformity or the opposite. Conformity was rewarded and hostility punished.

Survival within the system brings into play a number of mechanisms of accommodation which may be summed up in the statement rationalizing accommodation to the Stalin terror that we have already reported: "I had to believe it was right." The individual has no choice except to persuade himself to conform.

Accepting the impossibility of any action except conformity, even the essentially disloyal—that is, those who in a situation of free choice would reject or act against the regime—adopt mechanisms of accommodation to facilitate their adjustment. These self-induced mechanisms include: (1) generation of reenforcing images of society; (2) control over own communication; (3) control of own behavior; (4) control of own impulses; (5) psychological devices for the resolution of moral conflict.*

In emphasizing mechanisms of accommodation, we must not overlook the fact that while the goal of the manifold pressures built into the social order is, and continues to be, compliance, even under Stalin a number of safety valves for discharge of disagreement were provided. The satirical magazine, *Krokodil,* is a medium for vicarious expression of criticism of public figures and public policy. It abounds in cartoons holding up to public scorn the foibles and misdeeds of public officials, the head of the plant and the chairman of the collective farm. The satirical skits of the puppet show are another vicarious outlet.

One keen observer of the Soviet scene has pointed out that while expression of sexual impulse as such is taboo there, when seduction is portrayed in dramatic action or in dancing on the stage it is much more realistic than in our own or other Western countries, and no doubt represents another indirect expression of forbidden impulse. The newspapers invite criticism. As a matter of fact, there has recently been an increase in the number of correspondents whose business it is to report public misdeeds and unmask wrongdoers in public office. Sometimes the

* *Ibid.* Page 286.

stories carry the actual names of the wrongdoers; sometimes they are referred to in more general terms.

Another trend is the promulgation of legislative changes six months to a year in advance of the date of their enactment, and the encouragement of discussions of their merit in the various organs of the party and by professional groups in the field affected. One example of this is the widespread discussion of the features of the pension system some years ago and, more recently, of the education reforms promulgated in 1958. In many important details the original proposals for changes in the educational program were modified in the light of the opinions registered by the professional educators.

"Soviet officials have been urged to get closer to the people, to pay more attention to them. . . . Sessions of local soviets are being held more frequently . . . in some instances, agendas of meetings [of soviets] have been posted and public hearings held on the items under discussion." *

There has been a good deal of discussion of a new balance between the prerogatives of the trade union and management. Union committees have been set up to share in some of the decisions made by the manager. Presumably such committees have been encouraged to express vigorous opposition to management policies directly to management when necessary.

The changes we have noted, which portend a different relationship between the individual and the state, largely fall into two broad categories. One has been introduced as correctives to the extreme features of the system of social control and some of the excesses which it has engendered, e.g., the relaxation of the terror, the leveling up of income of the different occupational groups, the increase in the amount of consumer goods, the liberalization of housing provisions. The second group of changes, apparently intended to increase the partici-

---

* "Equality and Inequality under Khrushchev." Robert A. Feldmesser. *Problems of Communism,* No. 2, Vol. IX, Mar-Apr 1960. Page 32.

pation of the average individual in community affairs, is generally tied to the thesis that the era of communism is at hand.

The assumption underlying these social devices to promote more citizen participation is that they transfer more and more of the prerogatives of government into the hands of the individual. There is a growing tendency toward formalization of many activities which the regime proclaims as representing transfer of authority from the government to the people. The most recent example of this is the granting of greater authority to the "comrades' courts." Heretofore, these were informal organizations whose power was derived from the disapproval of the offender's colleagues. The legal status of these courts was clarified in 1961, details of their organization defined, their jurisdiction enlarged, the kinds of penalties they could impose and the consequences of noncompliance with their decisions clearly spelled out. They now are an integral part of the court system of the U.S.S.R.

Another set of sanctions enjoying increasing official approval may have more ultimate significance than has been accorded them thus far in that they may promise increased tolerance for expression of feeling. This new dispensation is exemplified in the encouragement of more elaborate celebration of anniversaries, festivals and holidays, with greater emphasis on the ceremonial aspects. It is pertinent to note that advocacy of these forms of public behavior is always coupled with the declaration that tradition is an important ingredient in life.

It is important to point out that students of Soviet life have not arrived at any consensus of the real significance of these new forms of participation in community affairs. Do they represent a consistent trend toward more freedom, or are they just instruments for harnessing the energies of the people, which have been made available by increasing leisure, for the achievement of public goals?

There is general agreement that the successors to Stalin have resorted to less coercion and that individualism has been allowed to express itself more fully and in many more forms. From some of the things we have reported, one has a right to conclude that the present regime recognizes that coercion excessively applied may negate the purpose it was designed to achieve. But, as in most societies, each swing in one direction brings its counterswing. And so we have a "mopping up" process—cleaning up the vestiges of the old order—which has taken the form of increased penalties for idleness, black marketeering, etc., and an extension of capital punishment. The ultimate balance is still a matter for speculation.

What is clear is that sufficient progress has been made in realization of the original economic and social goals of the revolution so that the kind of repression which Stalin resorted to is no longer necessary. This can be assumed to be the rationale for the degree of liberalization we have described rather than that a new political philosophy has replaced the old. Moreover, coercion often had consequences the opposite of those sought. The excessive regimentation and pressures to which the individual was subjected reduced his ability to contribute rather than heightened it. The concessions to the average individual thus far granted are seen by many students of Soviet life as intended to increase the individual's contribution rather than to enlarge his orbit of freedom or well-being, and these will stop at the point where they interfere with the goals of the regime.

PART TWO

SHAPING THE SOVIET MAN

Chapter 7

Conceptual Framework for Child Rearing and Education

ALMOST ANY VISITOR to the U.S.S.R. is struck by the appearance and behavior of the children he meets in the street, in the parks, in the children's centers and in the playgrounds. They are well-nourished, clear-eyed and well-behaved.

This is in contrast to what he likely to see in the classroom and in sharp contrast to what he will see in the home. In the classroom, he encounters both the poised and the tense. Seeing the child in the company of his parents and in his home, however, the good behavior so evident in the public situation may give way to the willful, self-indulgent manner of the pampered child.

The generally favorable appearance of children cannot be separated from the place given them in the national ideology. Conservation of child life is a major goal in Soviet national policy, and this is expressed in the priority accorded the child in the health and welfare programs. That the state depends on the strength and character of the future generation is universally affirmed. Yet closer examination reveals perceptible differences in the picture. The individual child is not an end in himself, but a means in social construction, and everything that is done with him, for him and through him is directed toward that end. More than that, as we will see, the methods relied upon to achieve a personality consistent with this goal are neither subtle nor scientific, but direct and elementary. Their primary concern is with external behavior, with the way the child behaves rather than the way he thinks and feels.

However, in spite of whatever blind spots may exist in the theoretical approach to the psychological development of the child, there are virtually no gaps in the arrangements for the care, education and protection of children in the Soviet Union. The universality and completeness of the various programs designed to conserve child life merit sincere tribute: the far-flung health system, which starts with guidance for the mother during the prenatal period and extends throughout childhood; the growing educational establishment with its many and varied resources, beginning with day care facilities for the very young child and extending through a network of child care and educational institutions. In truth, the variety of measures designed to help parents discharge their responsibility for the care and rearing of the child are probably more complete than most nations have achieved.

Admittedly, the Soviet plan of childhood nurture and conservation is an impressive example of completeness of arrangements for child care, education and protection. But we will see that it falls far short of embodying any consistent scientific or even theoretical frame of reference.

Both theory and practice are primarily instrumental and pragmatic, with elements borrowed from different cultures and systems of thought, and embodying different concepts of human development. The result is a mélange—some of the ingredients are idealistic and romantic, the heritage of the prerevolutionary liberals, others are realistic, reflections of revolutionary goals and methods. One stresses the realization of the child's potential as an individual and the other his role in achieving the communist state.

The diverse bits and pieces of philosophy and science which constitute the rationale for child rearing and education are given shape and character by the regime's purposes—the texture changing as these undergo change, with old ingredients dropped out and new ones added. As in all science in the Soviet Union, so in the science of human behavior, the primacy of ideology remains, both as to methods and content. If theories of heredity suggest immutability in human nature, then they must be proscribed because the ideology demands faith in perfectibility.

Educational theory and the building of communism

Marx himself did not elaborate principles for educating men for the new society. In his view, education had been used as a weapon in the class struggle in the nonsocialist state, and for this reason only under socialism, in which social classes no longer exist, was education on an equal basis possible.

He did not specify what this education should be, except that he assumed differences between intellectual and physical labor could be abolished while emphasizing the importance of combining both in educational practice. Accordingly, Marx advocated "polytechnic" education to equip children with broad knowledge of the basic processes of production as a first step in preparing them for socially useful work. The concept of "polytechnic" education is the single most important educational idea which the Bolsheviks took over from Marx and which has been consistently proclaimed as basic to Soviet educational theory.*

Central to Marx's political and economic plan for a more perfect society was the 19th century liberal belief in the worth and importance of the individual. In his view, socialism was to be established in order to create the best conditions for the free development of the individual and his potentialities, rather than to subordinate his development to the demands of the state.

In this respect, Marx's views approximate those advocated by the great 19th century Russian liberal thinkers and educators who also sought a more perfect society. Their discontent

---

* Counts, *op. cit.* Page 13.

with social conditions surrounding them was coupled with an immense faith in the potentialities of the people and in the importance of the individual. "Only a freely developed personality . . . can change life," * wrote Tolstoy. "The road to freedom and the welfare of the people lies in enlightenment," ** said another one of this group.

In the decades following the emancipation of the serfs, educators, especially the famous K. D. Ushinsky, demanded that school and intellectual activities be free from state control. The school and the teacher were called upon to shape a man's character and to form a personality capable of critical thinking. Political reformers of this time also concurred in the belief that the fullest possible development of the individual would benefit society.

While 19th century liberal ideas of the importance of the individual and the need for his rounded development are still sometimes cited in the Soviet Union as basic to educational theory, the attitude of today's rulers toward education owes at least as much to ideas held by the czarist governments.

The czarist rulers of the 19th century recognized, as the Soviet authorities also were to recognize, that education was an important weapon in liquidating Russia's industrial and intellectual backwardness. Although the czars were ambitious to play an important role in world politics in the 19th century, they were handicapped by the fact that Russian economic and cultural development lagged far behind her political rivals. Education thus became a practical tool to further state aims. However, then as now, education in Russia was also expected to promote and propagate official ideology, and schools and universities were expected to suppress any ideas which could lead to subversive action or even to subversive thought.

---

* *Ibid.* Page 21.
** *Ibid.*

The difficulty of educating young people while at the same time attempting to control their thought was evidenced in czarist times by constant student unrest and by the unremitting struggle waged by the government against the intellectuals. "The desire for education . . . everywhere growing," warned Uvarov, a czarist official who later became Minister of Education, " . . . should not be suffered to disturb in any way the existing class system, by awakening in youthful minds the impulse to acquire unnecessary knowledge, which cannot be applied in practice." *

The radical revolutionaries of the 19th century contributed little to educational theory. Relying as they did on violent action by a small revolutionary minority to shape the new world, they gave little thought to shaping the new men who were going to inhabit it. As the broad strata of the population were not needed to reform society or to choose the kind of society they would wish to live in, the need for education did not seem urgent to the revolutionary thinkers. Only Tkachev foresaw that education would have a crucial role in the new society, when he stressed the need to "reeducate man and change his very nature." **

The Soviet view of education contains elements from all these streams of thought. As Marxists, Soviet ideologists see education as a weapon in the hands of the ruling class in any given society; in a society which is "building socialism" it must be wielded by the proletariat in the battle for communism. As inheritors of the liberal tradition, they stress the importance of the individual and of the free development of all his abilities whereas, as inheritors of the ideas of the radical revolutionaries, they insist that these abilities and talents be used by and for the state, which alone is allowed to determine the goals of society. As propagators of a new orthodoxy and autocracy, they insist on unquestioning obedience to official ideology and pre-

---

* *Ibid.* Pages 16-17.
** *Ibid.* Page 28.

vention of the acquisition of "unnecessary knowledge." Finally, as reformers of society and planners of a new Utopia, they insist on changing man to conform to the new society, rather than changing society to conform to the needs of man.

While these elements remain constant in Soviet educational thought, officially proclaimed educational theory has shifted throughout the years of Soviet rule in conformity with the changes in political, economic and social policies. A brief recapitulation of trends in Soviet educational and psychological theory, as well as of the practical measures adopted, shows a development paralleling other aspects of the Soviet social order. Soviet educational and psychological concepts followed the same general evolution from active controversy and advocacy of differing opinions to the adoption of a single, rigidly defined orientation.

The first period after the Bolshevik revolution was marked by great ferment in the educational field. The majority of psychologists and educators at this time regarded man as a machine-like passive creature, activated only by his reaction to external stimuli. His behavior was determined by environmental or biological forces—the extent of the role of either of these factors was variously estimated by different theorists—and man's basic motivation was considered to be the maintenance of a state of equilibrium between himself and his environment. The role of consciousness in his behavior was completely discounted and the very concept was denounced as akin to bourgeois idealism and contrary to materialist philosophy. Man was conceived to be basically good, but helpless in the grip of forces which acted upon him. He could therefore not be held responsible for his acts.

Educational policies at that period were highly experimental. Pedagogues viewed the child as the product of his environment and held that educational measures must concentrate on creating the best conditions possible for his development. Thus, the school system was remodeled: in accordance with radical revolutionary doctrine a school system which had served the interests of the ruling bourgeoisie had to be destroyed completely. In its place, the Bolsheviks established the "unified labor school," a single system of schools, open to all, free of charge. The basis of all instruction was to be "labor," and polytechnic education was to be the guiding principle of the new school, but the curriculum for each school was to be worked out locally by the school itself.

In the first flush of revolutionary enthusiasm, the Bolsheviks expected that with the abolition of private property as the means of production classes would disappear and the communist society would be just around the corner. Some educators even expected to see the withering away of the schools as a formal institution.

With the introduction of the New Economic Policy in the 'twenties, these sanguine hopes disappeared. The realization that a class society still existed, and would continue to exist for a considerable time, meant that the educational system must again be re-formed—fashioned into a weapon for the new ruling class, the proletariat.

A new education act was passed establishing a school system which would provide preferential treatment for the children of the proletariat. A compulsory curriculum was worked out for all schools of the Russian Republic, thereby ending the extreme decentralization of the first period. Teaching was still to be based on the principle of labor and studies were to be built around the topics, "Nature, Labor and Society." Socially useful work was to play an even more important part in the education of pupils, with work and examinations to be carried out in groups. In both these early systems formal methods of instruction were abolished and discipline was considered to be actually harmful.

Psychology in this early period was a far-flung endeavor which undertook to investigate many different aspects of individual and social behavior. Research was carried on in industrial psychology, medical psychology and criminology. In educational psychology, the science of "pedology" gained great popularity. Pedologists devoted themselves to the investigation of the conditioning factors in child growth and development. Various tests and measurements were devised and questionnaires were administered to groups of children as a means of identifying and measuring the various influences on the child, and his reaction to them. This represented the practical application of the basic psychological concept of man as the helpless creature of outside forces. In spite of the dominance of this idea, however, psychological discussion ranged over a wide field in this period and a variety of theoretical positions were tolerated.

The first Five Year Plan and the decision to "build socialism in one country," required conformity of educational theory and psychology to the rigid line established for all intellectual endeavor. The decision in favor of active intervention in the economic and social spheres called for new psychological theories and educational measures.

From that point, on, the state could no longer afford to regard man as a passive creature, in the grip of external influences and not responsible for his acts. Activists, who were conscious masters of their fate and could be made to conform by the judicious use of rewards and punishments, were needed. Consequently the official view of the nature of man was changed to conform with the new revelation: the ideal Soviet citizen now had to be an active, purposeful human being, tenacious and courageous, able to surmount difficulties and take the initiative in fulfilling directions from above. He had to be truthful, honest and loyal to his country, conscious of the need for the demands made on him, and disciplined to carry them out.

Educational policies also had to be changed: no longer was it possible to allow children to develop their abilities freely, nor could the school be allowed to experiment. Skilled workers and qualified professionals had to be trained for the economy and good citizens had to be produced for the strictly regimented society.

A whole series of reforms was introduced to align educational theory and practices with the new requirements. The school system was reorganized, formal instruction was restored and individual responsibility replaced that of pupil brigades; the curriculum was once again divided into individual subjects and "stable" textbooks were reintroduced. The authority of the teacher was strengthened and discipline was again conceived as an essential part of the teaching process.

"On July 4, 1936, the Central Committee of the Party issued the decree 'on Pedological Perversions in the System of the People's Commissariat of Education,' " which condemned the theories of the pedologists. Yesterday's gospel became today's heresy as pedology was scored as a bourgeois doctrine, and condemned for stressing the importance of the "fatalistic conditioning of children's fate by biological and social factors, by the influence of heredity and invariant milieu." * The decree stressed the fact that the correct view was the emphasis on the possibility of *re-educating* men. Clearly, if the social system could no longer be blamed for social problems, the emphasis on environmental factors must cease. Psychology was ordered to cease its wide-ranging investigation over many fields and concentrate on creating the best methods for shaping the new man. "Today, virtually all of applied psychology is confined to developing techniques of education and to training the New Soviet Man. A limited amount of work is done in such areas of application as medical psychology, vast fields of applications are forbidden, and there is, for practical purposes, only one theoretical position allowed." **

---

* Bauer, Raymond A.: *The New Man in Soviet Psychology.* Cambridge, Mass.: Harvard University Press, 1959. Pages 123 and 124.
** *Ibid.* Page 5.

The consequence of this mandate was to constrict the scope of Soviet psychology from an extremely broad discipline which studied animal and human, normal and abnormal, child and adult subjects, to a narrow focus with most of its attention on the study of the normal human. In the only theoretical view now permitted, the individual becomes a creature of will and action, who is responsible for his actions and who must be consciously and purposefully devoted to the attainment of the officially prescribed goals.

Educational theory after Stalin

Since the death of Stalin, there has been a further shift in emphasis in psychological and educational thought. The period of the "extensive building of communism" has been proclaimed. The establishment of communism is assumed to lie in the immediate future, when coercive measures will disappear, as they will become unnecessary. The new Soviet man will then voluntarily and on his own initiative perform all necessary tasks and his social consciousness will be so highly developed that work will become a vital need for him and material incentives will have become superfluous. Consequently, Soviet educators and psychologists have been called on to devise new and more efficacious measures for the development of this ideal citizen.

As the economy develops and the militancy in the execution of economic tasks decreases, the emphasis for the new man in the blueprint is less on his ability to overcome difficulty, on courage and tenacity of purpose and on militant loyalty, and more on the special attributes of the "collective" man: the citizen of the communist society must be helpful, considerate of his comrades and, above all, ready to put the interests of the society above his own personal desires. Desire for personal advancement and success must be replaced by desire for the advancement and success of the group he lives with and works with.

It is significant that the new movement for "socialist competition" in the Soviet economy no longer stresses individual achievement as was true in the days of the Stakhanovites. The present emphasis is on collective accomplishment—the team. The heroes of the "movement for communist toil" are workers such as Valentina Gaganova, who left her place in a brigade which was outstanding and voluntarily went to lead one which was backward to bring it up to the level of her old one.

The new program of the Communist party of the Soviet Union emphasizes the moral code of the builders of communism, embracing such personal and social imperatives as:

devotion to the cause of communism and love of your own country and the other socialist countries;

conscientious labor for the good of your society;

high consciousness of your social duty and intolerance for infringements of social interests;

humane relationships between yourself and others and comradely mutual helpfulness;

You must be honorable, honest and morally pure;

Your private and public life must be characterized by simplicity and modesty;

You must sustain mutual respect in the family and the best care in the upbringing of children;

You must abhor injustice, parasitism, dishonesty and careerism;

You must seek fraternal relations with other socialist countries and the toilers of all countries, coupled with hatred of all enemies of communism.

Educational policies have been instituted to implement these ideals. The school is assigned an increasingly important place in the life of the Soviet child and is to exert an ever greater influence on formation of his character. The educational reforms instituted in 1958 are partly aimed at future citizens for the communist society who will consider collective toil as a vital need of life. The new boarding school is considered to be an entirely new institution with unique possibilities for shaping the new man. The Academy of Pedagogical Sciences has worked out a detailed "upbringing" program for all schools, with instructions to the teacher on how to develop the various desirable characteristics in the child at the different age levels. The problems of collective education and of character formation are being endlessly discussed in the Soviet pedagogical press and new methods to achieve the state's goals are constantly sought.*

The two men who probably have had the greatest influence on present-day Soviet educational philosophy and practice are I. P. Pavlov and A. S. Makarenko. Pavlov's experiments demonstrated the possibilities of conditioning human behavior and constitute an essential cornerstone of present-day Soviet educational theory, with its emphasis on the educability of the average human being and on external pressures as a way of molding human response.

In contrast to Pavlov, who laid the scientific basis which later provided sanction for Soviet practice in education, in psychiatry and all interpersonal relationships, Makarenko was primarily a practical educator. A teacher and educator in the Ukraine, his work was mainly with the *bezprizorniye,* the "wild boys"— homeless and unsupervised juveniles who roamed the country in large numbers in the years after the revolution and the civil war. Makarenko established and directed two colonies for such children. It was only in the later years of his life that he expanded his theories to include children living under ordinary circumstances.

Although Makarenko was a rather obscure teacher, his fame and influence in the Soviet Union have blossomed in recent years. This can be explained by the fact that he elaborated a technique of education aimed at achieving the goals embodied in the official policies at the time. At present, he is extolled by

---

* See Chapter 9. Pages 268-270.

his successors for articulating the concept of collective education which continues to serve as the ideal and inspiration for Soviet educators.

The basic tenet of Makarenko's theory is that a child must be brought up to live *in and for the collective*. In his definition, a collective is not merely a group which lives together or studies together; it must be united by a common purpose. He cites the example of his first colony, where the group spirit did not emerge among the youths until they were called on to organize a defense against marauders in the vicinity of their colony. Thus, every group of children must be given a common purpose, before a collective can be said to exist.

A true collective is a self-governing and self-determining organization, in which every member is responsible to the group for his actions. Collective living emphasizes mutuality of interests, mutual aid and oneness of purpose.

Makarenko also stressed the importance of submission to the will of the collective as the final authority. The child must be taught to subordinate his own selfish interests to the group interest. All the tasks he performs in the course of his life in the community are performed for the sake of the group. Communal living is a "balance of learning, productive work, self-government, and group ceremonial." *

Working as he did with the homeless and wayward, Makarenko gave a great deal of thought to the importance of discipline. Strict discipline was necessary if the interests of the group were to prevail over the interest of the individual member, and it had to be maintained and enforced by the group itself. It was the collective which defined the rights and duties of its members, rewarded special merit and punished infringements of the rules. According to Makarenko, it is of primary importance

---

that the will of the collective prevail. He cites a case where the will of the group was upheld by him even though it was contrary to the convictions of both himself and the representative of the MVD, the secret police ministry under whose supervision the colony was operated.

Loyalty to the collective and a sense of belonging were fostered by the structure of Makarenko's colony, by the institution of "socialist competition," and by the introduction of certain group "traditions." These colonies were organized into detachments, each with its own commander. Rituals and exercises were woven into the life of these units which grew into traditions and which fostered the feeling of belonging to a group. The detachments also promoted competition between each other, but the colony formed a closed group vis-à-vis the outside world. Each detachment commander was a member of a central "council" which exercised both advisory and executive functions.

In spite of his emphasis on the primacy of the collective, Makarenko did not deny the importance of the individual: on the contrary, he stressed the need to develop the grace, originality and beauty of the individual personality. He held, however, that only as a member of the collective could the individual attain the fullest development of his personality. An isolated personal destiny, outside a meaningful social group, could not have any significance and could not yield true personal satisfaction. The collective, Makarenko contended, provided the individual "with nothing less than a character and a role to play in life." It was his duty to develop his abilities to their fullest extent and to use them in the service of the community. This duty held, even if it went against the personal inclinations and desires of the individual himself.

Makarenko relates the story of a boy in his colony who was very talented in dramatics but wanted to become an engineer, as that was the profession which seemed most useful at the time. Makarenko believed the boy would become a better actor than engineer and invoked the authority of the collective, which ordered the boy to drop his study of engineering and study acting. Although Makarenko had some scruples about the action, he considered it to be justified, especially when the boy turned out to be an excellent actor. The question of which profession would have made the boy himself happier was not considered.

Makarenko believed that moral growth is attained by teaching the individual to recognize the moral claims of the community. Such growth is promoted by making increasingly difficult demands on the individual in the name of the collective. As he fulfills these demands, the individual is made to feel that his personal satisfaction, or "joy," derives from the performance of increasingly burdensome and important tasks for the good of the community.

The concept of "joy" is an important part of Makarenko's theory; it must come from "participating in collective strivings that involve the expenditure of work effort on behalf of common aims," * rather than from the gratification of personal desires. Every collective must be given a plan of "perspectives" for future development and a set of graduated tasks, which must be made interesting and absorbing for all members.

The significance of the individual in and for the group is summed up in the concept of "socialist humanism." It stressed the need of developing those qualities which would be most useful in achieving the aims of the state and the duty of the individual to develop such qualities in himself. Emphasizing as they did the role of the individual in a strictly regimented society, the importance of conscious understanding of duty, of training the will and the character and the utility of rewards and punishments, Makarenko's theories dovetailed with the philosophy propagated by the state. Moreover, Makarenko's emphasis on the importance of the collective in shaping the

---

* *Ibid.* Page 33.

life and in the character formation of the individual, and his concept of individual happiness as equated with social useful-ness, as well as his stress on self-discipline, reinforce the concept of the "Soviet man." From the foregoing it can be readily understood why his theories have gained such popularity in recent years.

Despite this, Makarenko's theories were not without their contradictions. While he believed in firmness and stern dis-cipline, he was conscious also of the value of the warm emo-tional relationship found in family life. While he believed in the paramount importance of qualities which would be useful to society, he clung to a romantic belief in the possibility of the fullest development of all individual abilities and talents. Al-though, in the case of the actor, individual inclination had to give way to group sanction when a conflict arose between them, Makarenko maintained that all personal abilities were valuable and should be developed.

In stating his ideas on education in the family, Makarenko tried to blend these contradictory attitudes into a unified creed. Even in the family, the first consideration should be the interests of society in the rearing of children. Parents were never to forget that they were responsible to the state for the upbringing of their children. They had to keep constantly in mind that they must bring up persons who would be useful members of a collective society and would be willing and anxious to serve the community. This principle was to be carried so far that parents were to have more than one child, even if material conditions did not favor it, since it was impossible, or at least difficult, to bring up an only child without making him into an egotist.

On the other hand, parents were urged to keep in mind that the new Soviet family was no longer the "autocratic" social unit it had been under the old regime. Fathers were to regard themselves as the guiding member of a collective—more as *primus inter pares*—rather than as the autocratic ruler of the family. Though parents must always respect the personality of their children, education in the family was to be stern, strict, disciplined and consistent, and parents had to guard against excessive love and sentimentality. In the relationship between school and family, the school was to have the guiding role and the principles of upbringing should not differ in the two institutions.

Makarenko's theory can perhaps be summed up best in his most frequently quoted precept: In education, there must be the greatest possible respect for the individual, combined with the greatest possible demands on him. In the demand for respect, the importance of the individual in the group is emphasized; in the demands which are made on him the paramount claims of the community find their expression.

In Makarenko's view, as well as in the official Soviet position, there can be no conflict between the individual and society. Personal fulfillment cannot be attained through experience opposed to the proclaimed aims of society. It can only be achieved through the realization of social goals. The individual must always be in harmony with society, and the values of individuality can be fully realized only within a meaningful social order.

This doctrine is supported by contemporary theories of cultural determinism—the theory that the personality does not exist outside of a cultural matrix. Still, in Western thought there is an allowance for the instability of the culture itself and for the individual's impact on it. Basically, Western society and Soviet society face the same issue today: How far is it possible to shape the individual through cultural influence and to make him the conservator of the culture, and yet still safeguard individuality and autonomy?

Makarenko's ideas represent an earnest attempt to achieve this goal for a collective society, but his theory cannot resolve all the contradictions inherent in it and, as yet, no reliable way has been found to change human nature in accordance with the planned blueprint for the Soviet man.

It is interesting to point out that while Makarenko was elaborating his theory in the Soviet Union, similar views were being tried out in the United States. Some of these American experiments may have preceded Makarenko's work. In *Youth in Conflict,* a book by Dr. Miriam Van Waters published in 1923, there is a description of El Retiro school for girls near Los Angeles, California, that experimented with a self-government organization which, in many respects, was like the collective Makarenko describes in *The Road to Life.* More than that, the George Junior Republics, which emphasized democratic student government, were founded in this country long before 1920. However, in spite of the similarity between these enterprises and Makarenko's, those in our country inevitably reflected our own view of the individual and the group in society just as Makarenko's reflected that of the U.S.S.R.

Within the relative freedom which characterizes the social scene in the United States, groups enjoy great latitude as to choice of interest and activities. In contrast, the activities of Makarenko's and other youth groups in the Soviet Union do not spring from spontaneous free choice but rather from a mandate which has been explicitly defined and to which they are expected to conform. It is also significant that in American enterprises of this sort the adult staff are aware that decisions of the peer group tend to be unduly severe and crush the individual. In such situations the staff intervene to temper them. Makarenko, on the other hand, defended decisions of the group as final.

With all the emphasis in the Soviet Union on the principle of collective education and on utilization of the group in the education of the individual, it is paradoxically true that Western educational theory has concerned itself more with examination and analysis of the influence of the group on the individual than has Soviet theory. It is impossible to discover in Soviet literature any detailed analysis of the philosophical and scientific elements in the concept of "collective education." The term is used both to designate a goal—the preparation of men for life in a collective society—and as a method of character development—the shaping of personality through the experience within the collective or the group. While the procedures for the conduct of collective group activities have been formulated in detail and heavily publicized in the Soviet Union, there does not seem to have been any significant effort to understand the process of group interaction in psychological terms.

Western theorists, like those in the U.S.S.R., emphasize the value of the group in the education and socialization of the individual. However, because of the difference in value systems, there is also a difference in views as to how the group may contribute constructively to the development of the individual. The West has gone much further in the effort to understand the group processes themselves, and although there is much yet to be learned about these processes, we in the West are beginning to accumulate a body of recorded observations of behavior of the individual in groups and of the behavior of the group itself. We have learned a good deal about the evolution of group structure, its hierarchical organization and the way in which stratification takes place. We have learned a good deal about the way in which the group confers leadership and how leadership is exercised within it.

Some common denominators run through the activities of all groups which we in our country sponsor and maintain. In all of them there is an emphasis on the individual and individual self-expression. We see the group as both sustaining and supporting the individual, as an instrument of release rather than one of repression. We see the individual participating in the fashioning of the group milieu rather than merely being fashioned by it. Thus, we design the therapeutic group so as to give support to anxious individuals through their identification of their own difficulties with the difficulties of others, a process which, in turn, gives them sufficient confidence to express their anxieties. Finally, through the response of others they develop some understanding of the deeper meaning of the ways in which they have come to terms with their problems.

We share with the Russians their convictions about the value of children participating in group activities and in doing things together. But the concept of what takes place is different. We see the individual measuring himself against others and retaining his difference, if he so chooses. In the Soviet view, however, the group is a microcosm of the social order and accordingly the will and the values of the group override those of the individual.

One other basic difference between ourselves and the Soviet Union is the extent to which we rely on the group as an instrument of character development. Here, too, we agree with the Russians in certain important respects but disagree in others. We acknowledge that groups which consist of children of the same age and grade, who feel and act together, influence each other's attitudes and values and no doubt have some effect on the moral character of their members to maintain and develop in ways appropriate to their age the values they have brought from home. But at the same time, we do not forget that group influence can also operate to break down such values and replace them with those less socially desirable. This is true of the deviant group or the gang in which the socially hostile or amoral leader may succeed in establishing codes of antisocial behavior.

There is no doubt that the peer group represents the psychological arena for learning many things, including moral behavior, particularly where the experience is reinforced by rewards and punishments which the group dispenses. Where we differ with the Russians is how far, how much and how fundamentally the group alone inculcates basic moral traits. We question whether the peer group is a pivotal factor in basic character formation, whether it is sufficiently strong to produce fundamental changes in character structure even though it has been operating through middle childhood and adolescence.

The group of American social scientists who devoted over a decade to the study of the moral behavior of a group of children from the ages of 10 through 17, and whose findings were mentioned in our discussion of character development, have come to the conclusion that while the peer group reinforces character traits that have been acquired earlier, no basic traits originate through the group influence alone. They have come to this conclusion after making full allowance for the nature and variety of the group's influences, including the fact that in the cases of those children who came from chaotic and loveless homes and families the peer group itself may serve as a matrix of character formation.*

The group established to achieve therapeutic goals—modifications of deviant or pathological behavior—may also be designed so as to recreate a family-like milieu, and where this has been achieved some basic changes in attitudes of the individuals toward themselves and others may take place. However, the recognition of this form of group influence does not modify the basic position these studies take, which is that the character structure, as well as the value content of each adolescent's moral code, came predominantly from the family. Moreover, whereas there were similarities in the values of the members of the group in the studies referred to, these could be directly traced in the individual behavior of the youngsters and their parents.

The social and moral adjustment of the adolescent is a reflection of the attitudes and behavior learned earlier in his home.

In their study of the character traits of individual children, the investigators established a direct connection between the quality of parent-child relationships and the character of the child. The child incorporates the attitudes and values of the adult whom he trusts and feels close to. This includes the

---

* Peck and Havighurst, *op. cit.* Page 141.

standard of moral conduct, what is allowed, disapproved and forbidden. The child's identification with the character traits of his parents lays the foundation for his self-control. External pressures do not effectively build such self-control. Persons subject to such influences achieve conformity as long as the pressures are exerted and cease to do so when they are withdrawn. This means, as far as our present knowledge goes, that we can only achieve a free self-directing personality through family rearing or through certain kinds of emotional experiences within an interpersonal milieu which simulates family life.

Our examination of Soviet methods of child rearing and education reinforces our thesis that the leaders have transferred to these functions some of the things they learned during the revolutionary experience—how to achieve unity of action on the part of the group; how the will of the group is impressed upon each individual and how this is achieved through the unchallenged authority of the ordained leader who wears the mantle of those who founded—or preceded him as exponents of—the correct view. They have learned the value of the utilization of the authority implicit in the hierarchical structure of the group and the power that this exerts, as well as the potential of the group as a medium of indoctrination.

The theoretical gaps and contradictions to which we have drawn attention have not yet resulted in any basic reformulation of the theory and practice of collective education. But this does not mean an absence of concern about many of its features on the part of Soviet educators. This is exemplified in anxiety about the unsocial behavior of many young people, the number of children who fail to achieve promotion and drop out of school at an early age, and the excessive supervision which may stifle creativity. While concern for the product of the system is widespread and appears in the daily press and in official pronouncements, there seems to be no beginning as yet of any fundamental evaluation of the educational system and its influence upon the personality of the child. The school and political associations continue to be relied upon as the principal instruments of implementation.*

But the child in the U.S.S.R., as in other cultures, begins life in his own family and he must be cared for as an individual before he can participate in the group experience. Even though some of the more orthodox Soviet theorists would limit the period of individual care to the minimum by rearing the child from the earliest years in the creche so that elements of group experience can be introduced in early life, almost all children in the Soviet Union at this point begin life as members of families and continue to be reared by their parents, at least during their early years.

Both we and the U.S.S.R. face many common problems about the future of the family. We, as they, are concerned with the dual impact of urbanization and automation, with the shrinkage of the size of the family, with the obstacles to the discharge of its traditional responsibilities, with the increasing employment of women outside the home. We and the U.S.S.R. have been deeply concerned about these changes and the impact on personality development of the loss by the family of the important role it now fulfills in child rearing. Moreover, the recent social changes have forced us to adopt many of the same measures as the Soviet Union—provision of extrafamilial institutions such as nursery schools, community centers, after-school supervisory arrangements, etc., which supplement the family's child-rearing capacity.

The difference between us and the U.S.S.R. lies in the way we look to the future. We are eager to find ways to conserve the essential indispensable contribution of the family to the development of the character and personality of the child.

The Soviet leaders, on the other hand, are moving in an entirely different direction. They would like to remove the

* See Chapters 4 and 9.

children from the home to community institutions for two reasons. First, they believe that professionals can rear children better than parents, and second, because for economic and other reasons they feel the mother should go to work. But the basic reason is that the family is the cradle of individualism and therefore cannot produce the group man. Having taken this position, they do not seem to be able to repress a note of anxiety as to whether the family's part in child rearing can be so drastically reduced without losing something irreplaceably valuable in the personality and moral development of the child.

The failure to rationalize with any degree of consistency the respective roles of family and school in the rearing and education of the child constitutes one of the weakest links in Soviet educational theory. No one knows whether this failure represents an undisclosed strategy calculated to achieve the contribution of both family and school during the transitional period. The fact remains, however, that the present situation makes for contradictory policies and seriously weakens Soviet practice in child rearing and education.

Chapter 8

The Family as a Child-Rearing Institution

THE RUSSIANS ARE baffled by the family. What to do with it remains an unresolved problem in their present social policy. While they have not been able to—and still cannot—manage without it, they are convinced that they will not fully achieve their ideological goals if the family continues to fulfill its traditional child-caring function.

Two opposing points of view concerning the family's role in child rearing have pervaded Russian thought and official policies since the beginning of the revolution. One stresses the potential contribution the family can make to the development of the personality and the character of the child, and affirms the value of rearing within the family. It is given practical expression in the development of many kinds of extrafamilial institutions to enable parents to keep their children at home, even though an increasing number of mothers go out to work.

The other point of view is reflected in the continuous criticism and downgrading of the capacity of the family to bring up children and the continued advocacy of the policy that children can best be reared in the residential nursery, kindergarten and boarding school, and that such facilities should be expanded as rapidly as possible to free the family from most of the responsibility for child care. The exponents of this point of view never fail to emphasize the essential connection between rearing within a group situation and preparation for life in a collectivist society.

As far as we know, there has been no considerate attempt to reconcile these opposing views and affirmatively define the partnership between family and child-rearing institutions, indicating the unique contribution which each can make and the responsibility which each may carry in terms of the child's age or certain aspects of his training and development.

159

Whatever form the final resolution of these differences may take, from a practical standpoint the Soviet Union cannot in the foreseeable future dispense with reliance on the family to rear its children. The institutions required for the alternative course are not yet available in sufficient quantity, nor are parents likely to be willing to give up their children to such institutions. However, this is not to gainsay that the architects of the future society may very well be correct in their view that the family remains the cradle of individualism and that the collective dream cannot be realized unless the state gains full possession of the mind and spirit of the child.

After describing the place of the family in Soviet life, we will return to a further examination of the official view of the social function of the Soviet family and its future development.

A. The Changing Status of the Family

As is true of all aspects of Soviet life, the changes in policy which the U.S.S.R. has adopted toward the family mirror the problems the regime has faced in its march toward communism in the last 45 years. The final balance represents a blend of traditional attitudes and communist ideology, both tempered by a variety of accommodations to practical realities.

Engels' conception of the family dominated official policies in the early days of the revolution. In Engels' view the husband was the equivalent of the exploiting capitalist and the wife, the oppressed proletarian.

There could be only one remedy—take the wife out of the home setting and give her a place in industry. This, in turn, calls for the "abolition of the monogamous family as the economic unit of society." Housekeeping must become a "social industry" and the "care and education of children becomes a public affair; society looks after all children alike, whether they are legitimate or not." * Further, the Soviet leaders were con-

---

* See Inkeles and Bauer, *op. cit.* Page 189 *et seq.*

cerned that children being reared by parents who were hostile to the regime would themselves continue to be antagonistic. The family was seen as a battleground between the old and the new —a battle in which the stake was the ideological orientation of youth.

Consistent with these views the revolution altered sharply the legal basis which supported the family as a social entity. The legal protection of the family was weakened; ecclesiastic control of marriage was abolished, civil procedures alone were sufficient; divorce could be obtained at the request of either party; *de facto* marriages were recognized as having equal weight and status with regular marriages.

By the early 'thirties there was a sharp reversal in these policies. The social and economic structure just could not dispense with the family as an economic unit or as the instrumentality for the physical, social and psychological nurture of its members. More than that, the radical change in the concept of relationship of the individual to the state, with its emphasis on conscious individual responsibility as an indispensable imperative in building the economy, also reaffirmed the responsibility of parents for the rearing of children and the role of the family as an economic unit.

The need to deal with the problems of child neglect which appeared in the wake of the war and the revolution generated further pressure for family stability and responsibility. A study of delinquency, which was completed in 1935, pointed out that the great majority of children spent much of their free time outside their home. Even those who remained at home during the period when they were not in school came from families where the mother and father were both employed. Study of the children in youth correctional colonies showed that approximately 50 per cent had been homeless.

In the light of these findings the Ministries of Education, Health, and Social Security were all ordered in 1935 to develop services to provide added protection for children. These included the establishment of children's homes for the orphaned—the *dietskie doma*—homes for handicapped children, youth reformatories for juvenile delinquents. The guardianship agencies of the local soviets were ordered to enlarge their programs and the hands of the police were strengthened by an authorization to fine the parents of children who commit acts of vandalism.

While the fundamental stake of the regime in the care of children remained unchanged, the immediate job of rearing children became the responsibility of the family.

All the propaganda media—movies, magazines, press, posters, radio—were mobilized to help stabilize the family. A lightminded approach to marriage was decried and people were urged to preserve family bonds. Incentives were offered to encourage large families. In 1941 a tax was imposed on childless persons and later this was also applied to those having no more than two children. A mother of 10 children was designated "Hero Mother," and corresponding honors and awards were given mothers with even as few as three children. These measures finally reached their culmination in the legislation of 1944 which revised the laws relating to marriage and divorce and the treatment accorded children born out of wedlock.

Registered marriage is now the only kind which is legally binding. *De facto* marriages are no longer legal and the spouse in such a relationship cannot inherit. The trial court by itself cannot grant a divorce; its duty is to reconcile the parties. Only when its efforts at reconciliation fail can the matter be taken to an appellate court. If that court finds the dissolution of the marriage necessary, a divorce may be granted. There are no specific grounds for divorce as such, only the criterion of necessity.

The laws now establish responsibility of parents for the support of their legitimate children. This obligation continues whether the child remains with both parents or, in the case of divorce, is in the custody of one parent. It also continues even where by reason of neglect the child needs to be placed in an institution or foster home. In 1944 a radical change in legislation transferred responsibility for the support of the illegitimate child from the father to the state. The latter assumed the obligation the father had previously carried by paying support to the mother. The rationale behind this reversal of policy is not clear. It may be to encourage procreation and offset both the extraordinary male mortality and the birth deficit suffered during the war years, or it may be intended to strengthen the family by relieving fathers of legitimate children of the added burden of supporting their illegitimate offspring. Or there may have been other reasons unknown to us.

Extraordinary requirements now obtain for support of each other by members of the family. Grandchildren must support grandparents, older brothers must support younger ones, and stepparents must support even stepchildren they have not adopted. Conversely, stepchildren must support stepparents.

These and other legal measures were intended to restore the family to its former status as a basic social institution. The government now supports marriage as an "indissoluble union" and the family is declared to be the very basis of society. The upbringing of children "is declared to be a sacred duty of parents in which they act as 'partners' of the state" in implanting qualities and traits of character which should constitute "the norms of behavior of every citizen of the Soviet Union." *

In recent years more impersonal pressures engendered by industrialization and growing urbanization are replacing legal dictates and social approval as primary influences in shaping family functions. The consequences have not been too different from those appearing in Western society. Thus, the continued march of women into industry is a social phenomenon appearing in Western societies as well as in the Soviet Union, although the rate may be higher in the latter, reflecting such factors as the drive toward industrialization, the loss of male population during

---

* Inkeles and Bauer, *op. cit.* Page 192.

the war and the need of the Soviet family for more earnings to achieve an acceptable standard of living.

Before the revolution, the pattern of family life had largely been established by the culture of the village community where 80 per cent of the population lived. The collectivization of agriculture broke up the old village commune, set in motion the movement of people from the farms to the cities and profoundly modified the economic functions of the old family unit. The size of the industrial labor force more than doubled during the first Five Year Plan and has continued its rapid growth ever since. As a result of this migration, many millions have been exposed to the conditions of living in crowded urban areas with negative implications for family life.

Closely linked in its consequences to those of urbanization was the war on religion fostered by the regime, which resulted in the closing of most of the churches and minimized the influence of traditional values on the young. The Komsomol (Young Communist League) became a potent force in disseminating scientific propaganda and in the atheistic indoctrination of youth. Urbanization brought with it an increase in the size and importance of white-collar occupations. It brought, as well, greater education and sophistication on the part of sons and daughters, which helped to widen the gap between them and their parents.

Urbanization, coupled with breakdown of tradition, has meant smaller families as well as the utilization of professional services such as nursery schools. We do not know what the total impact of urbanization on family life has been and whether on balance its consequences have been favorable or the opposite—whether it has increased or reduced separation or divorce; added to or diminished child neglect. We shall see that the Soviet regime has been very much concerned about the trend and has done what it could to counteract its harmful consequences.

This brief account of the principal influences to which the family has been subjected since the beginning of the revolution, and the changes in Soviet family life that have taken place, brings us to one important observation.

Without assessing the relative strength of these social determinants—tradition, freedom and discipline, the impersonal but powerful force embodied in industrialization and urbanization —their total impact on family life has not been as far-reaching as might be expected. It is a commentary on human nature that even during the decade when freedom in marriage and divorce was permitted, the family still remained together. Not everyone packed up and terminated his relationship with his partner. Similarly, the legal measures and other pressures for stability that have characterized the Soviet scene in the last three and a half decades have not brought universal conformity to puritan ideals.

The phenomena of separation, divorce and illegitimacy present clear proof of how human nature asserts itself despite efforts to harness it in accord with a rigid, strictly imposed set of standards.

Incidence of divorce

It is startling to find that in spite of the stringent legal restrictions on divorce, the admitted estimate of divorces in the U.S.S.R. amounts to as much as a third of those in the United States. It is also noteworthy that the literature on family life, as well as articles in the press dealing with family problems, is filled with references to separation between husband and wife and the need to provide for the children of such families.

We have no exact figures on divorce in the U.S.S.R. Kharchev, a Soviet authority on marriage and family life, points out that comparison of the divorce rate in the U.S.S.R. could not be made with information about divorce in Czarist Russia or with that of other countries in which divorce has been virtually forbidden.* If the comparison is made with the United States,

---

* "The Soviet Family Now and Under Communism." *The Current Digest of the Soviet Press,* Volume XII, Number 21, June 22, 1960. © Pages 9-12.

"it is far from favorable to capitalism. In 1957 the number of divorces in the United States," he affirms, "was almost triple the number in the U.S.S.R." However, it is not clear whether this finding relates to the absolute number of divorces or whether to the ratio of divorces to population in both countries.

What to do about divorce is one of the social problems about which there is a sharp difference of opinion in the U.S.S.R. On the one hand, so-called liberals feel that the present process of divorce is excessively complicated and that "when love has died no marriage certificate can bring it back to life." On the other hand, those who favor strict divorce laws point out that liberalization would put the state "on the side of the hundreds of bad marriages against the millions of good ones"—in other words, would tend to weaken family stability—and that despite the original view that freedom of divorce was integral to the emancipation of women, in the present Soviet society stable marriage is of great importance. They go on to argue that "if one studies carefully the conflicts that break up a marriage, it is easy to discern that there are no external causes . . . either in the economic or the political status of the person; the causes are rather to be found inside the marriage. In most cases those who divorce show clear defects . . . above all egotism." Since this is so, the answer must be stern condemnation of all who live "dishonest, thoughtless, libertine lives."

Perhaps what is more important about this reasoning is the admission that there may not be external causes, social or political, for marriage conflict; that difficulties in marriage lie within the personality, attitudes and values of the individual. This represents a startling reversal of the usual argument that asocial behavior, delinquency among children, crime itself, are largely the product of economic and social deprivation.

The reaction in the United States to the thesis that family breakup is due to personal factors is sharply different from that

(Condensation of article by A. Kharchev, "The Family and Communism," which appeared in *Kommunist,* May 7, 1960.)

of the author. It would be to try to understand what in the life experience of the individuals concerned led to the difficulties and then see what changes in their life situation, including appropriate form of professional help, might achieve change in attitudes and thereby avert divorce and family breakup. Kharchev, however, responds with a posture of stern morality, excoriating the individual for his "egotism."

At the same time, he admits that a change in the divorce laws is indicated. The present law "has fallen behind the moral development of our society." In his view, "such requirements as obligatory publication of the divorce notice and the requirement that both parties agree to the divorce do not help to strengthen the marriage but simply give rise to falsehood and hypocrisy in marital and family relations." He goes on to say: "It is wrong to think that all divorce is immoral. There are situations in which divorce is more moral than preservation of the marriage."

Size of families

We could not secure any exact figures on the size of families, although we were told during both our visits to Russia that the average urban family has two children and the rural family somewhat more. Because of the loss of as many as 40 million inhabitants during the last war, the government has had a strong natalist policy which has been exemplified by the discouragement of divorce and the prohibition of abortion.

The regime, however, seems to have accommodated to the natural resistance to large families by the greater part of the population and has yielded in two respects—the legalization of abortion in 1956 and the sale of contraceptives. The latter are easily obtainable and can be purchased without restriction. Abortion is still difficult to arrange, the operation requiring the approval of two physicians who must certify that it is in the interest of the mother's health.

The presence of social and psychological forces which counteract the regime's interest in larger families and population growth finds proof in the comparatively low and declining birth rate. The fact is that the birth rate in the U.S.S.R. in 1962 was 22.4 per 1,000 of population, a substantial drop from that of 25.6 in 1955 and the lowest ever recorded in that country. These rates compare with 44 per 1,000 there in 1926. What might be worth noting are the variations in birth rate as between the different republics. The Russian, Ukrainian, Latvian and Estonian republics registered birth rates in 1962 below the national average—that of Estonia being 16.1—while the culturally less sophisticated were substantially above the national average—e.g., Azerbaidzhan, 40.3, Turkmenia, 40.1, Uzbekistan, 37.2.*

However, the low average birth rate should not be taken to mean that the population is at a standstill or not increasing. As the table below indicates, the number of births exceeds the number of deaths, with resultant population increase.**

Illegitimacy

Writers on marital problems recognize the direct connection between the strict divorce laws and the amount of illegitimacy. Discussions in the public press point out that a husband and wife who cannot get a divorce will separate. Then either or both will go on to other alliances, produce illegitimate children, and then go to court with the plea that the only way the new family can be legitimized is by granting a divorce from the first spouse.

In discussing the seriousness of this by-product of the stringent divorce laws, one writer estimates that there is one illegitimate child for every divorce.

---

* "Natural Changes in the Population of the U.S.S.R." *The Current Digest of the Soviet Press,* Volume XV, Number 38, October 16, 1963. © Page 20.
** *Ibid.*

Birth Rates, Death Rates and Natural Increase
By Union Republics (Per 1,000 Population)

	Births		Deaths		Increase	
	1961	1962	1961	1962*	1961	1962
U.S.S.R.	23.8	22.4	7.2	7.5	16.6	14.9
R.S.F.S.R.	21.9	20.2	7.4	7.7	14.5	12.5
Ukraine	19.5	18.8	7.0	7.6	12.5	11.2
Belorussia	23.5	22.2	6.5	7.3	17.0	14.9
Uzbekistan	38.5	37.2	6.0	6.1	32.5	31.1
Kazakhstan	35.3	32.9	6.5	6.4	28.8	26.5
Georgia	24.7	23.6	6.5	7.1	18.2	16.5
Azerbaid- zhan	42.1	40.3	6.7	7.4	35.4	32.9
Lithuania	22.2	20.8	7.9	8.7	14.3	12.1
Moldavia	28.2	25.6	6.4	6.8	21.8	18.8
Latvia	16.7	16.1	10.1	10.8	6.6	5.3
Kirgizia	35.5	33.6	6.7	6.4	28.8	27.2
Tadzhik- istan	34.4	34.1	5.2	5.8	29.2	28.3
Armenia	37.6	35.1	6.5	6.7	31.1	28.4
Turkmenia	41.0	40.1	6.6	6.9	34.4	33.2
Estonia	16.5	16.1	10.6	10.9	5.9	5.2

While we have not been able to secure any statistics on the rate of illegitimacy, a report in the *Literaturnaya gazeta* of May 28, 1960, by a schoolteacher states that at least 20 per cent of the children are illegitimate.** The count is easy to arrive at because in the U.S.S.R. the birth certificate of the illegitimate child has a blank after the word *father*.

Teachers and other child welfare workers note that the illegitimate child is under a serious handicap. Apart from the denial of support from his father if the latter is already married, the child is ridiculed by other children.

* The figures for 1962 reflect a rise in the death rates resulting from the influenza epidemic in January-February of that year.

** "Marriage Law and Illegitimacy's Stigma: A Dispute." *The Current Digest of the Soviet Press,* Volume XII, Number 21, June 22, 1960. © Pages 13-15.

Discussions of the plight of the illegitimate child in the press acknowledge the suffering of many of the children, as illustrated in the following excerpts:

Yurka has no father. Or, rather, he has one but he has never seen him. Yurka's birth certificate has a line across the space for the father's name. He wanted to send his father his school description of himself, nothing more. He wanted his father to know that he had a good son. Perhaps the father would be sorry that he did not know him.

* * *

A fifth-grade pupil, 11 years old, tells the teacher: "What do you want of me? I'm a goner! Mother has three of us, and no one knows who our fathers are. My sister and I are papa's. We don't know him, of course. Now there is a fourth child on the way, 'Uncle' Valery's. All of us are fatherless." *

In his article Kharchev says:

It should be remembered too that as a result of the war it fell to the lot of many women to be single mothers and that tens of thousands of children are growing up in the U.S.S.R. without the influence of fathers. In our times our press has raised the question of eliminating the notorious "blank spot" in the birth certificates of such children. But this is only one of the half-measures. In order really to help single mothers and their children, it is necessary first of all to give public opinion a correct orientation.

He points out that a great many women were widowed and many could not marry at all.

When such a woman becomes a mother she should not be condemned; she and her child should be given moral support, for it would be unjust to deprive of the right to motherhood those who do not have a possibility of establishing a family. Yes, communist morality opposes extramarital ties in principle when they are the consequence of dissoluteness and a casual attitude, but the unmarried mother often has a different reason that has nothing in common with immorality—the desire to have and raise her own

---

* *Ibid.* Page 15.

child. The state helps such mothers. Boarding schools are one of the most important forms of this help.*

Other authorities who join Kharchev in his plea for a more lenient view of parenthood outside of marriage argue that it is absolutely essential to sanction this kind of parenthood in the light of the fact that there are so few men and so many women who seek motherhood as personal fulfillment. This adds to the birth rate and the population and therefore their conduct should be approved and praised.

Whatever changes in policy may lie ahead, illegitimacy remains a problem no nearer solution in the Soviet Union than it is in the "bourgeois" countries.**

B. Social and Economic Factors
Influencing Family Life

The regime has never lost sight of the many social and economic factors that handicap the family as a child-rearing instrumentality—the limited purchasing power of the average wage earner, the employment of mothers outside the home, the overcrowded housing, the difficulties in homemaking, the long work week, the amount of time taken from the home by the required participation of the parents in community activities.

---

* *The Current Digest,* Vol. XII, No. 21, June 22, 1960, *op. cit.* Page 11.

** *The Current Digest of the Soviet Press,* Volume XVI, November 11, April 8, 1964, in a copyrighted article entitled "Proposed Law on Marriage and the Family Described," published the complete text of the draft Principles of legislation on marriage and the family which were announced by the Council of the Union of the U.S.S.R. Supreme Soviet. It appeared in *Trud* on February 16, 1964 as a way of securing public discussion and reaction. Among others, the draft Principles propose a change in the procedure of registering births out of wedlock.

"It is planned that the birth certificates will not show a line drawn through the entry 'Father,' as is now the case. . . . provision is being made for the possibility of voluntary admission of paternity, and in certain cases for the possibility of determining paternity through the courts."

The other major change seeks to liberalize the procedures regulating divorce. It would abolish public announcements in the newspapers and would have divorce actions heard only by the people's courts.

All these factors help create serious problems in child rearing and child care, and the regime, well aware of this, continues to concern itself with measures to offset the resultant hazards to children. However, progress in raising the standard of living has not been in keeping with the widespread efforts on many fronts. The explanation lies in the fact that this goal takes second place to that of strengthening the industrial and defense establishments.

The problems faced by parents in making a living and the kinds of anxiety which these engender will obviously influence the kind of care they will give their children. We are persuaded that in spite of national policy, which brings basic necessities such as housing and medical care, and certain items of food—particularly bread—within reach of nearly everyone, the problem of making a living still constitutes a source of much anxiety to most heads of families in the Soviet Union.*

At this stage of the economy the standard of living that the average Soviet family can achieve can only be described as meager compared to that in most Western countries or even within the context of its own goals.

A factor that liberalizes the situation for some families and at the same time produces tension in others is the inequality in earnings in various sectors of the population. While this means that some families—the exact number cannot be estimated—are better off, it has also, as may be expected, meant a sharpening of the hunger of the economically less favored for more and better things and serves to spur the individual to give a better account of himself on the job so as to increase his earnings and purchasing power.

If we take for granted normal human desires to be decently dressed, to have one's children decently dressed and to have a

---

* In the autumn of 1963, because of crop failures, food was in short supply and the queues outside food stores were much longer than they had been latterly. Families with lower incomes have again had to tighten their belts; for them the standard of living has moved backward to a more austere level.

comfortable home with some degree of privacy, and the fact that these are unattainable by most but enjoyed by some, then dissatisfaction and resentment are inevitable.

It is difficult to describe the material aspects of family living without taking note of the wage and price equation. According to our own firsthand observations, as well as those of others, the average workman achieves a wage of about 80 to 100 rubles a month; a teacher's salary begins at 80 and eventually reaches 140 to 150; the average for doctors, 130; for engineers, from 80 to 130. In 1956, and we believe the same still holds in 1963, the actual buying power of the ruble for most commodities, except bread and milk, was the equivalent of 60 to 70 cents in American money.

Because prices are fixed by the government and economic plans have by and large called for diversion of industrial production into heavy industry and defense rather than consumer goods, prices of some commodities are extraordinarily high. Thus, in 1956 a pound of butter was equal to a half-day's pay for an ordinary worker; the price of a good suit of clothes equal to a month's wages. We cannot assume, therefore, as some do, that the Soviet citizens are satisfied because bread is cheap.

The problem the family faces is brought home to us by the fact that the cost of food for a low-income family is estimated at 20 rubles a month for each individual. This means that a family consisting of husband, wife and two children will need a total of 80 rubles, equal to the monthly earnings of many fathers, just for food. Then, although rent is nominal, it is still an item; transportation is another; cigarettes and liquor are also costly. It is reasonable to assume that the larger proportion of the income of the average family goes for food and other absolute necessities, and relatively little is available for clothing or furnishings.

There are no figures or data on diet or malnutrition. People look well-nourished, some are even inclined toward corpulence, which may be accounted for by the presence of so much bread in the diet.

What we have just reported is based on the assumption that there is equality in income. However, in many families there are two wage earners, with the husband and wife both working. During our visit in 1959 we were again struck with the tremendous variation in the earnings of people we got to know. The family of one of our guides had three wage earners and one pensioner. The father and mother were both professional engineers, the daughter, who was the guide, was a teacher, and the grandmother was a pensioner. Our estimate is that, in all, the earnings of this family might amount to as much as 450 rubles a month.

One of our Intourist chauffeurs was the head of a family which consisted of himself, his wife and a married daughter. He was earning 100 rubles, his wife was earning approximately the same amount, and their daughter was completing her training in one of the technical institutes and would also be earning approximately a like amount.

There are other factors which make for differences. In addition to the difference already noted between the laborer and the professional, and between the professional and the official, there is also the factor of piecework, which significantly raises the income of the more productive and skilled worker. Bonuses for successful managers or for the ordinary worker who exceeds his quota also make for inequality.

The legal protection of the right of inheritance would obviously have the effect of adding to the funds which the legatees may spend.

Two other important phenomena add to this picture of differences in income and buying power: the government's intensive campaigns to urge people to save and the extent of home ownership.

One sees numerous posters depicting the man who deposits money in a savings account and the many things he will be able to enjoy because of this—longer summer trips, the purchase of furniture and, lastly, the building of a house for himself. We were informed that one-third of the homes throughout the Soviet Union are now privately owned. Most of them are on the outskirts of the larger cities and in the smaller communities. The government encourages private ownership of homes and extends loans to those who wish to undertake their construction. Owners of private homes have the right to bring in members of their families as permanent tenants and outsiders on a temporary basis.

We have been referring to the condition of the relatively more favored Soviet families, those of the industrial worker or where one or more members have specialized skills or belong to the more advantaged occupational and professional classes, as well as those with more than one wage earner. We must not overlook the status of a very large segment of the population—as much as one-half—whose earnings are substantially below those we have portrayed. We refer to the laborers on the collective farms, pensioners, people living on minimum wages.

Only recently has the minimum wage been increased to 30 rubles a month, and the old-age pension for most is approximately 40 rubles a month. This is half, or less than half, of the 80 rubles that we have cited as average earnings for the industrial worker.

All available data establish the fact that the income of the rural worker is comparatively much less than that of his urban colleague. At the same time it is difficult to equate them because the worker on the collective farm has two sources of income: he gets paid for the number of days he actually works for the collective, and he owns what he produces on his own plot.

There seems little question, however, that even taking both types of income together, the collective farm worker's real income falls far short of that of the urban industrial worker. In many respects the collective farmer has not been fully in-

corporated into the Soviet economy and the incentive framework
within which he functions has not been as successful in mobiliz-
ing his participation as that of his industrial colleague. Some
observers have assumed that for these reasons the regime may
have favored the industrial worker.

Efforts are now being made to narrow the gap between the
actual earnings of the worker on the collective farm and the
worker in industry. This is to be achieved by a higher rate of
pay to the former. At the same time, however, his income is
being limited by a stricter enforcement of regulations governing
the size of his private plot.

Not only are there sharp gaps between the earnings of people
at the top of the occupational ladder and those at the bottom,
but there is also a great geographical variation in wages, so that
a substantial wage differential is offered to attract people to
Siberia, to the virgin lands, with the result that workers already
on the job in those sections of the country receive less than
the newcomers.

As a means of evening out and leveling up the economic condition of Soviet families, the state provides various types of
economic assistance, free services and benefits. These include
low rent and free medical care. Also there are low-cost cafeterias in the factories, and other benefits such as part-cost vacations. Furthermore, a broad system of social security which
includes many kinds of benefits—disability, old-age insurance,
etc.—is gradually and progressively being implemented. Thus,
a working mother who becomes ill receives disability insurance
even though her husband continues to work.

Another almost universal form of assistance is free education
for children and young people. However, it is important to
remember that some fees are still charged for care in the nursery
and kindergarten and until recent years a fee was charged for
the last three years of secondary school—the equivalent of our
high school. It should also be pointed out that the stipends for
students in technical and higher educational institutions are

generally insufficient to maintain them. We learned from students themselves that they can manage only because they receive monthly allowances from their parents.

The Soviet system of social insurance dates back to pre-revolutionary days and has gone through various stages of liberalization since then. Up to 1956 the economy did not permit more than partial implementation of the provisions. In that year, however, the present more liberal scale of payments was adopted and has since been fully implemented. This has given old-age pensioners, formerly condemned to slow attrition, a more adequate income, buttressed by nominal rents and free medical care. A parallel measure to raise the minimum wage to 30 rubles a month has, it is estimated, improved the purchasing power of almost one-third of the employed urban population.

These brief observations of the economic aspects of Soviet family life warrant the conclusion that in spite of efforts to level up and equalize buying power, to improve universal benefits, etc., making ends meet is still a serious problem for most Soviet families.

Housing

In spite of the fact that there is a great deal of construction of new housing going on in Moscow and other urban communities, and a good many small homes are being built in the rural areas and on the outskirts of cities, lack of housing remains one of the extreme social deprivations in the country today. It is undoubtedly an important factor in the quality of care which families can offer children. There are many references in the press to problems in child rearing that are the consequences of overcrowding and lack of privacy.

The housing norm for the U.S.S.R. is 9 square meters, or about 90 square feet per individual. The average available housing in Moscow is approximately 6 or 7 square meters, or about 60 to 70 square feet. This excludes the bathroom, kitchen and hallway, which are often used in common.

The great number of people one sees on the Moscow streets throughout the day and evening is, to a degree at least, accounted for by the overcrowding and the unpleasantness of remaining in the home. Space is still used on a twosome basis, with the same bed utilized by more than one person in the same 24 hours.

We visited one of the new experimental apartments. The family which occupied this apartment comprised father, mother and a son aged 13. The apartment consisted of a small kitchen —too small to eat in—a very small bathroom, and one room, 11' x 12', which served as dining room, living room and bedroom. The father, mother and son all slept in this same room, without any division by curtains or otherwise. The youngster slept on a cot which was put away in a closet during the day.

A chief engineer in a large industrial plant told us that his house consisted of a living room-bedroom, kitchen, and office for himself. One of the young women we met, who belongs to the privileged classes, before her marriage lived in an apartment consisting of three rooms, one of which was an office for her father. The father slept in his office and the mother and daughter slept in the bedroom, sharing the same bed.

Another impression of the housing situation is the tremendous size of the blocks of new buildings which are being erected. One of these complexes will house thousands of families. We could not help feeling that this new kind of living arrangement will dwarf the individual even more than he is now being dwarfed in the whole scheme of Soviet life.

From expert observers we learned that while new housing continues to be built at a consistent pace, it will take at least another decade to rehouse Moscow to any substantial extent.

Working wives and mothers

Employment of women in the U.S.S.R., as in other countries, has a direct bearing on woman's role as housekeeper, wife and mother. One of the original tenets of the revolutionary philosophy was that women were the equal of men, and one important way in which this equality could be expressed was equal opportunity with men for every type of employment.

In this instance, the practical coincides with the ideological. In line with its interest in expanding the labor force, the regime has consistently urged women to become workers outside the home. It expects that women will continue to work after marriage, and even after they have children. It buttresses this objective through the provision of maternity leave and other benefits to the pregnant woman and care in creches for the young child, on the assumption that these arrangements minimize the burden of being at the same time both a mother and an industrial worker.

The visitor to Soviet Russia is sharply impressed not only with the numbers of women working but with the kinds of occupations in which they are engaged. Street-cleaning is a woman's occupation, and women can be seen busy in this activity from early morning until after midnight. They work as motormen and conductors on street cars, they unload coal trucks, dig up street pavements with pick and shovel; and they lay railway tracks. Women are engaged in heavy labor as well as in all the trades and professions.

But it is also true that they are employed at what we might consider "made work." They are almost always the ticket collectors at theaters, in the parks, at expositions, and the number assigned to these jobs seemed to us out of proportion to the task to be done. We were reminded of the depression days in our own country, when many people were assigned to "made work" jobs.

Although by and large there is no discrimination as between men and women with respect to the occupations they may enter, there are professions, such as teaching and medicine, where women outnumber men; most of the direct patient care is done by women. What is also true—and this may represent a lag in the process of equalization—is that men outnumber women in the executive, managerial, top governmental and top scientific positions. For example, in the hospitals we visited it was more usual for the administrator to be a man and the chief of patient care a woman. Most of the chief scientists we met were men. In 1959 there was only one woman in the presidium of the Supreme Soviet, which numbered 15 members.*

We also encountered many contradictions reflecting traditional attitudes about man's superior role, as illustrated by the sight of a work gang on a truck hauling heavy building materials, with the women doing the loading and unloading, and the man sitting in the cab.

When the new pension scheme was recently revised, the government expressed the hope that women would gradually be taken out of the most burdensome and hazardous occupations. Moreover, women receive special consideration in the new pension law which lowers by five years the age at which they are eligible to retire in the three pension age categories. For example, a woman employed in a hazardous occupation, such as underground work in a mine, may become eligible for a pension at the age of 45, after 16 years of employment. Under similar circumstances, men must have worked 20 years and may not retire before the age of 50.

It is significant that the ratio of women employed in what is designated as "mental labor" is greater than that of men. Thus, in the 1959 census, of the 51,600,000 men employed, 42,000,000 were engaged in primarily manual labor and 9,600,000 in mental labor; of the 47,600,000 women employed, 36,600,000 were in primarily manual labor and 11,000,000 in mental labor. This means that within the group of employed women one out of four was engaged in mental labor, while of the men, one out of five was so engaged. Mental labor includes such posts

---

* Mme. Furtseva, the woman member of the presidium, was removed from the membership of the Central Committee of the Communist party in 1961.

as government officials, directors of enterprises—engineering and technical—doctors, dentists, nurses, librarians, lawyers, sales and accounting personnel.

It appears quite clear from public discussions of family life that, in addition to holding a full-time job, many women carry almost total responsibility for housekeeping, with the man enjoying his traditional rights of being waited on and served, even though housekeeping is more burdensome in many ways in the Soviet Union than in other countries. Long hours are spent in queues to buy food; much time is spent waiting turns in kitchens, laundries and bathrooms which must serve several families. Facilities themselves are still primitive and inefficient. In addition, the employed mother is expected to attend school meetings, political discussion groups, apartment house committees, shop committees, trade union meetings and after-work lectures at places of employment, not to mention Communist party meetings if she is a party member. Recent analyses of "free time"—what is left of the 24 hours after allowing for time at work, in sleep, time spent going to and from work, in shopping, household duties, child care—reveals that women have less free time than men.

How true is the view generally held in the United States that in the U.S.S.R. all able-bodied women work? Although expansion in the ratio of women in the labor force began even in Czarist Russia after the turn of the century, the trend was given renewed impetus under the first Five Year Plan, and as a result, from 1929 to 1938 "the proportion of women in the non-agricultural labor force rose from 27 to 38 per cent," and by 1959 had increased to 41.5 per cent.

Though there seems little question that the ratio of working women to the total who might be employable is greater in the U.S.S.R. than in our own country, the image of all Soviet women as being employed in industry is one of the widely disseminated errors about life in the U.S.S.R. It is a fact that a large number of Soviet women do not do remunerative work, limiting themselves to the role of housewife and mother. While the 1959 census does not give us any absolute answers, it clearly substantiates the fact that a large proportion of women of working age—perhaps one out of three—were not employed either in industry or collective farming at the time the census was taken.

The total population of the U.S.S.R. in 1959 was approximately 208,800,000. Forty-five per cent of this number were males, and 55 per cent females—approximately 94,000,000 men and 115,000,000 women. If the same ratio were to be applied to the total working population (men between the ages of 16 and 59 and women between the ages of 16 and 54), it would amount to 54,000,000 men and 66,000,000 women.

When we turn to the number of people actually employed, we find that they total 99,200,000, and this includes 51,600,000 men and 47,600,000 women. Thus, if we compare the number of women *actually* employed with the potential number, which is 66,000,000, we find that approximately 18,400,000 are not employed.

But the actual employed group includes women over the age of 54, and it is fair to assume that a substantial proportion of those employed—at least 5 per cent—would be in the latter group. If we deduct, then, 3,000,000 of the 47,600,000 employed, we get 44,600,000 employed out of 66,000,000 within the employable group. We can therefore assume that our estimate that one out of three employable women does not work seems warranted by the facts. At the same time, we ought not to conclude this analysis without drawing attention to the fact that the ratio of women in the employed group has been increasing and that it is the policy of the government to achieve a large increase in the ratio of the total number of employable women who are in productive work.*

---

* In the United States too, there is a consistent trend toward a greater proportion of women in the labor force. The government expects 6,000,000 more women to be in the labor force in 1970 than there were in 1960. This will bring

The official objective is to shift women from the kitchen and the garden to jobs in industry.

The Seven Year Plan calls for an increase in the number of workers and employees (this excludes collective farmers) by 12,000,000. This can be achieved by drawing women from housekeeping and auxiliary farming and men from auxiliary farming, and farming in general, into productive industry.

Discussing the movement of an increasing number of women into industry, the writer of an article in a Soviet journal in 1961 said:* "In the first place, the communal economy of the collective farms, the network of cultural, service and children's institutions and the trade and public catering enterprises have not yet been sufficiently developed." When they are further developed they will "enable all citizens to give up housework and auxiliary farming." In some districts, the writer points out, those engaged in housework and auxiliary farming constitute 25 per cent of those of working age. "We have not yet been able to create a network of children's institutions, public catering enterprises and communal and everyday services that would enable us to draw the overwhelming majority of women into social production."

The writer goes on to indicate more specifically what needs to be done. The number of pupils in the boarding schools is to increase; the number of new accommodations in kindergartens and nursery schools under the new Seven Year Plan (1958-1965) will be more than double the number added in the preceding seven years. "These changes alone will make it

---

their number to 30,000,000 in a total force of 87,000,000. More important, it will mean a 25 per cent rise in women workers while the number of men workers goes up only 15 per cent. This probably would mean that by 1970 one out of two women of working age in the U.S. would be employed as compared to two out of three in the U.S.S.R. in 1959. (See *The New York Times,* April 6, 1961.)

* "Plans to Shift Women From Gardens, Kitchens to Jobs." *The Current Digest of the Soviet Press,* Volume XIII, Number 5, March 1, 1961. © Pages 25-26.

possible to enlist at least 5 to 6 million women in social production."

The writer acknowledges that the transfer of child care to
community institutions, and housekeeping duties to catering and
other community enterprises will mean an increase in the total
number of working people engaged in the nonproductive sphere.
He points out, however, that the ratio of those who will be
released for productive activity will be much greater than the
ratio of those drawn into community services. What seems clear
is that the twin purposes of community care of children and
increased production reinforce each other. Placing children in
community institutions means releasing women for production;
as more women go to work, more children will be placed in
institutions. Nowhere in the article is there any expression of
concern about the wishes of the women themselves, or whether
the increase in employment of women outside the home would
be better for the children.

Family recreation and use of leisure time

The amount and use of leisure time is an important factor
influencing the quality of child rearing in the family. Even
though there is an active program for reducing the work week,
for most industries it is still 44 to 46 hours, five days of 8 hours
each, and 4 to 6 hours on Saturday. Sunday is the day of rest.

The general impression one receives is that leisure time is
more interwoven with the realities of living than in some more
materially favored cultures, such as our own. Women who do
not work usually do a great deal of sewing, either for their own
family or for the families of relatives where the mother is employed. Then, too, because of the amount of homework a child
is expected to do, parents naturally spend a good deal of time
at home while he is busy with his lessons, helping him with his
assignments or just being with him. Through our contact with
several families, we got the impression that a good deal of

leisure time is used up in visiting relatives which, we believe, often involves a great amount of reciprocal aid.

Although much attention is given to the organization of sports and leisure-time activities, many of them remain simple and informal. Visiting a small town on a Sunday morning one sees a large proportion of the population in the town square watching field events in which many of the young people are engaged. As one travels the highway on a Sunday morning one sees many people picnicking, others fishing. With the increase in the number of automobiles many people are out for a drive, either in cars or on motorcycles for two. One also sees a great many families working on their own private plots of ground.

The impression gained is that there is much less reliance on passive forms of recreation than in our country. There seem to be relatively few movie houses in Moscow, compared to the number in New York, Chicago or Philadelphia.

While it is difficult to estimate the proportion of the various uses of leisure time, there is no question that a great deal of time is taken up with mutual aid responsibilities or with volunteer community services. This is true for women who are expected to participate in parents' associations, in tenants' committees, in such activities as nursing neighbors who are ill, in supervision of playgrounds in the tenants' court. The men are involved in various kinds of duties on union committees and also in service as volunteer policemen, etc.

In visualizing the increased use of leisure time, the spokesmen for the regime and party theoreticians have expressed great concern that leisure time not be absorbed in "the private" aspects of living. They advocate expanding the community and mutual aid responsibilities of the average citizen so that leisure time is used more and more in participation in group activities such as sports or self-government, and in various kinds of civic responsibilities.

Under present Soviet living conditions, although a good deal of social intercourse takes place, it is hindered by several factors: the shortage of housing space and the resultant limitations on privacy and the capacity to accommodate visitors, as well as the burdens of housekeeping. With more adequate and better housing, with more mechanized household equipment, it is reasonable to expect that these obstacles to social intercourse would be minimized.

With the reduction in the work day to 7 hours and with some improvement in the distribution of consumer goods to reduce the burden of shopping, the average Soviet citizen will have more leisure. The question is, how will it be used? Will it mean freedom to establish private associations and increase social intercourse outside the control and surveillance of the party, and greater pursuit of individual forms of self-expression outside the organized use of time such as clubs and civic duties now offered to the Soviet citizen?

In particular, "controlled leisure" holds definite appeal for a party which aspires to create the "new Soviet man" and to make every citizen a public servant in the "stateless" Communist utopia of the future. For if working hours are shortened, the citizen will have more "spare time" which the party can then mobilize for the purpose of manning the "comrades' courts," the "volunteer militia," and other as yet unformed "public organizations" which, Khrushchev has intimated, will gradually supplant the existing state machinery as the "transition to communism" progresses. The party could also call upon the citizen to perform "voluntary" spare-time work on civic improvement projects, in scrap collections, and even communal housing construction. If doctrinal authority is needed to show that this would accord with the Communist conception of the ideal society, one may cite Lenin's statement in 1919 defining communism as "a system under which people become accustomed to the performance of public duties without any specific machinery of compulsion, when unpaid work for the public good becomes the general phenomenon."

There is evidence, also, that Khrushchev's version of the world's "highest standard of living" is more cultural than material: rather than corrupt the citizen's sense of values by giving him too many material comforts, grant him more leisure for cultural activities and recreation of a type approved by the party.*

In the early months of 1963 an elaborate study was undertaken to determine how much "free time" the average individual has, and consider what might be the most socially profitable use of such time.

After the amount of free time was estimated, the author discussed various choices for the use of this time: simple recreation that brings no social benefits as against self-improvement —going to night school, participating in cultural activities and as a volunteer in community services. Obviously the ground is being prepared for pressure upon the individual to use his free time, which has already increased and is likely to continue to, to achieve social goals.

*Governmental responsibility for
the protection of children*

The broad measures the regime has taken to protect child life are consistent with the premium placed on the health and well-being of children as the future builders of communist society.

In many ways, tangible and intangible, the Soviet government has tried to compensate children for the deprivation which the social and economic situation imposes. The protection of children is everybody's business: not only that of the designated official agencies and their staffs—the Health and Education Ministries—but of fellow-students, other parents, fellow-members of the parents' unions, tenants in the same apartment court, and officials of the Communist party.

Four ministries have an important role in providing services to safeguard children. These are the Ministries of Health, Education, Internal Affairs and Social Security. Moreover, the

---

* "The Outlook for the Soviet Consumer." William N. Turpin. *Problems of Communism,* Vol. IX, No. 6, Nov.-Dec. 1960. Page 34.

varied health, welfare and education services carried by the labor unions not only supplement those provided by the ministries, but also include many additional services not otherwise available.

As reported here, the republic ministries of health provide comprehensive health care for everybody from infancy through adulthood, through a variety of general and specialized clinical, hospital and institutional facilities. The protection of the health of the young child is not left to chance or to the will of the mother; homes are routinely visited by the public health nurse and the mother is required to bring the child to the clinic for regular checkups. Furthermore, the scope of responsibility of the health authorities is very broad and includes not only medical care but also health education and financial assistance. Health care of children in nursery school and kindergarten, both day and residential, is under the direct supervision of the health authority.

Among the ministries sharing directly in safeguarding the welfare of children, the educational authorities may be said to be the principal protective agencies; they carry many responsibilities beyond that of formal schooling. Child placement, foster home and institutional care for the homeless child, as well as protection of children from abuse and neglect, are but a few examples of child care functions of the educational authorities.

The Ministry of Internal Affairs is charged with responsibility in the field of child delinquency. It maintains the reception shelters and also administers youth reformatories or colonies for delinquent children.

The Ministry of Social Security is responsible for residential care of the imbecile and idiot child as well as some classes of the physically handicapped.

While it is outside the scope of our interest to assess how far trade unions in the U.S.S.R. exist in order to advance the interest of their members or how far they represent an arm of government to deal with problems of labor, it is clear that the labor unions play an important part in the lives of the people and in the protection of children. In each plant the union constitutes a protective and mutual aid association, and it carries many responsibilities affecting the daily lives of the average individual. It is active in the fields of housing and welfare. Much of the construction and management of public housing is closely connected with the operation of the plant and, except in the larger cities such as Moscow, Kiev and Leningrad, much of the housing is directly built by the plant, rather than the municipality. It is also customary for the plant to advance loans to workers who wish to build their own homes.

The unions operate cafeterias in the plants, with the union committee fixing prices and size of portions, and watching over the standards of service.

The Committee on Children's Work of the union is concerned with the sponsorship of the children's nurseries and in some instances, also, the kindergartens. The Committee on Social Insurance, which is concerned with disability and sick benefits of the workmen, is part of the plant administration. Such matters as admissions to sanatoria are also determined by committees of the union.

Having traced the principal responsibilities for child welfare of four ministries and the labor union it might be worth-while to turn to a brief description of the practical child welfare measures which have been provided. We have already indicated that every adult is considered responsible for doing what he can to protect children. While this is true in almost all other cultures, in the Soviet Union there is a greater insistence on this responsibility.

The tenants in the apartment building in which the family lives, or the neighbors next door, are supposed to report to the school authorities any evidence of neglect of a child. When this occurs, it becomes the responsibility of the children's inspector to make a formal investigation of the complaint—which might include such charges as immorality of the mother, phys-ical abuse of the child, failure to provide medical care. After investigation of such a complaint, the inspector may resort to warnings and admonitions, or he may arrange for one of the neighbors in the same apartment to look out for the child. If he feels that such measures will not suffice and the problem is so serious as to warrant either a more impressive kind of warn-ing or actual removal of the child, he will report the case to the Children's Commission.

The Children's Commission operates under the authority of the local soviet and its membership is made up of volunteers, with the actual staff work done by the children's inspectors. The Commission itself does not have the right to take the child away from his parents, but may go so far as to arrange for the placement of the child in a children's home or a foster home, and if the mother should refuse, then the matter is taken to the people's court.

Guidance for parents

Advice and help in child rearing are offered to parents in many different ways. The health, education, social security and other ministries literally bombard the family with leaflets and pamphlets offering advice on health care, habit training, growth and development, as well as directions for guidance which will produce the kind of character best suited for a collective society.

A parent troubled about the behavior of his child may turn to a number of different agencies for help. He may go to the polyclinic where the problem may be referred to the neurologist-psychiatrist. He may go to the teacher of the child or to the principal of the school. Or he may seek help from the party unit to which he belongs or the trade union of which he or his wife is a member. In the main, parents will turn to the child's teacher for help with behavior problems.

Child guidance as a specialized function, in the sense in which it exists in our country, is not known in the Soviet Union. The establishment of a special category of the teaching profession called the *upbringer* represents a beginning in the development of a special worker to carry the child guidance function. She now serves as the professional counselor in the children's institution and also carries special responsibility for shaping the personality of the child in the school setting. She is a teacher who has had additional training for the special tasks she carries as an upbringer.

One of the leading authorities in the Soviet Union on family life was very eager to learn about the child guidance function in the U.S., particularly our interdisciplinary approach in which the psychiatrist, psychologist, psychiatric caseworker and teacher all collaborate in the planning to meet special problems which the child presents. She felt that the present Soviet system was not satisfactory, that actually the upbringers were not sufficiently trained to handle the job.

Where children are reared
in the Soviet Union

It is widely believed in the U.S. that most young Russian children are reared in creches, or, if reared in their own homes, spend the greater part of the day in the day nursery or kindergarten. The general impression is that the mother is at work and the responsibility for rearing her child has been assumed either totally or for the most part by community agencies.

This is far from true. What always startles the foreign visitor and, for that matter, even some Soviet citizens themselves, is the fact that with relatively few exceptions children of all ages are reared in their own homes.

It is true that many mothers work, and it is also true that the regime is committed to a policy of day care in nursery or kindergarten for the preschool child, and camp and boarding school for as many school-age children as can be accommodated. However, many factors operate to limit the number of children receiving either partial or total care away from their families, the most important being the attitude of the parents themselves and the unavailability of requisite community facilities.

In the care of the young child we see a gap between official policy and reality. For example, while the health authorities strongly emphasize the importance of breast-feeding by the mother up to the age of eight months, the arrangements that have been provided do not generally make this possible for the working mother. Maternity leave with pay is limited to 112 days. Infant nursery facilities which would enable the mother to bring her baby to her place of employment, as well as a bus service to enable her to go home during the working day to maintain the feeding schedules, do exist, but are insufficient to meet the needs of more than a small proportion of the total group that might utilize these arrangements.

The gap in arrangements does not necessarily result in placement of the children. We know that even where the mother's employment makes it impossible for her to be with her child throughout the day, children are not necessarily placed in day nurseries. A great many are reared by grandparents or other elderly relatives. This practice accounts for a great deal of Soviet literature on the subject of old-fashioned grandparents, "aunties" and old women employed as homeworkers or servants. While some grandparents are esteemed by the state because of their revolutionary past, many are suspected of passing on to children ideas which do not coincide with those of the present regime: for example, acquainting children with religious ideas and practices. We think it is taken for granted that the older generation is more prone to make mistakes in rearing children from the standpoint of Soviet goals.

Besides being looked after by relatives, many children are left in the care of one of the other mothers or older persons living in the same court as the family. In one of the apartment courts we visited, the children who attended school in the after-noon were taken care of during the morning by some of the old-age pensioners.

There are many other arrangements to help parents with the care of children of school age. The plan for an extended school day enables the child to remain at the school from early morn-ing until 6:00 P.M. or later in the evening. In many respects this provides the school child with the same protection the nursery school provides for the preschool child.

The new apartment blocks now being constructed include a number of child care facilities—an elementary school, after-school rooms, nursery schools and play space. This means that the child who continues to live in his own home may participate in a variety of wholesome out-of-school activities until his parents return from work.

In this connection, too, it is important to refer to the summer camp to which almost all children, from the primary through the school years, are sent for a substantial part of the vacation period.

Bearing in mind that many children lost one or both parents during the last World War, and that the official credo of the regime is that children are best reared in community institu-tions, one may well wonder how many children are reared en-tirely away from their own people.

As far as we have been able to discover, the facts are as fol-lows: As of the summer of 1959, there were about 120,000 children in the boarding schools; 200,000 were in orphanages or *dietskie doma,* and another 600,000 to 800,000 were in various kinds of foster homes. These latter included homes where children were cared for on a relatively temporary basis while par-ents were ill or hospitalized and where the child would ulti-mately return to his own family. They also included children in "guardianship" homes where the child was permanently re-moved from his parents; also, children in adoptive homes. The figures cited are for the Russian Republic alone and add up to approximately 1,000,000 children in some form of substitute care. Taking the children in foster care and the total number of children in the population in the same age range, we find that no more than one out of every 18 children is reared in an institution or in a foster home.

It is anticipated that by 1965 the enrollment in boarding schools will reach 1,300,000 pupils, as against 120,000 in 1959. At the same time, however, one must remember that the new boarding school program envisages the transfer of the *dietskie doma* to the boarding school system, so that the net increase in the number of children living away from their parents would be less than the figures suggest. With the conversion of the *dietskie doma* into boarding schools, the population of these schools would be increased to about 1,300,000, and allowing for 600,000 children in foster homes, the total of those reared outside the family would be about 2,000,000. But even this would represent only about one in nine in the age ranges affected.

C. The Child in His Family

What the actual relationships of parents and children are today in the Soviet Union is not easily determined by a foreign observer. Few foreigners have had the opportunity to live with a Russian family, or to visit extensively in Russian homes. The glimpses we had of young children with their parents on the street and in the parks and playgrounds and, in a few instances, in their own homes, showed us more spontaneous, more outgoing behavior than we saw in organized groups such as nursery schools, kindergartens or Pioneer clubs. The parents seemed forbearing, kindly and indulgent. We perceived great warmth and comradeship between parents and older children. These observations give grounds for, as well as derive confirmation from, the indignant outbursts in the public press about "indulgent papas and mamas" and parents who do not set a good example for their children.

We interviewed many parents. Some of our well-educated guides and interpreters were parents. Parents spoke to us of their anxieties about their children and asked our advice. Almost without exception, observers of Soviet life report on the extraordinary warmth and attention that Soviet parents seem to lavish on their children. One observer said they are literally showered with caresses, both in words and action, not just by parents but by friends of the family, neighbors, and even passersby. The best is reserved for the children.

If we recall the legal provisions governing the rights and responsibilities of the parents and those of the state, we will recognize the sharp difference between the relevant governing principles in the United States and those in the Soviet Union. American and Soviet principles, in fact, move from opposing assumptions.*

In our country, the rights of the parent are paramount and the state intervenes only when and where it has been shown that the parent is unwilling or incapable of safeguarding the well-being of his child. It is then that the state exercises its rights as super-parent.

In the Soviet Union, as in the United States, the state is the super-parent but, in contrast to the U. S., in the U.S.S.R. the state sees itself as the primary parent and defines in considerable detail the profile of the future citizen and the kind of education and child rearing that will produce the type of character and personality that is embodied in the national goal.

Moreover, the Soviet Union is not content with a *laissez-faire* policy about parental responsibilities. Parents' obligations, both material and psychological, including the ideals which they are to inculcate, are carefully spelled out. These pages are replete with statements and comments on the image of the Soviet man and the responsibility placed on parents to rear their offspring in this image. We have already referred to the emphasis on

---

* Alts, *op. cit.* Page 94.

education, on achievement of skills, on productivity, on restraint, good behavior and social responsibility.

We have frequently drawn attention to the efforts intended to make every child politically conscious. Many books and stories for children glorify the leaders of the revolution who thereby become objects for emulation and identification.

A more striking difference between our child-rearing methods and those of the Soviet Union is to be found in the sphere of values. The widespread and incessant campaign to wipe out religion and religious training and substitute in their place secular morality rooted in party doctrine extends to family living.

It is not that traditional values, such as honesty and kindliness, have been scrapped or played down, but that the sanctions for such virtues have changed, with the good of the state replacing Holy Writ. And it follows that loyalty to the state must be accorded priority over loyalty to the family, and the authority of the family must give way to the authority of the teacher.

How these ideals are brought to the child, and their impact on him, obviously depends on the quality of the relationships between parents and children in present-day Soviet life—glimpses of which we have reported.

Two orientations to interpersonal relationships within the family can be discerned in current Soviet literature. One has its roots in what we have chosen to designate as the "romantic" approach to the problems of living; the other, the realistic and official.

The romantic approach is embodied in a vision of family life in which parents and children are very close to each other, sharing in many joys and discharging reciprocal responsibilities. Makarenko himself waxed inspirational in his portrayal of the relations between parents and children. A stream of articles and books are now appearing which idealize family living and suggest how it can be given greater meaning in the lives of parents and children. They address themselves to concrete suggestions as to how parents and children might live more happily together, and these include birthday and anniversary celebrations, and family outings. They also deal with more serious issues such as sex education and how parents may handle these subjects with their adolescent children.

In contrast to what we have called the "romantic," the official and realistic orientation hammers away at the role of the parent as agent of the state, at the responsibilities which have been entrusted to him.

We have read many Soviet books and articles written for children of various ages, young people and parents, representing both points of view. By and large, and this includes even some official publications by the government, they are all characterized by their idealization of child life, either romantically glorifying the ideals and values which children should be taught or delineating such ideals in hortatory fashion.

Characteristic of a publication which reflects both points of view is the illustrated book of poems for children written by V. Mayakovsky: *What is Good and What is Bad.*

On one page are illustration and accompanying poem showing what is bad, and on the next page are the illustration and poem showing what is good. The following two sets of verses are illustrative:

> When a boy's as black as night—
> Dirt on hands and face—
> We all know that's bad, all right,
> And a sad disgrace.

> If a boy is clean and neat,
> Washes every day,
> He's a lad we love to meet—
> He is good, we say.

> This one's frightened by a crow,
> Shame upon the lad!
> He's called coward, as you know,
> And that is very bad.

This one stops the nasty bird,
Though he's just a mite,
He's a brave boy, I have heard.
Now, that's good and right.

An official publication called "A Course of Lectures for Mothers," published in 1958, undertakes to help parents deal with some of the problems they encounter as their child grows up. This reveals not only the fact that the regime goes a long way beyond the emphasis on conformity, but also the Soviet concept of collective education as applied to the care of the young child.

It is also significant, in the light of our discussion of the extent to which children are still reared in their own homes, that this publication, meant for mothers of preschool children, sets forth schedules and routines that could only be carried out by nonworking mothers, as, for example, four meals a day and two fresh-air outings daily. Moreover, it is mothers and fathers who are instructed in the child's care in contrast to the earlier editions in which grandparents were frequently referred to. Actually, there is only one derogatory example of child care by a grandmother who infantilizes the child.

In this publication there is the usual insistence on the strict following of schedules at every age, the reason given being that this is not only best for the health and welfare of the child but that it also accustoms a child to the regular habits and responsible behavior which will be expected of him in school and in his adult working life as a Soviet citizen.

At the same time, the lectures point out that correct, careful training must be accompanied by parental warmth and understanding and sensitivity to a child's needs, but not by overprotection or leniency or demands which are not followed through.

The emphasis throughout is on constant habit training without a punishing attitude. Here are some illustrative excerpts from "Lectures to Mothers":

The child must be provided with a convenient place to play. In the child's corner all his playthings should be assembled. In no case should playthings be dumped into a box. Adults, together with the child, must put all toys in order: gather separate parts, place everything on the table or shelf: this develops in the child a habit of order and predisposes him to play. In families with one child, parents not infrequently view him as an amusement, a pet, they indulge him in all ways. In such conditions it is difficult to upbring a useful member of our society. In those cases children may grow up as egotists, little adapted to life and labor. . . . At an early age one must find work for children adequate to their development and which would hold their attention and interest. . . .

Children with poor appetites cause their parents many worries. The reason for a child's poor appetite, apart from ill-health, is the incorrect conduct of the parents. Sometimes the mother, in a hurry to feed the child, quickly thrusts spoon after spoon in his mouth, without waiting for the child to chew and swallow and to be ready for the next spoonful. Such feeding, when a child is thrust a spoonful into a full mouth or is forcibly fed . . . is very painful to a child. . . . A child's negative attitude toward feeding may persist, sometimes it is transformed into a morbid manifestation: there are cases when a child begins to vomit at the sight of food being prepared. The attention of children is usually highly deflected by their surroundings. Thus they should be fed in calm surroundings, the radio turned off, without loud conversations or the visit of outsiders. . . .

In the case of bad appetite, parents are often unable to hide their anxiety, their consternation is felt by the child and his appetite is still lowered. Apart from this, children of two to three years already are as if flattered by the anxiety they have caused in adults, they attempt to keep it up, and feeding becomes transformed into a violent scene, exhausting to both the adult and the child.

Many parents in urging the child to eat habitually make use of various persuasions: "For Father," "for Mother," "just this little bit more," "eat, or I'll give it all to the cat," or, "I'll give it to Sasha [another child]," etc. Sometimes, from loving persuasions and promises, parents change to shouts, menaces, spanking, and drive the child to tears. Or the parents strive to amuse the child by jokes and stories, sometimes succeeding to distract the child to the degree that he will eat mechanically, as if unconsciously, swallowing spoonful after spoonful. From the psychological, as well as the educational point of view, such methods must be considered incorrect. The child's attention must be on the food: this helps its digestion and forms the habit of good eating. . . .

The conduct of parents at feeding must be such that the child does not get the impression that his good or poor appetite presents itself as the center of interest to those around him, the source of their pleasure and grief, that having eaten a plate of soup or a cutlet, he may count on any reward.

The child eats best if at the proper time, already in his second year, he is given all possible independence. . . . When a child is already eating independently, it is best not to stand over him, not to hurry him, but to move away and watch only from a distance.

Good appetite is aided by a number of preparatory actions of the child. A child aged about 3 should, before sitting down at table, wash his hands, take his towel and having wiped his hands, hang it in its place, fetch his bib or napkin, bring his plate, spoon, bread, sit down at his habitual and convenient-for-eating place at table. . . . All those actions preparatory to eating attune him to food and undoubtedly raise his appetite.

As these excerpts from "Lectures to Mothers" indicate, while parents are admonished to deal with the child thoughtfully and to try to individualize his care, at the same time there is the emphasis on socialization, regularity and conformity. This is further illustrated in many articles by teachers and parents which suggest how socialized behavior should be implanted very early in the child's life. In an article by a "Hero Mother," she describes in detail how, when her child is two, she begins to teach him to take care of his own needs and to assume some responsibility for the care of his younger brother or sister.*

No account of the unique elements in Soviet child rearing can omit references to the traditional Russian practice of swad-

---

* See Chapter 9, D.

dling. The official professional position rejects swaddling; in actual day-by-day care of children, however, a modified form of swaddling is practiced both in the family and in the community child care institution. While the tightness in the binding of the child's body has apparently been given up, the child continues to be wrapped firmly, with the arms and legs held in position. This is true of the infants seen in the creches as well as those we saw in the arms of their parents on the streets. The persistence of swaddling, even though in modified form, may be related to the continued emphasis on conformity and submission of the child to the will of the adult.

Parent and child

As far as we know, the Russians themselves have made no study or analysis of the varied and opposing pressures and expectations to which both parents and children are subjected within their relationship: the obligation of the parents to rear a child who meets the high standards set by public policy—the obligation of the parents to instill the party ideology; the difference in the ideals taught by the school and Pioneer organization and those which the parents themselves may have acquired and hold.

Obviously, in no culture is there complete harmony between the general ideals and expectations which it presents to the growing individual and those held by the parents. This difference must be much deeper in the Soviet Union for many reasons. The value system for group and individual behavior is, as we have seen, sharply different from that which existed in prerevolutionary times, with the result that the parent himself is going through a rapid transition in his own views and ideals. There must inevitably be a lag in the degree of his acceptance of this newer view of what is important in living.

Our own observation, as well as that reported by other American observers, warrants the assumption that the majority of

Russian parents have, on an intellectual level, accepted the major thesis of the state about social ideals and social behavior. One result of this, which we have observed, is that this kind of parent becomes very anxious about any deviant behavior of his child.

"I worry that he is too boisterous," said Manya, one of our very intelligent and sensitive guides. "You would think he is overaggressive. Do you think I should send him to the nursery school? People tell me I should not keep him with us all the time." This was in reference to her 3-year-old son who was being brought up by his grandmother.

Manya's views can be assumed to be like those of most Soviet parents. They are subject to a barrage of propaganda in the form of articles in newspapers and magazines, and public lectures about the importance of teaching the child conformity to collective ideals as well as collective behavior. Any discussion of the subject without exception portrays the parent as the offending person in this respect, with the teacher and other professionals following a clear, consistent line in implementation of this policy.

Apart from the anxiety most parents must feel about their failure to live up to expectations, there is also the fact that the children, as we have seen and will see further, are subjected to the influence of the professional for many hours a day and throughout much of the summer. Moreover, the professional teaches the child a set of attitudes and a point of view without any concern as to how far these deviate from those the child has imbibed from his own parents. This undoubtedly creates distance between parents and children. We have read of instances where the child cites the attitude of the teacher and upbringer as the correct one, criticizing his parent for being wrong. The situation, however, becomes much more complicated when either the parent deviates from the official point of view or the child is skeptical of the official line.

On our first trip we encountered a number of young people who were distrustful of official policies and who spoke quite openly of their differences with their parents who, to quote one young person, "were just old-line Communists." The normal antagonisms between parent and child that characterize the growing up of young people are further intensified by basic differences in the degree to which either of them accepts or deviates from official ideology and expectations.

Kent Geiger, of the Russian Research Center of Harvard University, has published the results of a study of the role of the family in Soviet society.* This study was particularly concerned with the degree of difference and the degree of agreement between parents and children about Soviet ideology and the effect the differences had upon the parent-child relationships. The study sought to determine in what ways and at what point children, as they move out of the home and are exposed to the views of teachers and Pioneer leaders, come into conflict with the views of the parents who represent a different stage in sovietization. To a degree that has not been determined this conflict is assumed "prototypical" of parent-youth relations in totalitarian societies and has been designated as the "struggle" between family and state for the minds of the young.

The study was conducted by interviewing 141 young Soviet persons born in the period 1915 to 1929, and a group of individuals who were themselves parents in the Soviet Union and whose first child was born in the 1915-1930 period. Thus, in terms of age the adults interviewed correspond roughly to the generation of parents of young persons in the first sample. To quote from Geiger's report:

Of the 103 young persons who gave adequate responses [to the focal questions of the inquiry, "the role of the respondent's parents

---

* "Changing Political Attitudes in Totalitarian Society, A Case Study of the Role of the Family." Kent Geiger: *World Politics*, Vol. VIII, No. 2, January 1956. Pages 187-205.

in the development of his attitudes toward the Soviet regime and its works"] . . . 91 per cent came from families in which the parents had been at heart anti-Soviet in feeling while living in the USSR. This was a situation which posed a sharp problem for the parents: How, if indeed at all, should they teach their children to understand the real nature of the Soviet regime? How far should they go in transmitting openly their own attitudes and values to their children?

At the same time, the parents recognized that

other forces were at work—forces which served to restrict the parents' freedom of choice. Since school, youth organizations, informal peer groups, cinema, radio, and reading materials of all description strive to make the young person a loyal adherent to the works and symbols of the Soviet order, it is not surprising that children were regularly led in the direction of enthusiastic acceptance of Bolshevik ideology. In fact, within the anti-Soviet family there frequently appeared a young political activist who did not hesitate to display his sentiments:

> The child comes to the conviction that the Communist propaganda tells the truth, and if he hears from his parents the opposite opinion, he feels insulted and tries to explain these things to his parents, who are not politically conscious. In short, he becomes a convinced Communist, a Pioneer, fired by the Pioneer literature, activism, and so on.

It is startling that the study discovered that "one of the most widely cited norms of family conduct under Soviet conditions was the requirement that non-conforming attitudes were not to be expressed in front of small children":

Everyone was afraid of his children. A small child can betray his parents unwittingly, and therefore my parents were always careful in what they said before me and my brother.*

---

* *Ibid.* Pages 191 and 192.

The enormity of the problem which can result from differences of values between parent and child in the close and continuous interaction within the family is pointed out by Geiger.
Unlike the situation in other kinds of cultures,

> Under Soviet totalitarianism, however, it is clear that parents
> could not easily control the views of their young children. More-
> over, the problem areas in the parent-child relationship applied
> not only to matters which a Westerner would consider "political,"
> and in which, it might be argued, children have little interest or
> involvement, but to matters which had traditionally been of central
> importance to the parent-child relationship. . . . Consider, for ex-
> ample, the following comments:

>> . . . they told you you have no right to punish a child. And
>> if a child was punished, he would go and complain to the
>> authorities.
>> . . . in the schools they were developing a child of the worst
>> sort. There were denunciations, lack of respect for elders,
>> and denial of God.

The situation as it involves communication between parent
and child changes, according to Geiger, when the child reaches
the age of 14 or 15, becomes more aware of basic issues and
assumes some personal responsibility for his communications
with his parents. Parents then feel safer and are more ready
to trust the child with information which clearly shows "a gap
between family values and the official sponsored ideology." It
is also significant that many of the persons interviewed and
brought up in the Soviet Union told how they " 'knew' what the
parental view was." While the parents avoid direct talk on
political questions, one young person reports his father deflected
his attention from communism by making him "read classical
literature or other instructive and interesting books rather than
the Pioneer literature."

The report draws attention to the complicated issues which
parents had to face in the teaching of their children.

The first major conclusion . . . is that the regime was quite successful in opposing the anti-Soviet views of parents and thus in molding the attitudes of young people. Clearly, the first step in the process consisted in gaining the loyalty of children at an early age. The predominant reaction to this . . . was a feeling of fear and helplessness. Little could be done to prevent their indoctrination. As their children grew older, however, and developed a sense of responsibility for the welfare of their parents, it was possible to introduce them to non-conformist ideas. But as might be expected, and as these data indicate, by this time it was in many cases too late, and if the parents persisted in contradicting what the children had learned in school, conflict was likely to develop. Parent-youth conflict, actual and potential, then served as a social pressure within the family which often led to greater parental conformity with the attitudes and values of the new Soviet culture. It therefore actually served the purposes of the regime by helping to weaken the family as a source of opposition to Bolshevik ideology. . . .*

A basic conclusion is warranted. The family has on the whole not been a significant force in resisting the ideological indoctrination of Soviet young persons. While there is some evidence that politically tinged parent-youth conflict was a prominent feature in the prewar Soviet family, of equal or greater importance is the fact that Soviet parents so frequently minimized such conflict by their adaptive-conforming responses to the regime's ideology.**

The conclusion cited above is even more true today when so many parents are themselves wholly a product of the Soviet system of indoctrination.

The future of the Soviet family

A restatement of the official Soviet view of the role of the family in the social order is to be found in the article cited earlier.† Kharchev seeks to reconcile the contradictions which

---

* *Ibid.* Pages 200-201.

** *Ibid.* Page 204.

† *The Current Digest,* Vol. XII, No. 21, June 22, 1960, *op. cit.* Page 9.

have characterized Soviet policy and practice since the revolution. In attempting this he projects his view of the status and functions of the family when communism will have been established.

The author begins by noting the attitude of "bourgeois sociologists" who take the position that the Communists have always favored the abolition of the family. These sociologists, he states, claim that for 40 years a "fierce war of attrition" has been going on between the Soviet regime and the family, with victory alternating between one side and the other. They allege that the Communists are " 'irritated by the very existence of this institution which they do not control, this self-constituted and self-contained cell, this foreign body within the body politic.' "

Kharchev's position is that Soviet life completely refutes these claims of the bourgeois ideologists. He holds that the Communist party and the Soviet government are deeply concerned with measures which will strengthen and enhance family relations in *new social conditions.* He then proceeds to point out that, according to Communist views, the family represents a complex and many-faceted social phenomenon. "It combines the natural-biological relationship of the sexes with the social functions of raising children and ennobling the mind." Kharchev goes on to charge that bourgeois sociologists regard the family as an eternal and unchanging institution. In contrast, Marxism-Leninism affirms that the family arose historically and develops historically. "Change in the structure, the social functions and the economic and spiritual life of the family is determined in the final account by the development of the society's economy and change in the society's foundations."

The family, however, is not merely a reflection of economic forces. Since, Kharchev avers, the family includes moral as well as economic relationships, " it develops likewise under the strong influence of spiritual culture and cultural traditions and it possesses *relative independence* in its development. . . . Against the family based on property, Marxism-Leninism has always upheld a stronger and morally purer monogamous family—'marriage with love,' to use V.I. Lenin's expression." Kharchev proceeds to dispel one other erroneous assumption of the bourgeois sociologists—that free love is a leftist deviation. Socialism by no means frees man from a serious view of love, from the economic and moral obligations that matrimony creates, and from marital and parental duty.

Kharchev addresses himself at some length to consideration of the future of the Soviet family. He declares that

The genuine, real future of the family in connection with society's advance to communism will be determined by such factors as, first, the further development of social production and the transition to distribution *according to need* [our italics] and, second, the development of the individual personality and the intensification of society's interest in the correct, communist upbringing of the young generation. The rise of *the communist* family will also signify the gradual effacement of the economic-everyday-life distinctions between urban workers' and rural peasants' families as a result of elimination of the distinctions between the classes (of workers and peasants), between town and country, between mental and manual labor.

The first major consequence for the family of the transition to communism will be the socialization of everyday living, completely freeing woman from exhausting housework and enabling the family to grant considerably more time and effort to spiritual life and the upbringing of children.

What Kharchev means by "the socialization of everyday living" is freeing the mother of her burdens as a housekeeper. The family will get its food from restaurants, cafes; its clothing from tailoring shops; and other needs through other service institutions. But he no sooner projects the picture of the future than he proceeds to modify it. To quote him:

In no case will communism mean that a family will have to use social institutions always and in all instances to satisfy its everyday needs. Home dinners, suppers, parties and gatherings certainly will be preserved to the extent that the family wants them to satisfy its wish for "home joys" and contact with friends in the surroundings of the home.*

To continue with Kharchev's vision of the future of the Soviet family:

Along with the disappearance of many elements of the household economy and reduction of the family's economic activity . . . changes will take place in the family's moral-educational function. *Family upbringing* will be combined more and more with directly *social upbringing*. [Our italics]

Kharchev points out that it is well-known that the

U.S.S.R. already possesses the most extensive network of children's institutions in the world. In accordance with a decision of the 21st Party Congress, the construction of boarding schools has grown, and their number will increase manyfold by 1965. One of the purposes of the boarding schools in the present period is to give the family not only moral but material help in raising children. Only part of the cost of maintaining children in the boarding schools is collected from the parents. At the same time, the schools rely extensively on the experience and direct help of the parents. The result is that the parents' moral influence on the children is preserved but, in addition, such a strong factor in the formation of the child's personality as the collective of his coevals also goes into action. It must not be forgotten that in families it is sometimes difficult to guard children against the appearance of egotistic inclinations.

The next sentence in Kharchev's article epitomizes the present mode of thought on the part of professional educators and leaders of the regime on the molding of the personality of children. " . . . when the *parents'* experience is combined with the *teachers'* knowledge and the *student group's* sensitivity and impartiality, the effectiveness of upbringing is considerably increased." [Our italics]

---

* *Ibid.* Page 11.

The child, as can be seen, remains like a mass of clay rather than a feeling entity, which is shaped by parent, teacher and student group. As we have repeatedly pointed out, Kharchev, like leading Russian educators, does not openly acknowledge the connection between the emotional nurture which the child receives from his parents and the kind of person he becomes.

In the light of the many realities in family living and interpersonal relationships we have delineated, we may well ask how far Kharchev's projection of family life and child rearing is likely to be realized in the future. While he avoids the dichotomy between family and state, his orientation and values put him clearly on the side of community rearing.

Khrushchev, expressing the views of his official advisers on education, family life and child rearing, speaks of the "possibility that in the future all children will be reared in community institutions by professional workers." Running through all the official discussion of child care and child rearing is the conviction that if children are to be reared to be citizens in a cooperative or collective society, then they must be reared according to collective principles and as members of groups rather than members of families. Back of this, undoubtedly, are the recognition and fear that the family remains a private area, a small island of solidarity and loyalty within the totality of the national life. Nowhere has the family's place in character building been assessed and the dynamic elements in this process identified. Nor has there been any assessment of the role of the family's chief rivals—the school, the peer group, the camp. No one has outlined the limitations of rearing as a professional function rather than as an expression of natural human proclivities.

In this connection it should be pointed out that Khrushchev does not spell out in detail his policies on child rearing; we get fragments of a total plan. He does not say that young children should be totally removed from their families. The nation, in fact, is adding to its nurseries so as to enable children to remain at home while their mothers go out to work. Neither Khrushchev nor Kharchev spells out, except in general terms, what will become of the family's child-rearing responsibilities. They make no attempt to resolve the inherent conflict in their thesis of the attenuation of family functions and the continued role of the family in child rearing and social relations. Perhaps neither Khrushchev nor Kharchev is sure of the future direction beyond the fragmentary and contradictory proposals they both advocate. They have not yet separated ideology from reality.

Our own observations lead us to believe that the desire of Soviet parents to rear their own children is so strong that the regime does not at this point dare to propose, as did the old-maid schoolteacher whom we met in Sochi, that as soon as children are born they be taken away from their parents, who are incompetent to rear them. The extreme implication of the doctrinaire views advocated at this time is that parents should be allowed to produce children, but the rearing of them should be carried out by professional workers like our teacher in Sochi. There does not seem to be, as yet, any indication of how this contradiction will be resolved. There is no question that those who portray the vision of a new state move from the assumption that the family is the cradle of individualism. They believe that to leave the upbringing of children with the family not only means egotism or individualism, but also represents a hap-hazard policy allowing for chance and accident as against de-liberate planful child rearing.

Pitted against this view is that of the majority of the people we talked to on both our visits. They expressed very deep con-victions about the importance of having the child reared by his own parents, especially during his early years. These con-victions are so strong that we wonder whether the official views as expressed by Khrushchev and by Kharchev will not have to give way to the strong wishes of the parents themselves to rear their own children.

Not only did ordinary parents—taxi drivers, chauffeurs, guides, professional workers—express strong convictions about the importance of children being reared by their own parents, but they stressed their own personal feelings and desires to rear their own children. This was also true of some of the outstanding educators with whom we talked. On the other hand, the professional educators who rigidly follow the party line continued to repeat in almost parrot-like fashion the view that children must be reared in a collective if they are going to take their place in a collective society.

Our middle-aged taxi driver was quite sardonic in commenting on Khrushchev's views that the number of boarding schools should be increased and as many children as possible cared for in such schools rather than in their own homes. His comment was that this was Khrushchev's way of getting all the women to go to work. The taxi driver had one child, a married daughter; his wife was employed as a teacher; his son-in-law was finishing his education at a technical institute. The daughter was pregnant and her father was quite clear that when the child arrived his daughter would continue to remain at home and take care of her own child. He was not going to allow his grandchild to be reared in any "nursery school" or "babies' home."

A chauffeur who had been awarded the Lenin medal for bravery spent some time telling us about his family and his home life. We asked him whether his wife had gone to work while the children were young. He replied that she had never worked. "After all, the place of a mother is in her own home with her children."

The same attitude was expressed by a professional woman who was an active member of the Young Communist League and who was expecting her first child. She was quite determined to remain at home and take care of her child, at least during the early years.

The authority on family life referred to earlier felt very strongly that children should be reared by their own parents; she had reared her only son. A high official in the Ministry of Education of the Russian Republic believed that community institutions should help the family in the rearing of children but were no substitute for family rearing.

The case of our friend Gregory is in point. He has been wholly identified with the party and, in fact, has made his living as a professional worker in the Pioneer organization. Gregory has one daughter, who was reared entirely by her mother. She had never attended nursery school or kindergarten, and left home during the day only when she entered the elementary school at the age of 7. Not only was his child reared by her mother, but he also told us how he and his wife fought against the restrictions on visiting her at the Pioneer camp where she spent the summers, and how he was able to get around the regulations and visit his child.

In the face of the overwhelming desire of parents to rear their own children which we encountered, one may conclude that the regime cannot move quickly to transfer the care of children from the family to community institutions.

Our review of the status of the family as a child-rearing agency in the Soviet Union leaves many open questions. On the one hand, there are many beginnings and possibilities toward liberalization of many aspects of family life. There is general agreement that the economic aspects of family living are improving: the reduction of the work week, the gradual bettering of the housing situation, are but examples of changes which should help to ease the material and physical conditions of family life. Furthermore, the easing of economic pressures should also improve the psychological atmosphere by reducing some of the tensions and anxieties the family faces in this area.

Turning to another aspect of family life we find a growing recognition of the need to liberalize the divorce laws as a way of reducing the harmful consequence of the separation of parents. Similar benefits to children would accrue from a removal of the stigma of illegitimacy. The increase in freedom of expression and tolerance of ideological difference should further remove psychological barriers between parents and children.

The family will be further safeguarded by the expansion of extrafamilial child-caring facilities. We are referring to the creches, kindergartens, the "extended-day" school arrangements, the proximity of playgrounds to the family apartment, the variety of organized after-school activities. All of these are useful instrumentalities for the safeguarding of child life in urban society where partnership between the child's family and community institutions is indispensable.

What remains unresolved, however, is the role of the family as a child-rearing instrumentality. At the moment, official policy at best accords it a secondary role. And this role continues to dwindle in the ideology of men like Kharchev who are the heralds of the approaching realization of the communist society.

As we have seen, the notion that the U.S.S.R. is moving from socialism to communism appears in all discussions of social policy and has become a constant in present propaganda efforts. All the original ideological clichés have been dusted off and have again been released into circulation.

One cannot deny that from the standpoint of strict communist doctrine there is rationale for the view that in a communist society there may be no place for the traditional family as a child-rearing instrumentality. The implication of this position, however, has never been thought through in terms of the basic human needs of both adults and children. The Soviet thesis begins with the assumption that the family is bound to remain the cradle of individualism, likely to harbor and protect individual expression, and thus cannot but serve as a barrier between the individual and the state. How can it be reconciled, therefore, with a social order in which relations between the individual and the state must be direct, uncomplicated and unobstructed?

How children are to be reared and what social instrumentalities are to carry responsibility for this function remains an uncompleted part of the thesis.

Chapter 9

The Role of the School in Character and Personality Development

THE SCHOOL CONTINUES to be one of the principal instruments of the Soviet regime for shaping the child in the image of the Soviet man. The important role accorded the school, in contrast to the family, is consistent with the assumption that socialization can only be achieved through group or "collective" education and this can take place only when the child is participating as a member of a group in activities organized on a group basis.

Our special concern is with the school as a child-rearing instrumentality, with the interpersonal relations of the individuals involved—the relationship of the teacher to the pupils, their parents, and the pupils to each other. We are also interested in the way in which this complex of influences is brought to bear upon the child, the expectations set for him, and his response.

Because of the monolithic character of Soviet social policies and programs, any description of the psychological climate of the school must be incomplete unless it is seen as an integral sector of the total scheme of educational activities which permeates all aspects of Soviet life. Both the school and the child are subject to these wider influences.

In all countries, education is an instrument of national policy. In few countries in this as frankly acknowledged as it is in the U.S.S.R.

It is of primary importance to recognize that education in the Soviet Union is not a basic resource which undergirds the society, but a tool, fashioned, sharpened, and changed by the State in its own interests as those interests may be determined by the Party.*

There is no doubt that the Soviet educational program constitutes an extraordinary example of the possibilities of social planning and social engineering. The exemplary achievement of the Soviet Union in this endeavor has been so generally accepted by the world, particularly since the first Sputnik, that there is some real danger that it may be overrated and some of the shortcomings overlooked. The Russians themselves continue to make many changes in their educational program, but it remains without doubt a great achievement. What makes it even more impressive is that it is marked by continuous expansion in scope and coverage, and introduction of new emphases and direction.

Evidence of this accomplishment is seen in the unusual rate of growth of the educational establishment—the increase in the number of schools and teachers, as well as the student body— with the resultant enormous increase in literacy.

The percentage of literacy for all persons aged 9 and over in Russia rose from 24 per cent in 1897 to 81.2 per cent in 1939, with most of the illiterates, as might be expected, falling into the age group of 50 and over.** While the dislocation of the war called a halt to progress, the advance has been resumed in the postwar period.

In his article, "The School at the Present Stage of Building Communism and the Tasks of Teachers," Dr. Y. I. Afanasenko, Minister of Education of the Russian Republic, cites many facts about the growth of the school establishment in the Russian Republic.

---

* "Report on Higher Education in the Soviet Union." Pittsburgh, Pa.: University of Pittsburgh Press, 1958. Page 4.

** Florinsky, Michael T.: *Towards an Understanding of the U.S.S.R.* Revised edition. New York: The Macmillan Co., 1953. Page 184.

The enrollment in the senior grades of secondary general-education schools and in higher and specialized secondary educational institutions is now 20 times as great as in 1914. . . . [In 1960] there are more than 15,000,000 children in the first through the seventh grades of all general-education schools.*

Writing this in 1960, Dr. Afanasenko estimated that by 1962 there would be 19 million pupils, or almost four million more in the first through the eighth grades. By 1965 there should be 73,500 elementary four-year schools and 30,700 eight-year schools as against 72,700 elementary schools and 28,200 seven-year schools today.

In 1962, Dr. Afanasenko reported that the first forecasts had been substantially achieved.**

The Soviet concept of education is extraordinarily comprehensive and goes beyond the activities of the formal school. While we, too, recognize the newspaper, the television, the radio, the theater, the neighborhood center and the political club as educational media, we are much less consciously aware of their role as educational resources. Moreover, we do not as deliberately plan for the fullest utilization of these media; nor does our national government direct and control activities of this kind as does that of the Soviet Union. Unlike the situation in our own and other countries, where "cultural" media are taken for granted and are left to develop through the initiative of those members of society who have a special interest in them, in Russia they constitute part and parcel of the educational establishment and their scope and character reflect official goals and policies governing educational activity.

---

* "Russian Republic Schools a Year after the Reform." *The Current Digest of the Soviet Press,* Volume XII, Number 30, August 24, 1960. © Page 16.
** "Russian Republic Supreme Soviet Discusses Education." *The Current Digest of the Soviet Press,* Volume XIV, Number 30, August 22, 1962. © Pages 5-9.

Good theater is cultivated and widely appreciated. Ballet, opera, drama are not only well supported by the State but enthusiastically received by large masses of the population. In Tashkent, in Central Asia, we found a city of four hundred thousand people with six or seven theaters, one of which gives 200 performances of ballet and opera each year to a consistently filled hall.

Museums are crowded with audiences apparently representative of the population . . . a noticeable number of young people avidly taking notes which they claim to be for their own "development." . . .

Bookstores are crowded and interest in newly published materials is so great that, at least in Moscow, there is a black market in new paperback editions of both contemporary and classic works. Furthermore, statistics as to claimed holdings of general libraries are very impressive, although there is some question as to the interpretation of certain of the data supplied.*

This section of the "Report on Higher Education" concludes that these observations must be seen in the context of a far-reaching interest in cultural affairs.

It is not possible for us to conclude how much of this is spontaneous interest of the people and how much may result from encouragement by the Kremlin for whatever reasons may appeal to it in its total strategic political design.**

A. EQUALITY OF EDUCATIONAL OPPORTUNITY

Equality of educational opportunity has been one of the cardinal tenets in Soviet ideology and it still remains one of the slogans reiterated in every declaration of educational policy. Educational achievement is a basic requisite for assuring that the potential of skill, talent and energy is fully utilized, and as such is a road to national well-being. For most it is also the

---

* "Report on Higher Education," *op. cit.* Page 6.
** *Ibid.* Page 7.

road to individual status and success. As a consequence, educational achievement constitutes a source of pressure on every child to comply, to conform and to excel. Anything less than equality of educational opportunity is therefore a serious handicap to him in the race to achieve.

In the early days of the revolution, the Soviet leaders were eager to make educational opportunities available equally to all social classes, particularly those who had been deprived of this privilege under the czarist regime. In fact, such opportunities were then denied only to members of the former exploiting classes.

With the introduction of unequal rewards as an integral element in a new system of incentives, special educational opportunities became available to the privileged—those who had demonstrated their loyalty to the regime and were members of the Communist party or the Komsomol—with the result that many mediocre, unqualified though politically reliable, young persons were graduated from the higher schools. It was soon realized that industrialization called for a corps of well-trained intelligent individuals recruited on the basis of merit, regardless of their social class. Admission to advanced studies was henceforth to be based on scholastic ability, rather than on class or political considerations. Traditional teaching methods and discipline were reintroduced. Field designates this change as a "change from the Party to the report card." *

Ideologically,

. . . education was and is conceived as definitely social in its purposes. Its aim is to annihilate class differences, to do away with the psychological feelings of inferiority and superiority that separate different groups of people.**

---

* Field, in Bereday & Pennar, *op. cit.*
** Bereday, in Bereday & Pennar, *op. cit.* Page 61.

But beyond *ideology,* the principle of equality in education, according to Bereday, is reflected in three characteristics of the educational system: the establishment of comprehensive schools, a common curriculum and the Soviet attitude on coeducation.

Coeducation, which logically flows from the emphasis on the equality of the sexes, was suspended in Soviet schools during World War II, but has been restored. At present there seems to be no question about its validity. Boys and girls frequently sit together on the same benches in the classroom; in this way they are being prepared for an adult society in which jobs, honors and rewards are more equally distributed between the sexes than in many other societies.

A uniform, identical curriculum for all children throughout the Soviet Union is consistent with the theory of plasticity and perfectibility, the insistence on equal abilities, and the optimistic theories of heredity to which the Soviet Union has clung.

An interesting affirmation of the equalitarian principle was embodied in the decision as to the kinds of children who would be admitted to the boarding schools established in 1956. In the declarations advocating the establishment of these schools and in the prospectuses projecting their operation, the original concept was that of a model educational establishment which would produce the future leaders of the commonwealth, the model Soviet man. Once again a hoped-for ideal has been amended by a harsh reality. As it turned out, the schools have been used much more for children coming from poor homes where both parents are employed, and where the child may be in need of protection, than for children selected to be future leaders of society.

The equalitarian principle was once again threatened when it was proposed in 1958 that special schools for gifted children be established as part of the new educational reforms. This, too, was considered a violation of the principle of equality of opportunity and the proposal was abandoned. But this position has been hard to maintain. There are differences in human potential as well as motivation, and therefore differences in the degree of utilization of educational opportunities are inevitable. Thus, in 1962 a plan to establish so-called "differentiated" secondary education was gaining ground. This proposal is supported by the highest authority and is being tried out experimentally.

Many forms of inequality unrelated to capacity or motivation of the pupil still remain. These have their roots in the same equation between ideology and human nature that has produced the class system. Bereday charges that "Soviet pedagogical practice . . . refuses to make appropriate provision designed not merely to *further equality* but also to *circumvent inequality*." *

. . . the ever-increasing income differentiation, the wartime reintroduction of rank insignia similar to Czarist symbols and of uniforms for most civil servants, the introduction of different medals and orders for enlisted men and officers, and the abolition of the inheritance tax were all significant bench marks in the growing stratification of Soviet society, and presumably, in the monopolization of education by the upper and middle classes. It may be inferred, furthermore, that this trend, so contrary to some basic tenets of Soviet ideology, may have begun to cause the regime serious concern during the fifties. This concern seemed to stem from practical considerations as well as ideological ones. For once again, this trend, if allowed to run unchecked, would tend to limit the social base from which potential talent could be recruited and trained. In view of the importance of science and technology, such tendencies, over a long period, might have serious consequences, perhaps not as serious as the "class approach" of the nineteen-twenties, but serious nonetheless. Moreover, the ideological problem, caused not so much by the existence of income differentials and other status advantages, but by the ability of fathers to pass educational advantages to their sons and daughters, should not be overlooked. The existence of a "golden youth," of children having access to higher education because of their parents' position

---

* *Ibid.* Page 70.

(education therefore becoming a "social grace," a mark of status rather than the means to a fruitful occupation), the bribing of school officials to admit undeserving students of "good families," the refusal by many of these students to accept assigned posts in the countryside after graduation or to work at all, and the ability to use connections and influence to back up this refusal—these and other manipulations of the system for individual, nonsocial purposes were a flagrant violation of some basic Soviet tenets about opportunities being open to all and about the function of education.*

It should be pointed out that, in common with all societies, the emphasis on scholastic achievement as the door to a career and to additional material comfort, power and authority, is bound to create tensions in a country where education is the most important possession in assuring a career. These pressures for education are felt at all levels. The point of admission to universities is a particularly crucial area. It has become a cliché that there is only one place in the universities or institutions of higher learning for every four qualified students. Actually, this imbalance was cited as one of the considerations for the new educational reforms introduced in 1958 which, it was expected, would limit the number of general school graduates who would go on to the secondary schools and qualify for university admission.

Whatever the reasons may be, the fact is that a relatively large proportion of the children of the favored classes gain admission to the institutions of higher learning and go on to careers in the professions and industry. This is in contrast to the small proportion of the children of the masses, most of whom are destined for the more lowly tasks.

There are other specific expressions of inequality in the educational arrangements.

---

* Field, in Bereday & Pennar, *op. cit.* Page 181.

Elitist institutions of various categories have been established and still exist. These include military schools, which give preference to children of military personnel; in the Leningrad Ballet School, 60 per cent of the pupils are from families residing in the city itself; in music schools many of the youngsters are children of outstanding musicians.

There are still other kinds of inequalities. There is general agreement that the rural schools are inferior to the urban schools. There is constant complaint about the difficulty of getting teachers to accept posts in rural areas where reports indicate that the ratio of failures and drop-outs is higher. Undoubtedly, the greater opportunities to achieve a better education and higher social status are important factors in the movement of young people from the rural areas to the cities. Children in some of the union republics suffer an additional handicap: the need to acquire proficiency in the Russian language as well as their own national tongue makes for an extra burden and consequently a higher ratio of failure.

Inequality arises from other more subtle things. The children of favored families wear better clothes, have better manners, girls have smarter hairdos. Moreover, the children from educated families pronounce words differently. In some of the larger cities, because of the better housing enjoyed by the more favored groups, the neighborhood school is the school for privileged children. As a matter of fact, the insistence on proper speech, clothing and manners, the good form that is expected of the children, tends to highlight the separation of the refined from the unrefined.

The premium on "good form," coupled with the deeper implications in educational opportunity, is expressed in a basic psychological fact in Soviet life. This is the dislike for "black work," which harks back to the time when *muzhik* (peasant) and *chernorabochie* (black work, manual labor) were offensive terms. Even today, under Soviet rule, these words retain their offensive flavor and are identified with social inferiority.

However, as in most aspects of Soviet life so with educational opportunity, we continue to witness two opposing tendencies: the goal of an equalitarian society and, in conflict with it, sanctioned expressions of individual privilege and competitive drives provided for in the established system of incentives. Educational leaders are concerned about inequality and would like to see it wiped out. Though these efforts may modify its form or extent, inequality in educational opportunity will remain so long as the class system remains a feature of the Soviet social order.

B. THE ORGANIZATION OF THE EDUCATIONAL SYSTEM

The source of policy and control is an important distinguishing feature of the Soviet educational establishment. Education in the U.S.S.R. is still controlled from the top. The basic policy for all educational activities is decided upon jointly by the Central Committee of the Communist party and the Council of Ministers of the U.S.S.R. The ordinary elementary and secondary schools are administered by the ministries of education of the republics, with local and regional branches exercising day-to-day operational controls. The higher educational institutions are, except for some technical institutions which are sponsored by industrial establishments, administered by the All-Union Ministry of Education.

Curricula and methods of instruction in the elementary and secondary schools are uniform for all 15 republics. This is so because supervision of teaching methods, programs of instruction and related activities of each of the 15 republics are coordinated by the Ministry of Education of the largest, the Russian Republic.*

---

* Alts, *op. cit.* Page 176.

All, or nearly all, higher educational officials are members of the Central Communist party committees in their particular republics. Thirty-four per cent of the teachers are party members; *social science and history are taught only by party members;* with few exceptions, the faculty of Moscow University are members of the party. The principal of every school has to be a party member. Party members permeate all echelons of higher education.*

In a recent article stressing the party's responsibility for helping teachers to deal with current problems, the stake of the party in education is reaffirmed. The writer begins with the statement that "Soviet teachers are doing great work in carrying out the Party's directives. Considerable knowledge, lofty ideological spirit, a broad political outlook, some production skills and proficiency in teaching are required of them." **

The article proceeds from this declaration of the teacher's responsibility to the inference that "the teacher himself must study very persistently, and here he needs considerable help. The help is a matter above all for Party organizations. *Work with pedagogical personnel is the most important thing in party guidance of public education. . . .*" [Our italics]

In referring to the teacher's responsibility for child rearing and ideological teaching, the article states:

It must also not be forgotten that the teacher needs help in questions of child rearing. He not only teaches his charges and imparts a knowledge of the fundamentals of science to them; he rears the young person and forms his communistic outlook. . . . †

---

* "Report of the IIE Seminar on Education in the Soviet Union," November 19-20, 1959. Sponsored by the Institute of International Education. Page 7.

** "The Party and the Work of the Schoolteacher." *The Current Digest of the Soviet Press,* Volume XIII, Number 11, April 12, 1961. © Pages 20-21.

† *Ibid.* Page 21.

It is an objective of the party to familiarize young people more thoroughly "with the major tasks of communist construction and with the doctrines of Marx, Engels and Lenin . . . and of teaching them how to understand the problems of our times *correctly*." [Our italics] Beginning with the new school year 1961-62, there is to be a new course on fundamentals of political knowledge to be taught in the senior grades of the general secondary schools and technicums. The party's Central Committee and the U.S.S.R. Council of Ministers have adopted a resolution on certain changes in the teaching of history.

The article goes on to stress the importance of the "ideological-political" preparation of teachers. "Teachers," the writer continues, "are now participating more fully in propaganda, agitation and cultural enlightenment work."

In considering control of educational policy we must not overlook the role the Academy of Pedagogical Sciences plays in the conduct of research and in the formulation of educational theory and practice.

While organized as an enterprise of the Russian Republic rather than of the Soviet Union, by agreement the Academy serves all other republics which do not have comparable bodies. It is responsible for the development of methods for the teaching of individual subjects such as reading, writing, arithmetic, natural sciences. It is the Academy that carries responsibility for designing the curricula for the elementary school. It is also the Academy that developed in detail the round-the-clock schedule as well as the specific educational curriculum for the new boarding school. Many of its operational responsibilities are discharged through a number of institutes, one of the most important of which is the Institute on Defectology, which is concerned with the education of the physically or intellectually handicapped child. This institute maintains a variety of laboratories for the study of the psychological, auditory, phonetic and visual aspects of education.

The educational establishment

At the base of the Soviet educational system are two institutions for the preschool age group—the creche and the kindergarten. The first accepts children from one month through the age of 3; the second, from 4 through the age of 6. These establishments are primarily intended to serve children of working mothers and include day as well as residential programs. Responsibility for establishing and operating such institutions rests with regional or local soviets, but they may also be established and maintained by agricultural collectives and state farms, factories and other industrial enterprises. Their programs, which are supervised and guided by the republic ministers of health and education, are focused on the acceleration of the development of motor co-ordination and physical adequacy for the younger child, and provide nonacademic activities such as music, singing, gymnastics and arts and crafts for the older child.

All children are required to enroll in the elementary school at the age of 7 and are expected to complete the eight-year school by the time they are 15. At that point the child may go to work and continue his education through correspondence courses or by attendance at night school; or he may enroll in a technical-vocational high school, or go on for three more years in a secondary academic school which would prepare him for admission to the university or an advanced technical school.

In addition to the provision for general, specialized and professional education for all children in the Soviet Union, many special education programs are provided for the physically handicapped, the mentally retarded and the blind and deaf. It is our impression that the U.S.S.R. has achieved a high level of education for these special groups.

In our discussion of equality of educational opportunity, we referred to the special talent schools such as those for ballet, music and fine arts. These draw their pupils from the most gifted children and give them intensive training in their special field as well as the complete secondary education provided for in the general education school programs. Military schools for training officers for the army and navy also belong in this category.

Children attend school six days a week—200 days a year, as against 180 in the United States—and the school week varies between 27 and 36 hours. In addition, pupils are expected to do a number of hours of homework after school hours, the time devoted to this increasing with the progress of the child through the grades.

Consistent with its emphasis on educational achievement, the Soviet Union has always maintained compulsory educational requirements. Two concepts have been invoked: "universal" as distinct from "compulsory" education, one representing a goal, the other a standard to be enforced. Because of the shortage of schools and teachers and the need for the children to work in agriculture, official policy has veered between these two objectives, so that even now the law providing for universal eight-year schooling remains a declaration of a goal rather than an immediately enforceable norm. Official sources concede that the previously proclaimed goal of seven-year compulsory education has not been achieved.

Reports from the Russian Republic deplore the fact that as yet only one-third of the seven-year schools have been transformed into eight-year schools, that the building of new schools is not keeping up with the state plans and that boarding schools are not being established as rapidly as planned. Exact figures of the actual state of affairs are hard to come by, but it is safe to say that the fulfillment of the goal of eight-year compulsory education for all lies in the future.

There has been much discussion in the public press in our country as to the relative status of teachers in the Soviet Union and in the United States. It has been pointed out that in many ways the teaching load is not as heavy in the Soviet Union.

In the day schools, many of which are on a two-shift basis, there are usually two sets of teachers. In the boarding schools we visited, we found that a new group of teachers came on duty at 3:00 P.M. Some, however, work through the 12-hour day, but do so only for three days a week. They prefer the long day and fewer days a week so that they may have to make fewer long trips to and from their homes.

The schoolteacher's salary—as distinct from that of the university professors who are much better paid—begins at about 80 rubles per month. This is somewhat below that of a chauffeur. It ranges to about 140-150 rubles after many years of tenure. A fact frequently noted is that most teachers have two jobs. Some actually get extra pay within the school system itself. This is true of those who also serve as children's inspectors and carry these additional responsibilities after the regular school day.

The general impression is that the teaching profession in the U.S.S.R. seems to enjoy more public respect than in our country. However, while the children's regard for the teacher may be greater than it is with us and more like that which prevails in Oriental countries, the notion that Soviet teachers enjoy preferred status has not been generally accepted by American educators who have visited the Soviet Union. Many of them question whether the Soviet teacher has any higher standing either socially or in an economic sense than the American teacher.

C. Political Organizations as Educational Tools

The children's and youth organizations play an important role in shaping the character of the Soviet child, and maintain close ties with the educational establishment.

While the family carries the basic responsibility for nurture, and the school for teaching skills as well as inculcation of desirable character traits, the task of the political organizations is focused almost exclusively on character development. This is to be achieved through the identification of the child with the goals of the Communist party and the unquestioned allegiance to party and regime. Ideal character traits will flow from these attitudes on the part of the child.

For this reason, these organizations are regarded as important media for training young people in disciplined conduct and, in addition, constitute the recruiting ground for party membership and the development of party leaders.

Pioneer Youth

While superficially there appear to be certain similarities between the activities of the Pioneers and our Boy Scouts and Girl Scouts, it is actually an oversimplification to assume that the Pioneer Youth Organization is a counterpart of the scouting agencies in the United States and other Western countries. It is true that both the Pioneers and the Scouts are concerned with the development of the moral character of the child and with inculcating certain character traits and ideals. But there are many differences in the role which these organizations play in the child life of these nations. In the first place, almost all of the children in the eligible age group belong to the Pioneers; this is not true of the Scouts in Western countries. Most important, in the case of the Pioneers, the values taught are part and parcel of the ideology of the Communist party.

The Pioneer Youth is a far-flung organization and plays a more important role in the life of the Russian child than do the Scouts and similar groups in our own country. The Pioneer organization carries on many different kinds of activities. It publishes millions of copies of books and magazines for children, operates summer camps and Pioneer Palaces, and maintains units in every school.

By the time he has reached the age of 7, the Russian child will have joined the Oktobrists, the first formal association dedicated to the teaching of communism. At 10, he becomes a member of the Pioneer Youth and at 15, of the Komsomol (Young Communist League). Although in each case the number of those who move from one level to the next tends to shrink, it should be noted that at the present time, we were informed by the executive head of the All-Union Pioneer movement, at least 90 per cent of the children in the eligible age range belong to the Pioneer Youth.

The Pioneer organization in each school is led by a "council" of Pioneers elected by the membership. Pioneers in every class are organized in detachments, guided by detachment councils. Within each detachment there are several "links," led by elected link leaders.

In each school there is an adult who serves as director of Pioneer activities. Sometimes he is a professional devoting all his time to Pioneer activities, sometimes a teacher who combines the duties of a Pioneer leader with part-time teaching responsibilities, and sometimes he is a member of the Komsomol carrying leadership duties as a volunteer.

There are 50,000 professional and about 130,000 volunteer Pioneer leaders; those who devote full or nearly full time receive payment. In a school where there are 500 or more children there is likely to be a paid Pioneer leader.

Besides the work in the schools, the Pioneer organization maintains at least 3,000 Pioneer Palaces and houses, 300 stations for young naturalists, 200 camps, 32 children's railroads and a number of related children's enterprises. There are new forms of activities now emerging: for example, there are clubs of polar investigators, and a group of young technicians interested in space ideas is studying this field carefully for the development of additional activities for young people.

The aims and tasks of the Pioneer organization, according to its executive director, are determined by the aims and tasks of the state and party. "We try to bring up a new person for the new communist society. Those school children who are not able, or willing, or interested in the aims and tasks of the Pioneer Youth Organization cannot come into it."

The program for Pioneer members is organized on three levels, related to particular age ranges. The first is for children 10 and 11 years of age, who are generally in the third and fourth grades. The second is for youngsters of 12 and 13 who are in the fifth and sixth grades, and the third, for 14- and 15-year-olds who are in the seventh and eighth grades. For each step there are certain tasks and certain kinds of knowledge that must be learned.

The prescribed activities are focused on three objectives: the development of certain skills, the acquisition of knowledge that would increase the child's political understanding and strengthen his patriotism, and the constructive use of leisure time. Thus, the Pioneer in the first grade must know how to plant a tree; in the second grade he must do something more difficult, such as the cultivation of a flower garden. He must participate in the government of the collective, learn certain facts about Lenin and local Communist heroes, and read the Pioneer newspaper. He can improve his skills in sports, artistic activities or any hobbies of his choice.

Socially useful work includes making something for his class or keeping his school clean. Exercises in civic activities will include the organization of assemblies around certain lofty themes, helping to maintain discipline in school, seeing that there are no failures in the class.

Pioneer activities are supposed to take up at least two hours a day; the minimum is two 2-hour sessions a week, although we were advised that it usually went beyond this.

Training of Pioneer leaders is carried on in co-operation with the ministries of education of the republics. The curricula are developed by the Academy of Pedagogical Sciences. The students who take the training courses are also required to spend some time in practical training in the Pioneer camps. "We train our people to do other things than just talk," we were told by the head of the All-Union Pioneer administration. "Each leader needs to know thoroughly a number of other things such as dancing, sports, handcrafts, etc." All teachers are taught Pioneer principles and Pioneer methods.

The leaders of the Pioneer organization frankly recognize the risks of rivalry between the teacher and the Pioneer leader. According to the head of the movement, "This is our sore problem." In almost every class there is a Pioneer unit so "there are two bosses in the classroom—the Pioneer leader and the teacher." The teacher has the task of teaching the child, but the Pioneer leader has the more primary responsibility of influencing the moral development of the child. Collaboration in this task between the Pioneer leader and the teacher remains a serious problem. Attempts to meet it take the form of involving educators in the top administrative councils of the Pioneer movement. In 1959, the president of the Academy of Pedagogical Sciences served on the All-Union executive board. There are attempts to achieve this kind of co-ordination at the republic and regional levels. In its training curricula the Academy of Pedagogical Sciences seeks to harmonize the teaching function of the Pioneers with the general educational program and the responsibility of the classroom teacher.

The Komsomol

At the age of 15 a pupil becomes eligible for membership in Komsomol. This organization is, in the Soviet definition, "the aid and reserve of the party," and it is expected to promote any goal important to the Communist party. The Komsomol is modeled after the party, with primary organizations formed in schools, universities, factories and farms. Every primary organization elects a secretary, every larger unit a committee and a secretary. Membership is more selective than for the Pioneers.

Admission must be sponsored by two members of the organization or one adult party member.

With the recent increase in membership, now presumed to be 18 million—almost half the population in the eligible age range—the Komsomol is no longer a politically select group with revolutionary zeal, but begins to take on the character of a young people's community service corps, with its emphasis on the preparation of young people for their responsibilities as adult citizens. It acts as a propaganda medium in spurring its members, as well as others, to achieve economic goals—raise production or bring virgin land under cultivation. It also organizes drives and campaigns to promote atheism and does what it can to prevent its own members from engaging in any rituals or ceremonials of a religious character.*

Like the Pioneers and all peer organizations, the Komsomols carry on mutual aid as well as surveillance activities. Thus, they may help their members with material as well as tutorial aid. They will admonish their male members for being too free with the girls or both male and female members for going to the cinema too often.

The Komsomol organization injects itself into the most personal spheres of a young person's life. Not only are the religious activities of every member a cause for concern, but it has also been related by a visitor to the Soviet Union that the Komsomol organization of one university held a public meeting to decide whether one of its members had acted honorably in abandoning his steady girl friend for a new attraction. A Soviet film shows the dilemma of a young girl who has grown up with her mother, who married a second time after the girl's father was presumed to have died in the war. Suddenly the father returns and it must be decided whether he is to have his daughter or whether she is to stay with her stepfather. The Komsomol organization

---

* See "Antireligious Education of Soviet Youth," by Alessio U. Floridi (Pages 89-99) in Bereday & Pennar, *op. cit.*

she belongs to holds a public meeting to decide this question for her. In this instance, she refuses to go to the meeting and is censured by her stepfather, the hero of the film.

Besides its goal of enforcing the "Communist way" in private life, another function of the Komsomol organization is to encourage the movement for Communist toil, which combines socialist competition for better and more production with the aim of getting all workers to study and improve their qualifications.

Two responsibilities undertaken more recently are to round up hooligans by brigades made up of Komsomol members which co-operate with the local police precinct, and to help design and popularize special ceremonials for weddings, birthdays, etc. This latter is an attempt to offset the religious forms and ceremonials for the same occasions.

A function of special importance to its members is the collaboration of the Komsomol organization in the writing of the *kharakteristika* for each student or would-be student. This is necessary for job assignments or for admission to higher educational institutions. Compiled by the trade union and Komsomol organizations in collaboration with the academic or plant administration authorities, these documents have equal influence with academic achievements in determining a young person's career.

Just as in other peer organizations, offenders who do not mend their ways are reprimanded by the local group at the monthly Komsomol meeting and if that does not work, by the next group in the hierarchy—the regional and then the national—with the ultimate penalty of expulsion from the organization.

As far as we know, no one in or outside the Soviet Union has made any comprehensive assessment of the actual contribution these organizations for children and youth make to child rearing or in preparation for adult participation in a collective society. There is no doubt that they reinforce the influences which make for conformity and compliance and bring one more authority into the life of the child. There is no doubt, too, that the leisure-time activities which they provide for children are valuable in the development of skills and identity. More specifically, both groups—and particularly the Komsomols—serve as transmission belts for party ideology and as preparatory ground for party membership.

At the same time, however, it is fair to point out that despite the deep interest of the regime in these organizations and the constant reiteration of the importance of their functions in character development, a reading of the accounts of Komsomol meetings—with their preoccupation with the deviant behavior of some of their members, with atheistic propaganda, and with their peripheral participation in law enforcement—leaves one with a sense of much insubstantial and nonsignificant activity.

D. The School as a Psychological Milieu

The institution selected by the Ministry of Education for our first visit to a school is located in a Moscow neighborhood which our guide described as "proletarian." It is larger than most schools, with an enrollment of 670 pupils and a staff of 52 teachers. It is considered an ordinary school with presumably little that is special or different about it.

The physical plant is old and looks very much like the traditional American school building in an urban community. It is two stories high, with classrooms opening off each side of a wide hallway which runs down the center. The lower floor houses the principal's offices and gymnasium; the cafeteria is in the basement.

The appearance of the principal and teachers in this school seemed very much like many others we saw. The principal, a middle-aged, rather heavy-set woman, gave the impression of solid stability and maturity. She was simply dressed, with her hair pulled back tightly into a bun, used no make-up, and looked prim and businesslike.

She was quite ready to show us the classrooms and the clinic, and have us meet the teachers and pediatrician, and equally ready to supply us with many details about the school.

In this school there were approximately 35 children to a class. The teaching staff consists of three types of teachers: the classroom (homeroom) teacher, other subject teachers and the special arts and crafts and workshop teachers. One teacher alone carries total responsibility for the class up to the fifth grade. From the fifth grade up, the classroom teacher shares the burden of instruction with the subject teachers. In addition, she is responsible for handling problems of parent-school relationships as well as advising parents on better methods of upbringing. She presumably visits the child's home about once a month.

The school staff includes a physician who is responsible for the health service in this and one other school. Every child is examined once a year, and where health problems are identified the child is referred for corrective care to the polyclinic.

The student organization in this school was typical of most. It is representative of all the children and comprises all the pupil organizations—the Oktobrist, the Pioneer Youth and the Komsomol.

The principal was reluctant to answer our questions about what happens to children who present disciplinary or other serious problems. We could not pin her down to any figures as to the ratio of children who fail, drop out, or who might have to be dealt with because of misbehavior.

She admitted, however, that one of the most difficult problems the school staff faces is what to do with children who were not doing well, particularly those who managed to reach the fourth grade and were unable to go beyond it. When we pressed her as to what happens to this group she replied, somewhat vaguely, that "certainly there are organizations that supply work for such children."

As to truancy, she said they had very little. There are so many committees of parents as well as individual teachers who visit the home, and the many-sided pressure to which the child is subjected is so great, that he does not resort to chronic truancy.

Parents, individually and in groups, are expected to visit the school at regular intervals, to attend lectures on problems of upbringing at least once a month, and after such lectures, to go to the classrooms of their children and meet with the class organization and the classroom teacher.

The activities of the parents' organization take many forms. There are parents' committees concerned with problems of neglect and misbehavior. Committees of parents visit the homes of those parents who are considered neglectful or who do not set a good example for their children, or are lax in dealing with problems such as truancy. The parents' committees also manage the hot lunch program and provide financial assistance to children who need it. They provide help and funds for arrangements for concerts in the school or for attendance at such events outside. They assist the school administration with such projects as the school gardens. They maintain liaison with the neighboring industrial plants which perform many helpful services for the school and the child.

Union committees in the plant may sponsor school activities such as a dance or excursion, and buy equipment for the school shop. Often children are assigned for their vocational training to a neighboring plant in which many of their parents are employed. It is accepted practice for the school official to communicate with the chairman of a union committee in the plant where the parent is employed to bring to his attention problems which the child presents in school and to urge him to do more to remedy the situation.

The child's day

When we were in the U.S.S.R. in 1959 we encountered differences of opinion as to whether the Soviet child is subjected to extraordinary burdens. The question became the subject of considerable interest in our own country as well. Some Americans argued that American children who attend boarding schools where classical education is emphasized carry equal burdens. Be that as it may, the Soviet educators themselves have been very much concerned about the overburdening of the child.

The new program introduced in 1958 was intended to lighten the burden. In reality, however, it has aggravated it by adding vocational training and fixed periods of work in the factory or on the farm to the previous work load.

A picture of the school week of two children as we saw it at firsthand in 1959 will give some idea of the work load of the Russian school child. The school day of one 12-year-old girl we got to know is probably typical of the child aged 10 to 14 who lives at home and attends regular day school. This youngster gets up at 7:00 A.M., leaves for school at 7:45, and has six classes from 8:30 to 2:00. Then follow the extracurricular activities. She has Pioneers, drama, sports, and finishes the day at 4:30. She then comes home and has two to three hours of homework. We saw this child doing homework on a Sunday evening.

At the *dietski dom* (orphans' home) and at the *internat* (boarding school), the children begin their day at about 7:00 A.M. and retire at about 8:30 or 9:00 P.M. At the *internat* the children have calisthenics for about 15 minutes after they get up at 7:00, then they tidy their rooms, have breakfast and go for about a 15-minute walk before the school day begins at 8:30. They have six classes between 8:30 and 2:00, followed by a two-hour break between 2:00 and 4:00. During this period they have the principal meal of the day. After that, they must clean up the dining room and kitchen, and then they have a free period of about an hour.

The homework period begins at 4:00 P.M. They now go back to their classrooms and sit at their desks for two hours under the supervision of the teacher. The homework session is followed by a period devoted to technical education on certain afternoons and extracurricular activities such as music and dancing on others. Pioneer meetings also take place during this period. The scheduled day is over about 7:00 or 7:30 P.M.

The problem of overwork is now receiving widespread attention from Russian educators, and efforts to meet it include the improvement of teaching methods in the classroom, thereby reducing the burden of homework on the children.*

As we begin to examine the psychological forces to which the child is exposed at school, we encounter the same alloy of ingredients we described in the chapter entitled "The Carrot and The Stick." ** These include good example, rewards and punishment, identification with the same values and standards set for adults and the same social pressures to conform and comply. We also encounter some of the same consequences of the complex of influence and pressures in fear of failure or in outright emotional disturbance.

In the school, as in the club, on the street, in the park, in the comics and stories that are read to him and that he reads, the Russian child is surrounded by examples of exemplary behavior and outstanding achievement. The first thing that strikes the visitor on entering the hallway of a school are the photographs and exhibits obviously planned to exert positive influence on the child. Examples of achievement by the children are to be found wherever the children move about. In the *dietski dom,* for example, samples of crocheting, sewing and photography are to be found in the hallway and in the arts and crafts rooms in which the children work. The walls of the classrooms as well as the hallways abound not only in photographs of the leaders of the revolution, heroes in battle and the underground during the last war, famous inventors, scientists and athletes, but also in those of classmates who now lead or have led the class, or who

---

* As this book goes to press a 5-day school week is being advocated in the Soviet Union.

** Chapter 2, C and D.

excel in sports or otherwise. To emphasize the point, a poster on the wall may depict the best pupil as Sputnik and the worst as a tortoise, each symbol bearing the actual name of the pupil.

The walls abound, too, in posters offering advice about personal hygiene. In one of the schools we found an "international corner" with correspondence between teachers and students in the Soviet Union and those in other lands.

We sat in on reading lessons in three schools, and without exception the lesson dealt with the lives of scientists, astronomers, geographers, medical workers and inventors as examples of contributors to the common good. The story about the inventor was particularly interesting for, in response to the teacher's question, a pupil pointed out that he was a great and good man because he invented useful machines and was poor and a lover of the people. The examples the child should emulate are not limited to accounts of the lives of outstanding individuals, but also include instances of kindness to the aged, the weak and the helpless, as well as to schoolmates.

Films dramatizing these moral precepts are shown in the classroom. The stories of two of them will serve as illustrations.* One, entitled *The Find,* told of an old lady receiving a letter from her son with a money order in it. The story follows:

She cashed the order and put the bulging purse in her pocket. Then she walked home. On the way she got tired and sat down on a park bench. It was hot, so she pulled out her handkerchief to wipe her face. The purse fell out unnoticed. She got up and walked away.

Two boys, playing ball, found the purse. They hurried after her to return it but the traffic light was against them. When they were permitted to cross the street, the old lady had disappeared. The two boys decided to take the purse to the police station. While the boys were explaining their story, the old lady entered, very upset.

---

* "Character and Moral Education in a Collectivist Society," in *The Changing Soviet School*. Edited by George Z. T. Bereday, William W. Brinkman, Gerald H. Read. Boston: Houghton Mifflin Co., 1960.

The police officer returned her purse and, when she tried to embrace the boys, they were much embarrassed. They only did their duty. The film ended as they stood at attention and gave the Pioneer salute and slogan, "Always ready!"

The other film illustrates the spirit of comradeship:

Vasia, a little boy, brought home a dog, Sharik, and begged his mother to let him keep it. The mother agreed, if the boy would promise to take good care of the pet himself. He promised but soon he forgot about it. The dog was not fed regularly, he was not washed or brushed, and he was never taken for a walk. One day the dog found the door to the apartment open and he ran away. When Vasia came home, Sharik was gone.

While running the streets, Sharik was knocked down by a car. Another boy, Petia, picked him up and, as his owner could not be found, took him home and nursed him back to health. He found another name for the dog and the two became the best of friends. He took care of the dog and always took him for walks.

On one of these walks they met Vasia, who recognized the dog as his old pet. The two boys argued about whose dog it was and finally agreed to let the dog decide who his master should be. The dog would belong to the boy to whom he ran when he was called. He ran to Petia. Petia was most happy but he decided that it was only fair to let Vasia share the dog.

The film ended with the two boys shaking hands and deciding to be firm friends.

When we visited classes we generally sat in the back of the room and had a view of the teacher and all the children. The teacher usually stood at the head of the class rather than sat at her table. Our impression of her was that of a drill master who asks one question and after getting a reply proceeds to the next one. The children stood up to answer, and in some classes came to the front of the room to recite. Many children seemed to be daydreaming. Four at least, out of a class of 35 eight- and nine-year-olds, were sucking their thumbs, and this was in the afternoon.

One cannot escape the impression of an intense struggle on the part of the children to come up with the right answer and their fear of failure. There is a tautness in the air.

Another observer has reported this incident: A girl in the tenth grade of a secondary school was called up to the blackboard to recite. The child was obviously very nervous and hesitated a good deal with her answers. The teacher admonished her continually for being nervous and for not having enough self-confidence. Finally she reduced the child to tears. "I will give you a '3,'" the teacher said, dismissing the girl to her seat, "to teach you not to be so tense. If you had not been so nervous you would have done better." In a second-grade class, a boy was called up to the front of the class and publicly reprimanded. When the teacher had finished scolding him, she asked him whether he knew what he had done. The boy hazarded several guesses: "I talked." "I did not pay attention." All proved to be wrong. He was finally informed that he had raised his arm too high in demanding a hearing from the teacher, and was sent back to his seat.

In the *dietski dom* we saw a class of girls, about 13 to 14, when they returned at about 2:00 for their dinner. Here the director of the home was eager to have the children perform for us. This led to a considerable struggle, with the director finally winning out. Most of the children were bashful and loath to sing or recite. Finally one youngster, more outgoing than the rest, who seemed to be a leader, both sang and recited. After that there was some group singing, but it was not very spirited.

On our way out one of the little girls attached herself to us and insisted on accompanying us down the steps to the door of the taxi. We gained here, as we would in an American children's institution, a sense of the affectional hunger of these "orphan" children. The kind of assurance, sturdiness, pride, which one superficially assumes to be characteristic of the Russian child, seemed absent in this children's home. It is not the existence of this phenomenon in itself that is significant. No social order today is able to satisfy the emotional needs of its children with any degree of adequacy. What is significant is that the Russians are so reluctant to acknowledge the existence of emotional deprivation and hunger. In the boarding school where we spent an entire day we gained two distinct impressions: one was that children are strictly disciplined, and the other, a thinness of emotional expression—what might be described as a flatness of affect.

We were also very much struck by the apparent absence of any emotional ties between the teachers and the children. The whole atmosphere seemed to be one of impersonality, and this was true even though this was a model school and the staff impressed us as being above the average.

The impressions we gained in these three different settings (*dietski dom,* day school and boarding school) were of driven, fearful, tense youngsters reacting to excessive pressure to achieve, fearful of mates and teachers, and altogether overburdened. The free, self-assured, bright-eyed, hopeful child was not among those we saw in these groups.

The Soviet child has to reckon with certain realities which may impose adult choices and burdens earlier than in other modern cultures. There is still no scientific frame of reference by which to judge whether these are appropriate and growth-producing or premature and harmful. Judgment must still be based on one's scheme of values and on one's view of man in society.

An extensive set of rules to govern the conduct of children in the primary school has been formulated by the Academy of Pedagogical Sciences. They are grouped under such headings as "Elementary ideas of good and bad"; "Love of Motherland"; "Industriousness and frugality"; "Good social conduct in the school, at home, in the streets, and in public places." They spell out obedience to the teacher and parents, obedience to the rules of the Oktobrists and young Pioneers, the duty to follow the example of the best pupils, and so on.

The rules emphasize not only achievement in scholarship but also punctuality in attendance, proper deportment in the street and at home. For example, the child is expected to leave and to enter the home quietly and without banging doors; to ask permission to take something or permission to leave the house.

Although this has been omitted from the new rules, it is important to record that in stressing deportment the old rules included the following precepts: The child must sit erect during the lesson period, not leaning on his elbows or slouching in his seat. And he must salute the teacher when he meets him on the street.

Our observations in the classroom bear out the spirit of these injunctions both as to the conduct of the child and his attitude toward teachers. The teacher expects and, it is our impression, receives, respect and obedience from the child. Speaking of teachers, one observer gives as his impression: "Their matronly bearing and determined manner proclaim that they will tolerate no nonsense, and they obviously impress the younger children." *

The importance accorded formal examinations in the Soviet educational scheme strongly influences teaching methods and colors the psychology of the educational milieu. Tests and marks are the bases for promotion from one class to another, and more formal examinations for admission to technical schools and institutions of higher education. When we recognize this, we must also remember that in Soviet society today both status and economic opportunity and, to some degree, personal security, depend on educational achievement. One realizes how crucial is success in examinations when it is recalled that as many as

---

* "Impressions of Soviet Education," by Frederic Lilge. Berkeley, Calif.: *International Review of Education*, Vol. V/1959/No. 1, Pages 11-25 (Mimeographed, Page 1).

30 students compete for a single place in a technical institute and there are few educational institutions where there are not at least four or five students competing for one opening.*

One American observer has pointed out the contradiction between the emphasis on examinations and the rejection of tests of intellectual capacity, noting that the examinations in fact constitute a predicter of capacity to meet the demands of the more advanced curriculum. Whatever the theory, Soviet educators fail to see that in practice this combination of emphasis on marks and matriculation through examinations as criteria for admission to higher schools and the granting of stipends constitutes *de facto* tests of intellectual ability.

We can detect at least two consequences of the overvaluation of the examination. First, the student is concerned with the right answers, without knowing why they are right. In the second place, it mechanizes teaching; teacher and student alike are harnessed to detailed instructions for the teaching of the subject and for the examination, which the ministries of education promulgate. "Covering ground" is an appropriate metaphor in speaking of education in the Soviet Union, for it has been an education in extension rather than in depth.**

One characteristic of the Soviet educational method which is closely related to its emphasis on examinations, and which in itself represents another kind of pressure on the child, is the underlying assumption that knowledge is something exact, clear-cut and definite.

It is found in the head of the teacher and in the textbook currently in use. There is a correct answer to every question, a solution to every problem. At any rate, it is the answer that matters, not the way it is arrived at. . . . Things are true or false, right or wrong, and either-or. As the teacher enters a "5" for excellent or a "2" for bad work, grading the students frequently during the

---

* *Ibid.* Page 2.
** *Ibid.* Page 2.

lesson, she accompanies the notations with authoritative expressions of praise or blame to which the whole class is witness. Obviously, the conception of knowledge that is conveyed in such teaching is more appropriate to some subjects than to others. It has advantages in arithmetic and in Russian grammar, where there is little room for individual invention and where basic elements of knowledge have to be mastered. But in the teaching of history and literature it encourages the parroting of approved interpretations. I judge, of course, on the basis of a limited range of observation. Yet, I find my impressions confirmed by certain self-criticisms published by Soviet teachers in their own press. The teaching lacks "romance," one put it, because it does not take hold of the interests and imagination of many students.*

A report from a British observer who visited the Soviet Union in 1957 further confirms our own impressions of the mechanical, rote character of present educational methods there.

We saw seven-year-olds taking their first reading lessons. Every child had its book open at the same page, and was pointing to the same letter with a colored pointer. When they started to write, the class sat up straight, the teacher said "oo," the class took up their pens and made the appropriate letter, and then put their pens down again. The teacher then said "ah," and the process was repeated. The exercise books were ruled not only horizontally, but also diagonally from top right to bottom left, so that the writing should have the same slope. A twelve-year-old painting class—it was explained that the curriculum allowed water-color painting for the first time at that state—sat closely packed in desks with drawing boards before them, all painting a brown earthenware pot that stood on a table "out in the front." The paintings all seemed to be at the same stage of completion.**

It should be pointed out, however, that since the school reforms of 1958 Soviet educators have been reiterating the need for developing new teaching methods which would activate all pupils and have them all participate in the teaching process.

---

* *Ibid.* Page 3.
** P. Quince, quoted in Alts, *op. cit.* Pages 165-6.

Academic material should be made more interesting, they urge, by bringing it closer to the children's own experience and by tying it in with other practical subjects. The Soviet educational press contains numerous complaints that children are not taught to think for themselves, and gives instructions to teachers on how to achieve this.

Besides the pressure upon the child exerted by the system of examinations and the continuous marking of every element in his performance, there is also the underlying assumption, to which we referred earlier as the affirmation of equal abilities, which means that *you can accomplish anything if you want to.* If you fail to do so, you are subject to blame: You have failed morally.

One observer reports that the "teachers frequently exclaim 'Shame on you!' when a student does not give the right answer. During a visit to a school in Kharkov [the same observer] saw a young boy with a somewhat embarrassed mien standing outside his classroom, but [he] thought nothing of it. The deputy director accompanying [him] realized that the boy had been put there for some misdemeanor, and hissed at him: 'Now you have degraded us in the eyes of the whole world!' " *

We did not experience similar incidents in our visits, but we did see the constant pressure communicated by the teacher to the child. We have already reported how the girls were urged to perform for us at the *dietski dom.* A variation of the same pressure occurred at the boarding school when the teacher showing us around the shops turned to the head of the shoe repair shop and, in the presence of the children, asked: "Who is your best pupil?" And the head of the shop pointed the boy out. "Who is your worst pupil?" And again the head of the shop, in front of the other children, pointed out the boy who was the worst. In other words, humiliation of the laggard is an accepted weapon.

---

* Lilge, *op. cit.* Page 3.

Lilge concludes the report of his observation of the pressures to which the pupil is subjected with the comment: "Always to be at one's best and to be a worthy representative of the Soviet society would seem to put a considerable strain on young persons." *

Discipline in the school situation as a complex of many kinds of influences, including approval, disapproval, rewards, deprivation and punishment, is encountered by the child in a variety of relationships, those with his peers in the pupil organization and in the Pioneer group as well as with his teacher.

Though the way discipline is administered is more important than the reward and punishment per se, the catalogue of approved disciplinary measures may provide the reader with an additional sidelight on the psychological climate of the school milieu. Physical punishments are strictly forbidden; also the old-fashioned "shame" punishments, such as standing a child in a corner, putting a dunce's cap on his head and exposing him to public ridicule, are forbidden as offending the dignity of the child's individuality. The following are permitted:

> reproof in private) Either of these can be noted in the
> reproof in public) child's "daybook"
> warning
> private reprimand
> public reprimand
> lowering of the grade for behavior: this must be done after
>   consultation with the director of the school and is a severe
>   punishment
> warning of expulsion
> expulsion from school

Before any punishments are administered, however, teachers are urged to find the cause of the child's bad behavior and remove it.

---

* *Ibid.* Page 3.

If a child does particularly well, he should be encouraged:

> expression of confidence in the child by assigning him some
> responsible task
> encourage the child in his work
> praise the child before his parents
> praise the child for a special good answer, or work well done
> praise the child and give him a prize.

This means of encouragement, it is specified, should not only be used for achievement but also for effort. And not only individuals, but collectives as well can be praised.*

Within the school, pressure to conform to rules, to measure up to expectations, is communicated through the teacher, the Pioneer leader, and through the organization of pupils in class committees, general student councils and Pioneer groups. All of these share in the authoritative supervisory and guidance structure. Outside the school there are billboards, newspapers, slogans and do's and don't's everywhere, to say nothing of the Communist party itself, whose influence seeps down to the youngest child.

We have already sketched the amenities that characterize the relationship between the child and the teacher, the obligation of respect and obedience on the part of the child toward the teacher as the representative of the organized community and an authority for what is right or wrong, good or bad.

Our first encounter with the Soviet variety of social pressure occurred on our first visit to the U.S.S.R. in 1956. During a tour of a psychiatric dispensary in Moscow, we were ushered into the dining room of the children's residential unit at lunch time. Here we found about 50 children between the ages of 6 and 10 drawn up in squads of 10 or 11 each. A serious little boy of 8, wearing eyeglasses, stood some distance from these

---

* *Pedagogika* by Yesipov and Gonsharov. Uchpedgiz 1950. (Textbook for pedagogical schools.) Chapter 15.

squads. As we watched, a child would step out of each line in turn, advance a couple of paces toward the little chief, salute, report, salute again and step back into line. We inquired and learned that these were the monitors of each dormitory group reporting to the chairman of the children's council on the behavior of their groups during the morning.

The same type of social pressure is brought to bear in the school. In its simplest dimension the procedure is as follows: A child is not doing well, his marks are bad. As a first step, the teacher asks some of the *aktiv* pupils to discuss his shortcomings with him. His work fails to improve. The class monitor then brings the matter up at the monthly meeting of the student group. If this still does not bring results, it is brought up at the regular monthly meeting of the parents and children of his class. The principal of a school explained to us that the parents take a report of their child's misdeeds more seriously when it comes from other children than from the teacher alone.

Another step is posting the child's name on the bulletin board with a statement of his failures. And in case this whole disciplinary process fails, the matter is brought before the whole school body to determine appropriate measures for dealing with the situation, measures which might range from shame and humiliation to expulsion from the student group and, finally, from the school itself.

It was in the boarding school that we gained additional impressions of how the student council operates. Suroja was a handsome 15-year-old boy who was eager to spend time with us because he happened to be very much interested in learning to speak English. He walked around with us for at least an hour and a half between 6:00 and 7:30 in the evening, while the youngsters were in the shops or performing their Pioneer assignments. He made it very clear that by moving about from one part of the school to another and by going in and out of classrooms, he was making sure the children were behaving and doing their work properly. Thus, as he accompanied us through the assembly hall he pointed out the "brigade" of little girls who were polishing the floor by shuffling up and down with polishing pads on their feet. One of the little girls was a *starshi* (sergeant) who was responsible for the brigade. He explained that the children's soviet decided on the work assignments. It is the soviet that determines which child will polish the floor during a particular month. This is a very important prerogative, since in the boarding school the children help with all the housework—in the kitchen, dining room, etc.

An article in a Soviet educational journal includes an account of the efforts of the Pioneer organization to achieve the reformation of two pupils in the sixth grade who were failing in class:

. . . It was suggested to them that they reform. This did not help. Then the squad leader together with the class instructor went to the boys' parents. They both lived in good conditions, but the parents paid little attention to the conduct and studies of their sons. The question of the boys was presented in squad meeting to which their parents had been invited. At first the parents had been offended: "What is this, are *we* called to attend Pioneer meeting?" (But they came.) One Pioneer after another stood forth and spoke to S. and K. of their misdeeds. When the squad raised the question of whether the boys should be in the squad any longer, then the boys pleaded hotly not to be expelled. They said the squad was dear to them and promised to reform. At that point the parents admitted their guilt in not interesting themselves in their sons sufficiently. Now S. and K. have changed their attitude, started to behave better at home and in school, to prepare their lessons. . . .

Teachers are constantly urged to utilize the Pioneer as well as the student organization in maintaining good order.

The Pioneer organization is the best aid to the teacher in his difficult job, though there are still some teachers who do not sufficiently help Pioneer work, but keep aloof and underestimate it.

The very participation of children in Pioneer organization obligates them to study better, exerts on them a powerful educational influence, mobilizes their will, mind and emotions for the struggle for high achievement. "You are a Pioneer and therefore you have no right to have a negligent attitude towards study, you have no right to be rude, undisciplined, misbehave in class, etc." In this spirit the organization brings up Pioneers from the very first days of their entry.

While proclaiming its virtues as a character building and disciplinary medium, Soviet educators are troubled about the abuse of power by the collective, recognizing that the penalties the children mete out to each other can be cruel and excessive. When we discussed this with the head of the boarding school, she explained that she tried to keep in touch with the head of the student council so as to temper, where she believed it necessary, the punishments decided on. It will be recalled how strongly Makarenko felt that the authority of the collective must be upheld, and that where there is a conflict between the view of the educator and the view of the collective, the latter should govern, even though its views may appear unjust to the educator.

Makarenko's championship of the collective as the only body that successfully and fruitfully enforced discipline was so congenial to the philosophy of a collective society that it has continued to enjoy the approval of educators to this day. Indeed, a Makarenko story epitomizes this conviction. It is the story of a boy who had engaged in stealing and was taken to task in private by the teacher. When the teacher proudly told Makarenko that the boy had repented, he was severely reprimanded. Only the collective should have the power to make a culprit repent; repentance not accompanied by public shame is of no value. In fact, the practice instituted by Makarenko is still followed in Soviet schools. When the collective is to discuss the case of a culprit, its members assemble in a ring around him.

The "accused" is made to stand in the middle, in full view of his comrades, and await judgment in the glare of publicity.

From our talks with educators we believe that many of them have mixed feelings toward the collective. We infer this from the references in articles in educational journals to the failure of some officials to support the collective, and also from the acknowledgments by educators in their talks with us that the judgment of the collective can be harsh.

An example of what group pressure may mean to the individual child is revealed in the case story of a 15-year-old boy cited in a book of lectures on child psychiatry.* The author reports that this child was suffering from a paranoidal reaction caused by inner conflict between two motivations: a feeling of duty to inform on a comrade and a fear of doing so. When, after several days of indecision, he did report to the school authorities he immediately became sick and manifested psychotic reactions—extreme fear, guilt and the expectation of being beaten up.

Socialist competition is another means by which the group exerts pressure on the individual to support group goals and participate in collective enterprises.

Competition between pupil groups and classes may be for the highest marks in school subjects, for top rating in cleanliness and orderly conduct. The daily performance of the competing class is scored on the bulletin boards in the hallway, indicating the standing of the competitors. If one grade leads all the others for a week, it may win a banner; or if it maintains its lead for a month, the children may be rewarded with tickets to the children's theater. "The individual child is made aware that the standing of his group depends on his performance." **

---

* Sucharevya, G. E.: *Clinical Lectures on Child Psychiatry*. Translated by Elena Calas.

** Lilge, *op. cit.* Page 4.

This principle is well illustrated in *Seventeen,* a novel for young readers. The action revolves about a tenth-grade secondary school class which decides to sign a pledge that it would graduate without failures or bad marks as one of the top classes of the city. One girl refuses to sign the pledge—signing is voluntary—explaining that she is in no need of the help of her comrades or of any special prodding, as her marks have been consistently good and she is one of the top pupils of the class. The entire book is devoted to the cause of bringing this girl to see the error of her ways in isolating herself from the collective. This is finally achieved by ostracizing her completely for the rest of the school year.

We had a long talk with a senior member of the faculty of the Institute of the History and Philosophy of Education, who is an outstanding authority on Makarenko. He is also the author of an authoritative book on discipline.

We were interested in ascertaining the professor's approach to the problem of discipline. What were his views as to the causes of deviant behavior and how should it be handled? We came away with the impression that he was essentially interested in disciplinary devices rather than in what lay behind troublesome behavior or how basic attitudes between teacher and child influence the child's conduct. Although he speaks kindly of children, his approach remains basically intellectual. He sees the process of discipline as a complex of reward, punishment and approval. While an awareness of the importance of interpersonal relationships breaks through, it is not apparently integral to his basic philosophy.

"Sometimes," he said, "undisciplined children are very clever and therefore not satisfied by the school program; some overrate themselves and their poor behavior is a reflection of their feeling that they are too bright and therefore find fault with the curriculum."

The professor also recognizes that mental illness may be at the root of some troublesome conduct. He goes on, however, citing Makarenko: "If a child's behavior is bad, then it is the teacher who is bad, or it may be the methods of education, or the parents. Sometimes it is not exactly that way, the problem being a much broader one—the total psychological atmosphere surrounding the child may be wrong. This is proven by the fact that a child may behave badly in one school and may behave better after he is transferred to another."

When we kept pressing for his views as to the importance of the relationship between child and teacher, he cited an article about a girl in a children's home. In this situation the teacher scolded the child because she left the bedroom hurriedly and in disorder. Later they found that she had done this because she was running to get her raincoat. In this instance, the child's feeling of being scolded and treated unfairly was the important point. In another example, the professor spoke of a child who may feel that his companions are unfair, and can then become very much upset about the way in which he is treated by the whole group. He says that everyone knows this is so, but in practice it is not always taken into consideration. The tendency is to say the child is the devil when there is trouble.

The professor agrees with Makarenko who always found good in every child. Our talk was concluded by his declaration that the problem often lies with the teachers or with the children's organizations, rather than with the child.

As is true of the other educators whom we interviewed, the professor seemed to have little familiarity with psychiatric theory and the significance it might have for the education of the average child.

What is perhaps even more significant is that the professor's field of vision seemed to be limited to overt transactions between adults and children, and children with each other, rather than the emotional quality of the basic interpersonal relations within which these transactions take place.

E. New Developments in Soviet Education

Two developments in Soviet educational affairs since 1955 highlight the kinds of problems which those who shape Soviet educational policy are grappling with. They clearly attest to the concern of the regime over the failure of the educational system to realize the goals set for it: the fullest transformation of innate potential into useful skills and the shaping of the kind of personality required for fruitful participation in a collective social order.

1. *The boarding school.* The establishment in the autumn of 1956 of the new boarding school by the Soviet Union was a highly significant step from the standpoint of basic philosophy of child rearing and education.

The decision to establish this educational institution had been made at the 20th Congress of the Communist party held during the spring of 1956. The plan had the blessing of the highest leadership in the Soviet Union, especially of Khrushchev. In September of that year 170 boarding schools were ready to open in the Russian Republic.

The *Report on Public Education in the Soviet Union,* issued by the government in 1956, recites the reasons for the establishment of the boarding school as follows:

The family and the school remain, no doubt, the most important nuclei of socialist education of children. But this can no longer be considered sufficient. In the prerevolutionary past, in addition to the general schools, the *ruling class* had their own privileged system of educating the young generation, a system which corresponded to the existing regime and to the spirit of the time. . . .

These tasks of making child education incomparably better and more perfect are to be solved by the boarding schools. . . .

Children are to be enrolled in the boarding schools only at the request of their parents. They will live at the schools and their parents will visit them on holidays, during vacations or after school hours. . . .

Fine teachers equal to the lofty calling of engineers of the souls of the growing generation will be selected.

The new boarding school is visualized as fulfilling two basic functions—that of an ideal educational facility and that of an instrument for child protection. The boarding school is to become a laboratory for the molding of the ideal Soviet citizen of the future and also the resource for solving many of the educational problems which the ordinary elementary and secondary schools have been unable to solve to the satisfaction of the regime. Development in its pupils of strength of character, initiative, creativity, and dedication to Soviet ideals—this is but one of the goals the new boarding school is expected to realize. The child protective function is to be realized by providing residential care to those children whose home situation is inadequate.

The unique feature which differentiates these institutions from the ordinary school is the opportunity they offer the educational authority to plan and control the child's total experience during the entire 24 hours of the day. In this way, the non-directed rearing in the family would be avoided and prescribed educational and child-rearing methods given full scope. To what extent have the objectives of the proponents of this educational facility been realized?

First, how many schools are there and how many children in them? In the period between 1956 and 1962 in the Russian Republic there were 1,179 such schools, with an enrollment of 400,000. This constitutes about 2 per cent of the enrollment in the regular day schools for the same age span.

While thus far we know of no full-scale evaluation of the extent to which the boarding schools are achieving the objectives set for them, the general attitude of educators is that they have proven themselves, and consequently their pupil capacity should be increased so that ultimately all children will receive their education in schools of this sort. Present plans call for increase of the number of children cared for in such schools in the

Russian Republic to 1,340,000 by 1965, which would be about 7 per cent of the children in the age range covered.

One of the unresolved questions at the time the schools were established was the balance in their functions as educational laboratories and as child protective agencies. Thus far it appears that the boarding schools have given preference to enrollment of the so-called neglected children—children from homes in which the father is absent, or children whose parents are unstable, alcoholic, or otherwise incapable of providing the right kind of child rearing and character training. The increasing number of students attending them may therefore be a reflection of increasing concern about child neglect resulting from family breakdown.

In our talks with educators there seems little emphasis on the boarding school as an educational laboratory or a model educational institution. The emphasis is entirely on the boarding school as a child care facility, as a substitute for family care. This is given point in the recent merger of the network of *dietskie doma* with the boarding schools.

Originally, the boarding schools were to enroll children who had living parents and the *dietskie doma* were for orphans. This distinction has now been wiped out, and all children who need substitute home care because they have no families or because their families are not able to provide the care they need will be eligible for admission to the boarding school.

Some criticisms of the quality of education in the boarding schools are beginning to appear. One is that the children in these schools are being oversupervised, thus militating against the expression of creativity on the part of the child. Another is that boarding schools are becoming "closed institutions," cutting children off from life outside and even, in some cases, from their parents.

It is worth noting that the cost of care in the boarding school is about ten times that of ordinary schooling, and this may very well be a factor in slowing down the expansion of these schools.

However, in our opinion, the extent of the use and the number of boarding schools will be determined by the readiness of parents to send their children to them, rather than the cost. The regime is so strongly committed that it will undoubtedly be prepared to meet the additional cost involved in substituting them for day schools.

Another child care program which reflects the concern of the regime for the protection of children is the combined educational and child care plan embodied in the "extended-day" school.* This stems from the recognition that the expansion of the boarding schools would of necessity take time and that many children will continue to live in homes where the mother returns from work long after the regular school day is over. The "extended-day" school program is intended to serve the dual purpose of keeping within the school setting children who would otherwise be unsupervised until their parents returned from work and of extending the influence of the school in the life of the child by increasing the amount of time the child spends in the school setting. The activities in the additional hours spent at school are to include homework, recreation and rest. No facts are available as to how many children have been taken care of in such programs, but it is safe to say that the number is constantly increasing.

2. *The educational reforms.* The educational reforms launched in 1958 rank along with the boarding schools in their potential impact on education as well as character development in the Soviet Union. The principal changes they usher in are the emphasis on productive work and technical skills as a component in all education, the establishment of eleven-year rather than ten-year schooling as a universal standard and the leveling upward of the compulsory education requirements. The elementary and intermediate divisions of the general school to-

---

* See Chapter 8, Page 193.

gether now constitute an eight-year program, compulsory for all children. The secondary school which previously covered the eighth to the tenth grades now covers the ninth to the eleventh grades.

In advocating the new program, the principal goals emphasized by its proponents may be paraphrased as follows: To achieve a more rounded personality, the intellectual and the practical must be unified. It may be of interest to note that this goal happens to be identical with the viewpoint of Karl Marx which is presumed to be based on his observation of the combination of education and work in London in the mid-19th century.

The greater emphasis on physical work in educational theory and practice is intended to meet the problem of the growing class consciousness of the professional and the intellectual and their disdain for ordinary work. On our last visit we encountered young people who expressed their scorn for physical labor as follows: "Finish the ten-year school and spend your time driving a tractor!"

The new reforms also reflect the general disappointment over the attitudes of the young people that the educational system has produced. At the same time, they are also regarded as an indication of the decision of the regime that the Soviet Union has been successful in producing a sufficient number of scientists and other professionals and that no increase in the ratio of these classes to the population as a whole is needed.

It may undoubtedly be assumed that one of the gains of the new program would be the acceleration of production and the gradual rise in economic standards that would result from drawing younger people earlier into the productive labor force of the nation.

While it is not clear whether better education, from the standpoint of personality and character development, or an enlarged and improved labor force were both among the original objectives of these reforms, there is no question that an improved labor force is bound to be one of the results if the changes are carried out as projected.

The new program provides that after the child completes the eighth grade he may go to work and continue his education by attending night school or by taking correspondence courses, or he might enroll in a trade school or continue in the academic program through the eleventh grade.

Six types of schools are specifically provided for:

(1) evening, seasonal or correspondence schools that will give part-time education to the majority of young people who are working on farms and in factories; (2) polytechnical labor schools offering occupational training and closely associated with industry, state farms and technical repair stations; (3) technicums that will continue to prepare specialists and technical personnel of middle rank; (4) boarding schools . . . are to be increased, and will furnish the model for all other types of schools combining instruction with productive labor; (5) special schools for the arts will be continued; (6) special schools for young people highly gifted in mathematics and the sciences are envisioned, but not definitely established for the moment.* No special mention is made of a type of school with a predominantly humanistic curriculum, although some educators to whom I talked in the spring thought that such a school would find a place in the new plan. The whole reorganization is expected to meet the demands of both ideology and industrial expansion. Its purpose is threefold: to restore the respect for labor that is supposedly a distinctive attribute of a socialist society; to combine more successfully than before a general education with occupational training; and to supply the skilled manpower required for fulfilling the new seven-year plan.**

---

* The number of boarding schools has been increased to 1,179 and special schools for the gifted in mathematics and physics have already been established. (See Page 259.)

** Lilge, *op. cit.* Page 9.

It is pertinent that even those children who go on to the academic schools are expected to work at least eight hours a week in a nearby factory. Those who go on to professional schools are expected to work at least during the summer before enrolling in the professional school.

There has as yet been no evaluation of the new program. In his article Afanasenko details many of the practical problems involved in the implementation of its provisions. He points to the need to develop special methods for teaching the older children who have left school at an early age and who now in increasing numbers will be terminating their full-time education by the age of 14 or 15. This calls for the development of new types of evening schools, correspondence schools, adaptation of curricula for the older child.

A good deal of difficulty has been encountered in arranging for the practical work of those children enrolled in the intermediate and secondary divisions (from the fifth to the eleventh grades).

Vocational training in the last three grades of the secondary division is not always successful, as schools often train pupils in skills which are not needed in the region where graduates are likely to be employed. There are numerous complaints that the school administration does not clear its plans for vocational training with the local planning agencies, or that skills taught in the schools are so narrowly specialized as to be virtually useless on the labor market.

It was originally hoped that satisfactory arrangements for work for the pupils could be made at neighboring plants, but because of the lack of planning it is reported that the children often stand around watching the adults work. The men in the plants who are attuned to the fulfillment and surpassing of norms are reported to be annoyed by the youngsters, whose presence reduces productivity.

No doubt it will require many years before the problems of implementation of the work program have been solved. Only then can there be any real evaluation of the objective of these reforms and the extent to which they are achievable and being achieved.

It is not clear at this point what the impact of the program has been upon the enrollment of pupils in the three upper years, or whether the emphasis on work and the move from the eight-year school to jobs in industry is reducing the number in these grades and thus the number who consequently become eligible for admission to universities and higher professional schools. There seems to be a difference of opinion as to whether the number of children enrolled in the upper grades has been reduced during the first year of the program, with some evidence to support both points of view.

F. New Trends and Unsolved Problems

The educational program in the Soviet Union engages a great deal of public interest and concern. Letters from readers, as well as articles, appearing in daily newspapers and educational journals criticize teachers, teaching methods, classroom procedures, and discuss the merits of proposals for changes or innovations which are being advocated or have been introduced. They express great pride in the extraordinary achievement in training of technical and professional personnel and in increasing the literacy of the nation. But at the same time they point to existing shortcomings and suggest means of overcoming them.

These public discussions highlight a number of unsolved problems which cover a wide range of important issues in the educational program beyond those which the educational reforms of 1958 were designed to solve.

As we have already seen, much of the anxiety is focused on the character defects of the products of the system—the young people. In the press, in discussions among professionals, in cartoons appearing in *Krokodil,* the egotism, the Westernism, the softness and also what we would call "Momism," are pointed to and condemned over and over again.

It is important to note, however, that the catalogue of character defects which troubles the Soviet leaders does not coincide with the critical reactions of American educators who have recently visited the Soviet Union. The limitations represented by overconformity, compliance, lack of curiosity, rigidity, have rarely been covered in past Soviet self-criticism. Only now is some concern about them beginning to emerge.

Moreover, while criticism of many aspects of education is freely expressed, none of the basic assumptions are being questioned. Thus, the postulates that we have referred to as "equal abilities" and "unlimited perfectibility" have not been challenged, even though there seems to be a growing anxiety about the children who fail to achieve promotion as well as those who drop out of school too soon.

On both our visits we found a tendency on the part of the educator to draw a curtain over the fact of underachievement. We found reluctance to discuss the labor brigade, a program for the child with relatively little schooling to his credit who is to be absorbed into the labor force, where training primarily takes the form of apprenticeship.

As we traveled about the country we saw girls who appeared to be no more than 14 or 15 working on highways. We asked our guide to tell us how girls of that age had been selected for this kind of work. We were told that they were girls who had misbehaved or who did not get along well at school.

It is no secret, after all, that the rate of failure of pupils in individual subjects, especially in Russian language and mathematics, is still high in our country. Every year more than 1,500,000 pupils in the country schools are not promoted. . . .

Many children experience emotional trauma on failure of promotion. Some of them drop out and never complete their schooling.*

Afanasenko cites figures which show that approximately 5 per cent of the children who enter the first grade are left behind during their first year. Many of the children who fail do not reach the fifth grade until they are 13 or 14. They then come to be known and regarded by the other children as backward pupils. They become ashamed of themselves and look for any excuse to leave school which they have grown to hate. Moreover, it is those who are left behind who are the first to drop out of school.**

He deplores the large number of young people who have not completed seven-year schooling.

In the Altai territory, for example, more than 4000 children and adolescents did not go to school in the past school year and more than 5000 dropped out of school. The situation is no better in Tyumen, Astrakhan and a number of other provinces. Such a situation indicates that some workers directly responsible for general education have become accustomed to the fact that every year a large number of children fail to attend school.†

He is loath to accept limitations in the child's ability and places the responsibility for failure on the doorstep of the teacher, pointing out with approval that some teachers achieve 100 per cent promotion of their classes, and some districts succeed in enrolling all children required to attend school.

The introduction of eight-year general education now depends not only on the solution of organizational questions [he means school buildings, supply of teachers]; it is more and more becoming a pedagogical problem.††

---

* *The Current Digest,* Vol. XIII, No. 11, April 12, 1961, *op. cit.* Page 20.
** *The Current Digest,* Vol. XII, No. 30, August 24, 1960, *op. cit.* Page 17.
† *Ibid.* Page 16.
†† *Ibid.* Page 17.

There is much concern not only about the competence but also the dedication and ideological education of the teachers. The sensitive teacher who justly evaluates each child's knowledge and behavior, who creates an atmosphere of mutual trust and respect, and whom the children grow fond of, is contrasted with the teacher who is indifferent to his work and to the children, to their joys and sorrows. This latter kind of teacher engenders a rift in the relations between teacher and pupils which later widens into dislike for the teacher and unwillingness to study. "As a result," Afanasenko says, "there are pupils who are left behind . . . even in the first grade."

He proceeds with a plea for better teaching with the following exhortation:

Without Creative Effort, Without Daring, One Cannot Be a Teacher.— . . . There are a number of reasons for the absence of a creative base in the work of certain teachers. In the case of some teachers it is a matter of lethargy, of a lack of the pedagogical fervency that should be characteristic of a teacher; in the case of others, it is a result of insufficient training. . . . But frequently we ourselves push teachers into a rut. As long as a teacher's work is appraised not on the basis of the results of this work, not by the knowledge and *good breeding* of the students but merely by the *percentage of pupils who receive passing marks* . . . it will be difficult to turn all teachers onto the path of creative quests. . . . * [Our italics]

Afanasenko cites the fact that within the Russian Republic alone there are 1,000,000 teachers but of these, 10 per cent do not have the necessary formal preparation. He draws attention to the fact that in the pedagogical institutes much more emphasis will be given to courses that increase the teachers' skill in upbringing. In these institutes the times assigned for all forms of teaching practice have been increased, and now total a full

---

* *Ibid.* Pages 19-20.

year. Work in the ideological and political training of teachers is being intensified.

The high demands made on teachers and child-rearing personnel call for *stricter selection* of young people for admission to pedagogical institutes. . . . [Our italics]

Raising the qualifications of teachers already working is of special importance. . . .

It is necessary to intensify work on enlisting in correspondence courses all teachers who do not have a higher education. . . .

At the same time, the task is set of ensuring that within the next three or four years all teachers are enrolled in courses, seminars, practical training classes and other forms of study; it is also necessary to overcome the shortcomings that, as stated in the theses, lie in the fact that all this work is one-sided, of a purely methodological nature, with the result that the teachers are not being sufficiently familiarized with the latest achievements of science, culture and technology.*

Afanasenko goes on to touch on many related problems in educational practice. The question of homework also needs to be clarified. Instruction must be so organized that "the pupils assimilate the new study material mainly in the classroom. Until this is done, overloading of students with homework will not be eliminated. But we cannot abandon homework entirely, as some people suggest."

He discusses the recording of marks: " . . . the keeping of records should not become an end in itself; it is impermissible that 30% to 40% of the study time should be spent on it."

He then proceeds to discuss tasks of upbringing, pointing out one serious limitation in the present situation. This is the "practice of excessive supervision of Young Pioneer and particularly YCL [Young Communist League] organizations that exists in some schools." He points out that the members of the YCL are not the immature youngsters they used to be.

---

* *Ibid.* Pages 20-21.

"They are already working in a workers' collective, participating in the production of material values. The task of teachers of pedagogical collectives is constantly to rely on and support the prestige of the YCL and Young Pioneer organizations. . . . "

On our first visit we tried to elicit a picture of the philosophy and practice of the special disciplinary institutions for children with behavior problems, for the delinquents, and for the mentally ill. What we found was that the approach to re-education of these children was basically the same as that employed in the education of the average child: the same emphasis on good example, the same pupil organizations to exert pressure upon the individual child, the same marking as a measure of performance. Perhaps the only difference was the greater emphasis in both the disciplinary school and the school for the disturbed and mentally ill on *work as therapy*.

We were interested in learning on our second visit whether there had been any change in the approach to the re-education of these special groups. Although some "break-throughs" in philosophy and perhaps in practice are taking place, it is our impression that these have not yet reached the architects of educational practice. Certainly they are not reflected in any basic changes in attitudes or practice of the teacher.

There is still little open discussion of the more basic problems in education and child rearing. There has been almost no recognition of the problem the child faces in trying to achieve a balance between self-interest and altruism, the polarities of the Soviet incentive system. There is still no concern for the most fruitful division of labor in child rearing between the family, the school and the political organization.

The report of a commission on shortcomings in education, established by the Academy of Pedagogical Sciences, was completed in 1959, but by 1961 had not yet been made public nor is there any evidence that its recommendations are being carried out. Whether the findings of this commission will lead to a re-evaluation of theoretical postulates—less emphasis on external pressures, on rational and intellectual processes, and more on release of impulse, more on feeling and positive interpersonal relationships—or to an intensification of present methods, is too early to tell. There is as yet no convincing evidence of any fundamental reorientation.

This brings us to the present status of educational and psychological research in the U.S.S.R. The organization of research in these fields follows closely the pattern of organization and control of all scientific inquiry in that country. Like all other aspects of Soviet life, research activities are carefully planned and objectives established for stated periods in the future—5, 7, 10 or 15 years. Research objectives and research concentration must be part and parcel of the total national effort and designed to advance that effort. This means that research is focused upon certain specified objectives in contrast to the "peripherally regulated free-ranging multiplicity with which we are familiar." *

To make sure that the research undertaken adheres to the generally agreed upon objectives, workers in a particular field are notified of the over-all plan. The chief of an individual laboratory or institute will design a program for himself and his subordinates that will contribute to meeting one or more of the stated objectives. After a review at various levels it is submitted for final approval to the Academy of Medical Sciences or the Academy of Sciences or, in the case of educational research, to the Academy of Pedagogical Sciences.

At this time all research must conform to Marxist-Leninist-(Stalinist)-Khrushchev doctrines, and must avoid any theories or assumptions that challenge these. It is for this reason that at the famous conference in 1950 Pavlovian theory was accepted as the basis for psychological research, because, "This

---

* Kline, *op. cit.* Page 182.

theory holds that man is a product of his environment and by suitably modifying the environment a new type of man can emerge." * This is an example of the need to have science support ideology, rather than ideology proceed from science. It explains why the Soviet government took sides in the dispute as to whether acquired characteristics were inherited. If the acquired characteristics are not inherited, a number of the assumptions on which the Soviet government is operating are false, destructive and nonsensical.

From 1936 until this conference in 1950, psychology was in disrepute, although neurophysiology continued to flourish. The psychologists were given an impossible task—to develop a discipline that would be scientifically productive and fertile but still within the framework of dialectical materialism.**

Pavlovian theory is ideologically accepted as the basis for interpretation of human behavior and as the foundation of educational theory and practice.

This theory holds that nervous systems out of which the intellectual (neural) process evolves vary in strength, stability and balance. These qualities constitute the child's neural-physiological quotient. If this basic neural-physiological equipment is defective, the mental process is bound to be defective, and it is so because the basic material out of which it grows is impaired to begin with. Accordingly, they diagnose deviations in behavior from the standpoint of where the defect lies in the nervous system, and whether there is some way of overcoming it.

A child with a well-balanced neurological system who does not do well in school is usually, according to the sanctioned orientation, a victim of faulty teaching practices in the early grades. Once the proper diagnosis of this difficulty has been made, it is possible to remedy the defects. The Soviet psychol-

---

* *Ibid.* Page 185.
** Report of IIE Seminar, *op. cit.* Page 48.

ogists and educators are convinced that they are producing a genuine science of child development which will enable them to solve all their educational problems and build the new Soviet man.

On our first visit to the Soviet Union, we were very much impressed with the research and experimentation carried on by the Institute of Defectology of the Academy of Pedagogical Sciences, which was concerned with the improvement of methods for the education of various classes of mentally and physically handicapped children. The research embraced the mentally retarded and mentally defective, as well as the deaf, blind and crippled. We were similarly impressed with the caliber of the professional personnel engaged in these activities, their knowledge of methods in other parts of the world and the relative freedom of experimentation which they were enjoying in the defined spheres of their activity.

Most dramatic of the work which we encountered was that carried on in the Institute by a scientist who has devoted a lifetime to the development of methods for educating the deaf-blind, the Helen Kellers of the world.

We returned to this Institute on our second visit, and as we saw more we were even more impressed by the extraordinary progress the scientists there have made in developing methods for teaching such severely handicapped persons. It seemed to us then, and it still does, that perhaps the Soviet specialists in this field are further advanced than are those in our country.

In addition to extensive research in the education of various classes of handicapped children, there is also a large amount of research in methods and materials of instruction, but thus far almost none at all on the impact of the educational program on the children themselves. Then, too, a great deal of the research being done has been characterized as "gadgety" in quality: learned discussions of the best kind of classroom desks; new illustrations in textbooks and new passages in textbooks to replace existing ones; and questionnaires asking teachers and pupils if they like the new materials.*

The educational psychologists are very much interested in mechanical apparatus of all kinds, such as electronic recordings, a 30-channel polygraph, and the like. The Institute of Psychology developed an apparatus for making X-ray films of the voice box simultaneously with the recording of speech.**

On this second visit we were particularly interested in learning about any research that might have been carried on in the social sciences, particularly that which is concerned with basic assumptions in social organization and the relationship of the individual to the group of which he is a member. In spite of our many inquiries both at the Academy of Pedagogical Sciences and at the University of Moscow, we did not uncover anything of interest. In fact, we encountered a good deal of reluctance on the part of the professional workers with whom we talked to help us in our search.

We learned that most of the research in the social sciences is of an historical nature. The reason for this is obvious: the Soviet specialists must stay away from empirical research that would cast any doubt on the communist conception of the ideal society.

A recent article in a Soviet journal undertakes to survey the various theories of social structure now held in Western countries, particularly in the United States. Though it begins by pointing to the incorrectness of the basic underlying assumptions of these theories, at the same time it stresses the benefits which the Soviet Union could derive from fuller employment of some of the specific technologies developed by the social science field in the West—survey methods, public opinion polls, study of population problems.

---

* *Ibid.* Page 50.
** *Ibid.* Page 51.

A subsequent article advocates the establishment of a sociological research institute, stressing the values of developing better technologies for the study and analysis of social phenomena. One cannot but assume that the increased attention to current social phenomena will inevitably result in concern for the underlying social processes themselves.

The work of the newest department of the Academy of Pedagogical Sciences, the Department of Contemporary Education in Schools Abroad, may be expected to yield a broader theoretical approach to educational problems. This unit, whose area of interest is comparable to an institute of comparative education, has a staff of 13 professional workers engaged in studies of education in foreign countries. Consistent with their responsibility, members of this group are eager to learn all they can about American methods of education. In the years since our visit we have responded to numerous requests for information about American theories and methods, particularly those concerned with assessment of personality traits and character changes. But the inquiries have gone beyond that to such problems as treatment of delinquents and emotionally disturbed children.

On our last visit we had the impression that in the psychological field there were a number of beginnings of movement into heretofore forbidden or closed areas.

There is a beginning recognition of emotional disturbance as being distinct from mental illness. On our first visit we learned that children were considered either sick or well. The delinquent was either a healthy child whose behavior reflected bad upbringing, or he was a mentally ill child. There was no concept of the emotionally disturbed as an in-between group. Mental illness was the result of defects in or injuries to the central nervous system. Deviations in behavior not amounting to illness were the product of wrong upbringing. Neurosis among children is a product of traumatic life experience, discrimination and deprivation and, we were told, was disappearing as socialism was being achieved in the U.S.S.R.

On our second visit we discovered some revision of these tenets. This was exemplified in the establishment of two schools in Moscow for "borderline" or "asthenic" children. The concept of "asthenic" is not synonymous with our "emotionally disturbed"; it is used to describe the flaccid, withdrawn, fragile child and not the acting-out misbehaving child. We visited one of these schools and while their programs, on the whole, followed very much their traditional practices of education in the regular school, they do represent an attempt to provide education which may be thought of as therapeutic. This is reflected in the staff organization in this school. While the director of the school is an educator and not a psychiatrist, his second in command is a psychiatrist.

At the same time, we must report that in reviewing with us some of the case histories of the children, the psychiatrist tried very hard to interpret the child's difficulties as the result of some defect in the central nervous system. The modifications in the educational and treatment program included some slowing down of the pressure upon the child, the use of vitamins and sedatives, with the addition of psychotherapy.

It is significant that on our second visit we found a much more general acceptance of psychotherapy by the professional workers treating the mentally ill child. Another development in the same direction is embodied in the point of view of one of the leading psychiatrists who has recently published a revision of her lectures on child neuroses.* Without admitting it, it is apparent that she finds that Pavlovian theories are no longer adequate to encompass human behavior and must be revised and amplified to constitute an adequate conceptualization of human activities.

---

* Sucharevya, *op. cit.*

This psychiatrist borrows many concepts from dynamic psychiatry as these have been developed in the U.S. and other Western countries. She discusses psychoanalytic theories, rejecting classical psychoanalysis but expressing approval of some of the "neo-analysts," particularly for their emphasis on cultural factors in social behavior. She reports that 70 per cent of the children appearing in the psychiatric clinics in the Soviet Union are suffering from "borderline" states. In her lectures she is very much concerned with the life history of the child and with the significant events which the child may have experienced. While she stops short of any theoretical formulation which would show why certain incidents in the life of the child produce the symptoms, at the same time she engages in an extensive study of the history of the child-rearing experiences.

Without attempting to summarize the psychiatrist's basic assumptions in these lectures, a few points of view are worth highlighting. In discussing the usefulness of her classification of the types of "borderline" disturbance, she points to the absence of accepted nomenclature which makes clinical study of these disturbances difficult. She points out that it is her intention in these lectures to systematize psychogenic, reactive conditions and psychopathies, not only by clinical symptoms but also by psychogenetic factors.

She rejects Freud's position that sexual factors are the basic cause of the neurosis, because in her view this impoverishes the human personality and ignores the complexity of emotions by reducing all to a blind instinct, primarily sexual.

At the same time, she recognizes conflict as an etiological factor in neurosis, pointing out that even in children the nature and content of conflictual emotions varies. Already in preschool and school ages conflicts may arise in connection with unfavorable interrelations in the family and at school. She criticizes Freud because he takes no account of the personality in which the pathological syndrome develops, the somatic factors and the social milieu in which the child is reared. She refers with approval to neo-analysts who see the cause of neurosis in "culture" and "civilization" which hamper the development of the normal instinctual expression as a consequence of which neuroses arise.

In this psychiatrist's view, "neuroses are those morbid states in which psychic trauma serve as the etiological factors which determine not only the cause of the illness but also its symptomology and its course. . . . Some forms of neuroses develop mostly in the presence of inborn or early acquired nervosity. . . . The pathogenic significance of a psychic trauma and its clinical manifestations may vary in accordance with the action of the trauma being sudden and acute or gradual and long term." As a consequence, she proceeds to consider it "possible to use the general principle of the intensity of reaction as a criterion of a preliminary grouping of psychogenic reactions in children." She has divided the latter phenomena into three groups depending on the acuteness and intensity of the reaction to the psychic trauma.

First group—acute shock (and sub-shock) reactions. Those arise in the presence of acute and sudden psychic trauma and often take their course during an unclear consciousness.

Second group—sub-acute psychogenic reactions (psychic trauma in this group does not act as suddenly). The cause of the psychogenic reaction is a difficult life situation, conflictual emotions. The content of the psychic trauma is comprehended by the patient and an intellectual elaboration is resorted to. To this group belong the basic clinical forms of psychogenic reactions (both "situational" and "personality" according to the terminology of different authors). Those can be considered the true basic "kernel" form of psychogenic reactions.

Third group—the psychogenic reactive states develop gradually under the influence of a prolonged traumatization (connected with incorrect upbringing) or because of repeated psychogenic traumas. The clinical manifestations in those cases develop slowly and gradually, there arise long-term reactive conditions, and sometimes the incorrect formation of a child's character.

Between those three groups of psychogenic reactions there is no sharp borderline.

Other examples of "break-throughs" are worth mentioning. One which may have basic significance is reported in a recent article in which the writer attacks the proposal that tests be used to assess the child's attitudes. If this proposal were adopted, the child would be given a test such as one that offers him the choice of helping his fellow-pupil who is behind in his homework or going out to play. Presumably this would be a way of determining whether or not the child's attitude was social. The writer strongly attacks this proposal for new tests, no matter how clothed, as being a reversal or throwback to pedology.

The same article attacks another proposal which may have significance equal to or greater than the use of tests to determine the social component in the child's attitude. According to this second proposal, each school would employ on its staff a psychologist whose business it would be to group the children according to their ability, and their education could thus be geared to their capacity. A similar new development is represented by increasingly frequent demands that some ways be found to determine vocational aptitudes in children and find some means of directing them into the professions for which they are best suited.

While these emerging concerns may be considered as straws in the wind, at the same time they indicate the possibility of a re-evaluation of many educational practices and, if the trend continues, the basic assumptions of collective education itself.

PART THREE

Chapter 10

The Outlook

WHEN WE BEGAN our review of the experience of the Soviet Union in molding the Soviet man, we had hoped to achieve a clearer view of the problem—to weigh the success of the effort and to assess the meaning that this might have for the U.S.S.R. itself as well as for the rest of the world.

Having come to the conclusion of our survey it is fair to ask: How far have we gotten? Are we in a position now to say whether the Soviet Union has been able to achieve a new kind of motivation in its citizens—to produce a more socialized human being? Is the Soviet system coming nearer to the achievement of a state of harmony between man and society? Have its efforts to mold the Soviet man brought any change in its objectives or in its practical measures?

When we examine such psychological phenomena as the degree of personal security or anxiety, the degree of altruism or self-interest, all we can say is that if there are differences between the products of the Soviet and those of other educational systems, the differences are not yet sufficient to be considered basic or decisive.

What seems clear is that the Soviet Union has achieved a sufficient degree of conformity to mobilize human energy in the interests of national goals and to create tools for civilized life—a relatively stable economy, a comprehensive system of education, health and welfare—and a defense establishment the equal, apparently, of any other in the world.

One recurring theme that strikes the ear of those interested in Soviet affairs is the Soviet claim that it has accomplished the first phase of its march toward the final goal—the collective social order. This declaration is coupled with the promise of the ushering in of communism, with "the withering away of the state" as an integral step in establishing the ideal society. But the observer cannot fail to hear another voice—perhaps not as loud but possibly even more significant in its immediate implication. It is the stern voice of disapproval and condemnation of all unsanctioned conduct, a voice which seems to deny the degree of progress claimed, and which is accompanied by extension of punitive and coercive measures.

This voice cannot but remind us of the great price that has been paid for the positive achievements we have enumerated. The price exacted derives sanction from a system of values in which the end justifies the means, expressed in coercion that included imprisonment, deportation, slave labor, and the liquidation of millions of peasants who stood in the way of the collectivization of agriculture.

Although the achievements are indisputable, social phenomena which according to Marxist theory should have long disappeared mock its prophecy by their continued persistence. Moreover, these are gradually being accepted as permanent features of the national life. We refer to crime, mental illness, divorce and many other forms of personal and social disorganization. The Russians do not seem to have solved the basic psychological issues of man in society any more than we have.

It is becoming increasingly evident that the problem the U.S.S.R., no less than capitalistic nations, faces at this time is essentially a psychological one. The question is how soon the Russians will begin to recognize this and see that modern industrial society must rely more and more on mental rather than physical labor.

The well-integrated, stable personality, free of major psychological pathology, thus becomes much more crucial to society than the strong person free of major physical defects. Complex production and scientific problems are increasingly resolved by brain work, and more and more energy or power becomes available to replace the "hand." *

Will this mean recognition that the mental health of the worker as an agent of production cannot be separated from the mental health problems of the worker as a citizen, a father and a husband? This obviously means more attention to the issues involved in the development of personality and more and more psychological and psychiatric research, more attention to functional neuroses—more than the Soviets have thus far been willing to give to these aspects of their social situation.

For the Soviet Union, as well as for the rest of the world, much depends upon how and in what ways the regime will face the human problem and the many factors that enter into it. The regime is finding it increasingly difficult to explain nonconformity, egotism and crime as results of deprivation in the economic area or as the consequence of other environmental forces or "survivals of the past."

The basic question is: Will the existing contradictions between dogma and reality lead to the recognition that the ideal of a collective society may be unattainable and then to modifications or revisions in the ideal—either basic changes in direction or radical changes in pace, timing and method?

Soviet policies governing its relationships with the outside world are bound to influence and be influenced by what is happening in the domestic orbit itself: its success in harnessing human energy to attain national goals, the way in which it meets the various manifestations of social and psychological dynamisms within its own borders. How it resolves the struggle between the assertion of individualism and restrictive social control is bound to influence its attitude on the international scene and may intensify the struggle for power and dominance or the reverse. Then, too, if it feels beleaguered by the outside world it may be

---

* Field in Bereday & Pennar, *op. cit.* Page 190.

less ready to concede greater freedom for the individual within its own borders. We can only hope that the fuller appreciation of the human problem it faces may yield a modification in its national goals and, with this, many of the sharp differences between it and the Western world will diminish.

Obviously, too, both the domestic and the international posture of the Soviet Union will influence, and be influenced by, the way in which other nations come to terms with social problems within their own borders. Increased urbanization, with the unloosening of the traditional ties of the individual to his family and his kinship groups, and the weakening of social control are universal phenomena which have been intensified since the last World War.

The upsurge of technological changes, the shrinkage of space, taken together with the emergence of the new nations in Asia and Africa, will inevitably compel some *de facto* world government in the form of increasing international control over the individualistic prerogatives of nations. Increasing restraints upon the exercise of sovereignty of individual nations may in turn reinforce the internal balance between the individual and the social order in all societies. Greater equality of access to natural resources, as well as all the tools for civilized life, will not only reduce the existing material differences between peoples, but will undoubtedly further force a re-examination of the relationship between the individual and the state, with increased freedom for the individual in some societies and more control in others.

From the broad perspective we have sketched as a starting point, what clues, if any, to future directions does our examination of Soviet life yield? What has been the response of the regime to the problems we have identified? Is the nature of the response likely to lead to greater objectivity and greater readiness to examine the facts, to more doubt about absolutes, about such concepts as totality and perfectibility? Does the response presage more *Lebensraum* for the individual constricted by the heavy hand of rigid state control?

To begin with, it is important to note that in spite of what appears to be an unchanging ideology, the history of the Soviet Union during the four and a half decades of its existence has been characterized by a great deal of change: new lines of action adopted, pursued, abandoned and modified. Sometimes changes were made because policies did not achieve their goals; sometimes because the goals themselves were modified. We have described important changes in educational theory and practices. We have seen one concept of the family and its child-rearing functions give way to another.

Some of these changes give promise of greater freedom and scope for the individual. This is true of the emphasis on more open discussion of matters of public interest. The proposed provision in the new educational laws for special schools for gifted children even though originally advocated by Khrushchev, had to be temporarily abandoned because it was unacceptable to the majority of educators and to the public itself.

An even more tangible evidence of this trend is the reduction of the number of penalties for the infraction of work rules by the worker in industry, the efforts to reduce the inequality in wages between the different kinds of work and professions.

The recognition of the part which traditions play in the lives of human beings probably belongs in the positive column, even though, in the main, the motivation for the establishment of ceremonial days to replace religious holidays is to fight the persistence of religious observance. At the same time, Soviet writers who discuss the desirability of establishing these new kinds of ceremonial events parenthetically comment on the importance of tradition in the lives of human beings.

Within the field of our special interest we have noted many break-throughs toward a clearer recognition of the nature of the psychological problem. Among these are the expressions of anxiety over moral shortcomings of youth, about selfishness of the product of the educational system, the failure of children to achieve promotion, the disapproval of competitiveness as an instrument for inculcating altruistic motivations, the concern about creativity.

We see faltering admissions that human behavior cannot be completely explained as a product of external influences. We have encountered the view that the personality and behavior of the criminal are not only a product of the life experience to which he has been subjected and the impact of the social situation in which he finds himself, but that, in turn, the experience to which he is exposed is refracted by him in accord with his own particular personality and life experience.

We have also encountered the acknowledgment that "incompatibility in marriage is a private affair." Moreover, it is increasingly being admitted that the failure of children in school may be due to differences in their abilities, and the problem might be mitigated if there was more grouping of children according to their innate abilities as indicated by intelligence tests.

What is perhaps more significant than these break-throughs is a broadening of the etiological concepts of neuroses as these appear in the recent publications of a leading Soviet child psychiatrist: approval by her of the views of the American "neo-psychoanalysts" because of their acceptance of the role of culture in fashioning personality. However, in her approval of this element in their theories she does not, as yet, accept their emphasis on feeling as a dynamic in human growth and development.

Thus far it is difficult to discern to what extent the tendency to take observable phenomena more fully into account and the trend toward a broader theoretical foundation for human experience are likely to influence official thought and action. There is reason to assume that in the long run this is inevitable. What is difficult to predict is how long before these changes in point of view will make themselves felt in public policy. Until now, the basic ideology has resisted revision or modification. The anxiety over the failure of collective education to achieve a model child has not led to any reappraisal of basic educational theory and methods. What is more, it is hard to say whether the new educational reforms constitute an example of a course of action adopted after a systematic appraisal of experience or a sweeping measure intended to solve many problems in one fell swoop, with results that may include both those that were sought and others which contradict the original intent.

While no one questions that socially useful work, the focal element in the new program, can be a potent influence in personality development, it is important to recognize that it does not in itself go to the heart of the more basic issues in educational theory and practice to which we have drawn attention. It leaves untouched what we consider to be core problems in the development of the personality of the Soviet child: the duality of values which characterizes the dominant ideology and the conflict between the family, the school and the political organizations in the child-rearing responsibility assigned to them. The new educational reforms leave these basic issues untouched.

Our survey has indicated two clearly identifiable but opposing views about the role of the family in child rearing. On the one hand, we found professional educators glorifying the positive contribution of the family to the development of character of the child—and we believe that this view of the majority of the thoughtful and responsible educators is also reflected in a great deal of the writing to be found in pedagogical magazines. The opposing view, embodied in pronouncements of official policy, is the one elaborated by Kharchev, which, while glorifying its virtues, accords the family no clear place in the rearing of children but advocates that this function in the main be entrusted to community institutions.

The voices of those educators who advocate that young children should be reared by their own parents seem weak in comparison to official spokesmen like Kharchev. Whether or not these voices will finally win out over those opposed to them depends on the depth of conviction of parents themselves as well as of the dominant leaders in education and in the psychological sciences.

If the importance of family rearing, at least for the younger child, is accepted, then many practical implications follow. It would mean that the mother would remain at home during the infancy of her child and the role of collective education would be limited to extrafamilial institutions such as the day nursery or the day care program in the schools or summer camps. On the other hand, if the regime holds to the position that education in groups is the only sound child-rearing method for the future citizen of a collective society, then all children would have to be removed from their parents as soon after birth as practicable to be reared entirely in such community institutions as resident creches and boarding schools.

If we look at the practical measures that are now being taken in the child care field we find that they reflect conflicting ideological positions. Many kinds of new facilities are being developed to help parents keep their children at home, even though the mother goes out to work, while at the same time the capacity of the boarding schools is being expanded.

The layout of the new apartment blocks provides space for community health clinics, nurseries, kindergartens and elementary schools, recreation rooms for after-school activity and suitable play spaces—an impressive array of supplementary protective arrangements to help parents in the care of their children who remain at home.

While this is being done, the government is increasing its budget and programs for the expansion of the boarding schools and residential creches. Although the boarding schools are still used primarily for the neglected child, the plans provide for extending their use to the average child.

One may speculate as to which of these competing child care designs will win out. Will it be the family plus the extrafamilial facilities, or will it be the substitutes for the family? It seems quite clear that parents are today opposed to giving up their children. We see a race, therefore, between two competing rather than supplementary programs—one to help the family take care of its children at home with the help of community facilities, and the other to expand over-all substitutes for family care.

Closely related to the arrangement for the care of children is the status of women and the improvement in their lot, with which Kharchev and the regime are constantly concerned. Is the only answer to the full equality of women the removal of the care of children to child care institutions and of household chores to household service institutions? If it should become clear that care of the child by his own mother is preferable to that by the creche, then the emancipation of women could be advanced by reducing their work day during the years their children need their care.

The family and school and child care institutions will continue to weaken each other's efforts in the rearing of children until Russian educators address themselves to the question of the optimum division of responsibility between these two types of child-rearing instrumentalities. They must reach agreement on what each can do best for various ages of children. Only in this way will the basic conflict between them disappear or be minimized. However, the contribution of the family to child rearing can never really be fully assessed as long as there is so little acknowledgment of the part feelings play in the development of the human being and in individual fulfillment and realization. Closely related to the clarification of the role of the family and the place of feeling in psychological nature is the need for the Soviet educator to understand more precisely the kinds of personalities which are likely to result from the more impersonal rearing through the collective.

We have drawn attention to the studies of group-rearing that have been undertaken in various countries in the last decade.

They have been concerned with the personality of children brought up wholly, or nearly so, in nurseries and creches. These studies warrant the assumption that the rearing of young children in a group situation without adequate personal mothering results in impoverishment of the personality in the children and in adults who show a lack of feeling for a meaningful personal relationship. There is no evidence that Soviet educators have given weight to these findings or have been influenced by them.

Clarification of the respective roles of the family; the school, the kindergarten and creches; and the political organization is, in our opinion, one of the important steps the Russians would have to take to achieve more nearly their professed goals, to achieve social motivation without any—or with a minimum of—coercion. How this problem will be resolved may very well influence the quality of Soviet life and its relation to other nations.

As a way of delineating the problem it may be worth-while to sketch briefly other issues in the field of child rearing and education that we believe the Soviet educators need to grapple with if they are to get closer to their objectives. First they must recognize the meaning of human experience: that life transcends theory and that there are no theories yet to explain the totality of human experience. They must devote more time to examination and appraisal of observed phenomena. Doctrine must give way to results of experience which can be studied and observed. In other words, dogma must give way to science. Some specific things which Soviet leaders need to tackle follow.

Concepts like perfectibility and "equal ability" must be subjected to critical analysis, which cannot be done without, at the same time, taking a new look at the facts of heredity. The failure of children to gain promotion in school, on the one hand, and the search for potential leaders, on the other, should in due time force recognition of individual differences and the need to adapt educational methods to take account of these.

Psychological research must address itself to a wider range of human experience, the irrational and nonrational, as well as the rational. The Soviet psychologists need to take a fresh look at instinctual drives as these are expressed in the development of the individual, in his personality structure and his moral character.

Another important configuration of theory and practice which needs reappraisal is group process, with its underlying theoretical assumptions. It is paradoxical that the Russians, who place so much reliance on the group as a medium of character formation, have done so little to study the processes of social interaction within a group. The emphasis has been on the mechanics which sustain the group activities rather than on their content and quality.

One of the undeniable facts established by our survey is that basic human nature is beginning to exert powerful influences on the implementation of the goals of the Soviet regime in the area of family life and human relations. This is true even though it has not yet resulted in any notable modification of theory or goals and thus far is merely a source of general concern.

In our opinion, however, this phenomenon, which may be thought of as the dynamic of the contemporary Soviet social scene, has far-reaching implications. Unless many tendencies in Russian life which can be identified as individualistic can be checked, we are likely to see an extension of the more liberal social climate which has in varying degrees been tolerated since the death of Stalin.

The question remains, will this trend continue and expand, or be reversed?

Will the emphasis on conformity and restriction become stronger, or will the areas of individual expressions be allowed to grow?

At what point in its material and scientific progress will the Soviet Union feel safe in relying less on coercion, and more on identification of individual interest with the common good—on a vision of a co-operative society in which the power of the state is reduced and the prerogatives of the individual enhanced?

Nor does this necessarily mean surrendering entirely the dream of a free society. It may mean modification of the original blueprint, allowing more time for its realization and in the meantime being content with a less than perfect reality.

Before we go further in this projection of the forces which will contribute to greater freedom in social relations, we must ask ourselves whether the more liberal trends appearing in the U.S.S.R. will be accompanied by a new ethic. Economic progress and technological change may provide a starting point for changes in social relationships. However, it is hard to visualize any basic change in the quality of such relationships without a change in the system of values, and without a radical revision of the thesis that "the end justifies the means."

We must recognize that the realization of these and other possibilities we have projected will take time. The past persists in the present and changing social forms do not quickly wipe out habits of thought, traditional values and modes of behavior. New social sanctions will not immediately achieve the eradication of the ethic which expressed itself in the inhumanity of the Stalinist tyranny.

Only when we and the Soviets come closer in our concepts of human worth shall we be able to move closer together in dealing with common psychological and social issues which confront society in the present world.

The Soviet Union is not alone among the nations striving for a better social order and an optimum equation between the individual and the group. More and more, all human societies face common problems which contemporary civilization has produced. Growing urbanization is a universal phenomenon. The role of the family is changing in all contemporary societies, even though the nature of the changes may vary. Women in all cultures are increasingly becoming part of the labor force. The Western societies, as well as the Russian, are developing more extrafamilial services for the protection of children.

The Sputniks dramatize the oneness and smallness of the universe. They also promise great new sources of energy which will reduce the demands on man for physical labor. Inevitably, this must mean that the striving to secure the physical necessities for living will be replaced by other aspirations and uses of human energy. In our frame of reference we assume that this will enhance the value placed on self-awareness and self-realization—a recognition that the uniqueness of the individual constitutes the basis for cultural diversity and enrichment.

There seems little question that the Soviet social planner, as well as our own, must concern himself with psychological as well as social issues, and they are more likely to move closer to each other than further apart.

As the Soviets move toward more individualism, we in the United States are likely to move toward enlarged expressions of community of interest on the part of our total population. We are likely to move closer to the use of the group as a medium of socialization as the Soviets move toward greater freedom.

An ever-important place in the social order will likely remain for the family. No doubt we, with the Soviets, will need and continue to develop other kinds of social institutions that will help to sustain the individual in a society made up primarily of isolated individuals in contrast to one made up primarily of family and kinship groups.

No one today knows what the future of the family is likely to be. It has changed a great deal in the past and may still change a great deal more, without losing its primary function in the rearing of children. No one knows how much further it may change and whether and how far it can be replaced by new kinds of intimate human associations which may take over more of its psychological function.

One can only speculate how far the perceptible movement toward liberalization on the part of the Soviet regime means a transformation in values. Stalin resorted to liquidation of human beings as a means of collectivizing agriculture. While substantial change has taken place in the practice of the regime since then, still there is no assurance that this marks a more certain trend toward liberal policies. The extension of capital punishment, severe penalties for parasites and idlers, though they may merely represent a mopping-up stage on the presumed road toward communism, nonetheless constitute a reversal toward a more punitive and coercive approach to social control. Moreover, the strengthening of the role and authority of the comrades' courts, the involvement of more and more of the populace in the exercise of police powers and in the surveillance of their neighbors, all portend less rather than more freedom.

The basic power structure has not been modified since the days of Stalin and whatever liberalization has taken place represents the will of a very small clique—or even of a single person —in control of the party and the regime, rather than the organized expression of the will of the populace. No mechanism for such expression as yet exists. Power over the nation still rests with the Communist party and the sources of authority in the party are controlled by a small clique headed by a single individual. The possibility that one man's decision could reactivate all the repressive and punitive mechanisms of the Stalin regime is ever present.

We can only hope that the shrinking of our world in space and time will yield greater freedom in communication and exchange of ideas and this, in turn, will bring a more objective examination of human experience. Such examination should produce a social order which will enable men and nations to live more harmoniously on the road to freedom.

Perhaps this is *all* we can hope for.

Index

Abortion, 167

Academy of Medical Sciences, 271

Academy of Pedagogical Sciences, 146, 227, 233, 234, 245, 270, 271, 273, 274, 275

Accommodation, to social demands, 123-32

Acquired characteristics, inheritance of, 272

Activism, concept of, 33-34

Afanasenko, Y. I., 217-18, 264, 267-70

Agriculture:
backwardness, 66-67, 70-71
child labor, 229
collectivization, 30, 31, 33, 164, 175-76, 183, 284, 296

Alcoholism, 102-3

All-Union Health Ministry, 118

All-Union Ministry of Education, 225

All-Union Pioneer administration, 234

All-Union Pioneer movement, 232

Alt, Herschel and Edith, 9n, 225n, 248n

Anarchism, 24

Animal Farm, 71

Annals of the New York Academy of Science, 118n

"Antireligious Education of Soviet Youth," 235n

Anti-Semitism, 47, 49-53, 91

Anton Semyonovitch Makarenko—An Analysis of His Educational Ideas in the Context of Soviet Society, 147n

Apparatchiks, 73

Armenians, discrimination against, 47

Arts, and artists, 60-62, 85

"Asthenic" children, 276

Authority structure, 38

Autocracy, influence of, 28-29

Azerbaidzhan, birth rate, 168

Bakunin, Mikhail, 24

Balinsky, Alexander S., 69n

Bauer, Raymond, 36n, 38n, 70, 76n, 78, 127n, 143n, 160n, 163n

Belinsky, Vissarion, 27

Bereday, George Z. F., 41n, 71n, 220n, 221, 222, 235n, 242n, 285n

Bezprizorniye, 146

Birobidjan, Jewish colonization in, 50

Birth control, 167

Birth rate, 168

Birth Rates, Death Rates and Natural Increase (table), 169

Black market operations, 104

Black Sea sanatoria, 116

"Black work," 224

Boarding schools, 145-46, 171, 183, 194, 209, 212, 227, 230, 245, 258-61, 263n

Bolsheviks, 21, 23, 28, 30, 31, 137, 140, 141

Bookstores, 219

"Bourgeois criminologists," 108-9

Bribery, 104

Brinkman, William W., 242n

British vagrancy laws, 107

Calas, Elena, 255n

"The Canons of Art," 61n

Capital punishment, 104n, 132

Catechism of a Revolutionary, 25

Central authority, belief in, 28-29

Central Committee, Communist party, 38, 143, 225, 226, 227

Central Committee, 22nd Congress (1961), 180n

The Challenge of Soviet Education, 26n

"Changing Political Attitudes in Totalitarian Society, A Case Study of the Role of the Family," 203n

The Changing Soviet School, 242

"Character and Moral Education in a Collectivist Society," 242n

Character development, role of schools in, 216-79

297